Mapping a New World Order

Mapping a New World Order

The Rest Beyond the West

Edited by

Vladimir Popov

Central Economics and Mathematics Institute, Moscow, Russia

Piotr Dutkiewicz

Political Science Department, Carleton University, Canada

Edward Elgar
PUBLISHING

Cheltenham, UK • Northampton, MA, USA

Published by
Edward Elgar Publishing Limited
The Lypiatts
15 Lansdown Road
Cheltenham
Glos GL50 2JA
UK

Edward Elgar Publishing, Inc.
William Pratt House
9 Dewey Court
Northampton
Massachusetts 01060
USA

A catalogue record for this book
is available from the British Library

Library of Congress Control Number: 2016962583

This book is available electronically in the **Elgar**online
Social and Political Science subject collection
DOI 10.4337/9781786436481

ISBN 978 1 78643 647 4 (cased)
ISBN 978 1 78643 648 1 (eBook)

Typeset by Servis Filmsetting Ltd, Stockport, Cheshire
Printed and bound in Great Britain by TJ International Ltd, Padstow

Contents

List of contributors   vii
Acknowledgments   ix

Introduction   1
Vladimir Popov

 1 Convergence? More developing countries are catching up   7
    Vladimir Popov and Jomo Kwame Sundaram

 2 World hegemonies and global inequalities   23
    *Sahan Savas Karatasli, Sefika Kumral, Daniel Pasciuti and
    Beverly J. Silver*

 3 Why growth rates differ   38
    Vladimir Popov

 4 Lessons from China and East Asia's catch up: the new
    structural economics perspective   53
    Justin Yifu Lin

 5 Why the 'Rest' doesn't need foreign finance   71
    Luiz Carlos Bresser-Pereira

 6 Global 'disorder' and the rise of finance: implications for the
    development project   91
    Jayati Ghosh

 7 Capitalism and India's democratic revolution   123
    Prabhat Patnaik

 8 Latin America's development: a short historical account   137
    José Antonio Ocampo

 9 Russia and the European Union: the clash of world orders   161
    Richard Sakwa

10 Contemporary imperialism   181
    Samir Amin

Conclusions   196
Piotr Dutkiewicz

Index   207

Contributors

Samir Amin, Third World Forum (Forum Tiers Monde), Dakar, Senegal

Luiz Carlos Bresser-Pereira, Getulio Vargas Foundation, São Paulo, Brazil

Piotr Dutkiewicz, Political Science Department, Carleton University, Canada

Jayati Ghosh, Centre for Economic Studies and Planning, School of Social Sciences, Jawaharlal Nehru University, New Delhi, India

Sahan Savas Karatasli, Princeton Institute of International and Regional Studies, Princeton University, and Arrighi Center for Global Studies, Johns Hopkins University, Baltimore, USA

Sefika Kumral, Department of Sociology and Arrighi Center for Global Studies, Johns Hopkins University, Baltimore, USA

Justin Yifu Lin, National School of Development, Peking University, and All-China Federation of Industry and Commerce

José Antonio Ocampo, Economic and Political Development Concentration, School of International and Public Affairs; Committee on Global Thought, and Initiative for Policy Dialogue, Columbia University, New York, USA

Daniel Pasciuti, Department of Sociology, Georgia State University, and Arrighi Center for Global Studies, Johns Hopkins University, Baltimore, USA

Prabhat Patnaik, Centre for Economic Studies and Planning, School of Social Sciences, Jawaharlal Nehru University, New Delhi, India

Vladimir Popov, Central Economics and Mathematics Institute, Russian Academy of Sciences, Moscow, Russia

Richard Sakwa, University of Kent, Canterbury, and Russia and Eurasia Programme, Royal Institute of International Affairs, Chatham House, London, UK

Beverly J. Silver, Department of Sociology and Arrighi Center for Global Studies, Johns Hopkins University, Baltimore, USA

Jomo Kwame Sundaram, The Institute of Strategic and International Studies, Malaysia, and Khazanah Research Institute, Kuala Lumpur, Malaysia

Acknowledgments

The editors would like to acknowledge the many people who gave their time and efforts to help this volume materialize. We are grateful to Carleton University's Faculty of Public Affairs and Justin Li, Director of the Confucius Institute at Carleton University, for support in partial funding of the technical editing of this volume. We are most grateful to all contributors for their very effective and remarkably problem-free collaboration. Piotr Dutkiewicz is grateful to Ewa Hebda-Dutkiewicz for her time and encouragement. It is our pleasure to also acknowledge the great support we received from Edward Elgar Publishing.

Introduction

Vladimir Popov

There is no shortage of predictions that the twenty-first century will see the bridging of the gap between the rich (the West) and the poor countries (the Rest), and especially predictions of the rise of Asia, notably two Asian giants – China and India. The goal of this book is to analyse factors behind the recent rise of many developing countries, to try to predict changes that may result from the continuation of this trend and plot possible scenarios of future development. It is argued that the 'rise of the Rest' would not only imply geopolitical shifts (the rise of Asia) but could lead to the proliferation of the new growth models in the Global South (à la East Asian dirigisme) and profound changes in the international economic relations (new world economic order).

Many growth promoting instruments that are now regarded as unfair are likely to gain legitimacy: industrial policies, including protectionism and undervaluation of the exchange rate ('exchange rate protectionism') to promote growth; freer transfer of technology from North to South, including the weakening of the protection of intellectual property rights; restriction on foreign direct investment (FDI) (such as requirements to ensure exports and technology transfer); restrictions on short-term capital flows to reduce volatility; barriers to brain drain from the South, but freer international migration regime for low skilled workers; increase in development assistance and creation of new international financial institutions to manage aid of the West to the South; creation of international stabilization funds for resource commodities; adoption of preferential environmental, labor, safety and other standards for developing countries (proportional caps on emissions, for instance, are unfair to the South, where per capita emissions are much lower than in the West).

New rules of international relations may explicitly limit the use of force only to cases of severe violations of non-political rights (that is, mass repressions, hunger, ethnic violence and so on) and prohibit the use of force against liberal authoritarian regimes (just for the sake of 'establishing democracy'). There is likely to be a reform of the United Nations (UN) institutions, including the Security Council, and greater respect for the prohibition of unilateral military interventions (without the consent of the UN). There are also certainly going to be 'surprise' changes in the world economy and international relations that we cannot predict today.

The chapters of this book examine the factors behind the 'rise of the Rest', discuss how robust these trends are, speculate about implications and consequences, and analyse possible scenarios.

Chapter 1 (Vladimir Popov, Jomo Kwame Sundaram) examines the trajectory of growth in the Global South. Before the 1500s all countries were roughly at the same level of development, but from the 1500s Western countries started to grow faster than the rest of the world and gross domestic product (GDP) per capita (purchasing power parity (PPP) based) by 1950 in the USA, the richest Western nation, was nearly five times higher than the world average. Since 1950 this ratio has stabilized – not only have Western Europe and Japan improved their relative standing in per capita income versus the USA but East Asia, South Asia and some developing countries in other regions have also started to bridge the gap with the West. After nearly half a millennium of growing economic divergence, the world seems to have entered the era of convergence. The factors behind these trends are analysed and scenarios and implications for the future considered.

Chapter 2 (Sahan Savas Karatasli, Sefika Kumral, Daniel Pasciuti and Beverly J. Silver) seeks to understand the significance of contemporary radical changes in world income distribution (most notably the recent rapid rise of China, India and a handful of other peripheral countries) by comparing the present with other periods of world-hegemonic transition. The empirical core of the chapter examines the interrelationship between the rise and decline of world hegemonies and changes in the global stratification of wealth (between-country inequality) from the sixteenth century to the present. It is found that (like the contemporary period) past periods of world-hegemonic crisis and transition have been characterized by radical transformations in the global hierarchy of wealth, although there are fundamental differences in the nature/direction of change in each transition. The chapter draws on world-systems theories of global inequality and hegemonic cycles to conduct a comparative-historical analysis of the dynamics underlying the long-term empirical patterning in the global distribution of wealth and power. The authors analyse the implications of their findings for the ongoing debate about whether we are in the midst of an impending 'great convergence' or on the verge of a major reversal of fortunes favoring the global North/West.

Chapter 3 (Vladimir Popov) argues that the single most important factor determining growth rates is institutions and that state capacity depends on the trajectories of institutional development. There are two major groups of developing countries: one (East and South Asia, Middle East and North Africa (MENA)) has relatively low inequalities, strong state institutions (low murder rate and share of shadow economy) and high savings and investment rate; the other (Latin America, sub-Saharan Africa, Russia and some former Soviet republics) has high inequalities, weak state institutions (high murder rate and shadow economy) and low savings and investment rate. Quite predictably the first group grows faster than the second. Shadow economy and murder rates are regarded as objective measures of institutional capacity of the state and it is shown that economic growth rates are strongly correlated with these objective measures. The greatest threat to the ongoing 'rise of the Rest' is the increase in income inequalities within countries from the 1980s. The continuation of this trend could result in social upheavals. As large masses of the population become disadvantaged due to increased inequalities, there may also be a rise of nationalism as rightist political groups blame all the disasters and misfortunes on globalization. This may lead to conflicts, if not wars, between countries, with collapse of international trade and capital flows, like in the 1930s. The world may go once again over the familiar twentieth-century historical track and there may be a pause in or even a reversal of globalization, as during the Great Depression when the outburst of protectionism led to the decline of the international trade and capital movements.

Chapter 4 (Justin Yifu Lin) examines what are the good policies for engineering an economic miracle. For a developing country to use the advantage of backwardness is to follow the comparative advantage determined by its own factor endowment in the industrial upgrading and technological innovation in a market economy with a facilitating state, as practiced in the East Asian economies and elaborated in the new structural economics. Regrettably, under the drive of nation building and the influence of prevailing structuralism, the governments in most developing countries adopted an import-substitution strategy in an attempt to defy their comparative advantages and jump directly to develop the advanced industries prevailing in the West. To implement the strategy, their governments have introduced all kinds of interventions and distortions to protect/subsidize the non-viable firms in the priority industries. Their economies became uncompetitive, growth unsustainable and crises hit frequently. Instead of advantage, the backwardness becomes disadvantage in achieving rapid, sustained growth. On the contrary, China and the East Asian economies have been lucky in not following the inappropriate prevailing thinking in their development and transition policies due to the constraints of poor resources and the inherent pragmatism in their culture. Their success reveals the nature and causes of a developing country's attempt to catch up

with the West. The new structural economics intends to theorize the East
Asian economies' successes and the failures of the 'Rest.'

Chapter 5 (Luiz Carlos Bresser-Pereira) argues that the 'Rest' will only be
able to catch up and grow more than the West if it goes against a 'received
truth': capital-rich countries should transfer their capitals to capital-poor
countries. This is the mantra that the West uses to occupy the markets
of developing countries with their finance and their multinationals. Yet,
New Developmentalism tells us that developing countries will invest (and
save) more if their current account is balanced, if not showing a surplus.
Starting from a balanced current account, the decision to incur deficits or
grow cum 'foreign savings' – actually, foreign finance – will appreciate the
exchange rate in the long term and discourage investment. In consequence,
we will have a high rate of substitution of foreign for domestic savings,
and foreign funds will finance consumption, not investment. Yet, developing countries have difficulty in realizing this, first, because the West and
their economists are adamant in recommending current account deficits;
second, because such a policy is consistent with high preference for immediate consumption; and, third, because economists in developing countries
are unable to criticize the 'growth cum foreign savings policy.'

Chapter 6 (Jayati Ghosh) explores the conditions in international trade
needed for countries wishing to industrialize and complete their development project. Essentially, when countries are open to external trade in a
world in which increasing returns activities are significant, the chances
are greater that such trade will cement existing divisions of labor between
countries because those countries with small or infant industries will be
unable to compete with the competition from larger or more advanced
industries elsewhere. When these trade patterns get disrupted, either
through conscious commercial policies in some countries or because of
other factors (such as wars, global recessions and so on) there are greater
chances of some countries breaking out of the existing division of labor
to diversify into higher value added increasing returns activities. So
'instability' in global trade can indeed generate possibilities for industrialization under certain conditions – though it should be noted that the implications vary greatly depending upon the domestic economic conditions
and policies adopted by such countries.

Chapter 7 (Prabhat Patnaik) looks at the recent seemingly successful
development in India and argues that high growth has been accompanied
by such an increase in economic inequality and such a process of 'social
retrogression' that the country faces the real threat of social disintegration.
The neoliberal regime, even while it increases economic and social inequality, creates a constituency for itself which additionally has a vested interest
in perpetuating the inequities of the social order. Neoliberal capitalism, in

other words, far from dealing destructive blows on the old social order as commonly expected actually plays the role of strengthening the inequities of the old social order, of worsening its fault lines. Capitalism in 'newly emerging societies,' in other words, does not just arrest the democratic revolution, in a world conjuncture, which facilitates a rapid growth and consolidation of capitalism, it tends actually to roll back the democratic revolution. Hence, advancing the democratic revolution, and even retaining the democratic gains already made, requires, in societies like India, a resistance against the capitalism that marks the current conjuncture, that is, 'neoliberal capitalism.'

Chapter 8 (José Antonio Ocampo) explores three essential features of the economic history of Latin America. The first is that it was the part of the developing world (together with the Caribbean) most deeply transformed by colonization, as well as the first to become politically independent in the early nineteenth century (with the exception of Cuba). The second, which it shares with other parts of the developing world, has been its position within the world's economic system as a commodity producer, a feature that, a few countries aside, it has been unable to overcome despite the industrialization drive that took place in particular from the 1930s to the 1970s. This has made the region vulnerable to trends and fluctuations in commodity prices. This vulnerability, which has been enhanced in different periods by highly unstable and pro-cyclical access to external financing, has given rise to severe crises when these two factors have coincided. The third is that it is, together with parts of sub-Saharan Africa, the most unequal region of the world.

Chapter 9 (Richard Sakwa) looks at the two models in Europe that have been in contestation since the end of the Cold War – Wider Europe and Greater Europe. The tension between the two is a central facet of the cold peace that has predominated for the last quarter century, and has colored Russia's relations with the European Union (EU). Wider Europe is based on the tried and tested model of the EU, whose arc of good governance, economic liberalism and societal welfare was projected ever further to the East. The Greater European project sought finally to end the division of the continent, respecting the various cultural and civilizational traditions yet united on the principles of free trade, visa-free travel and the assertion of a multipolar but united continent in world affairs as a moderating force. This 'Gaullist' vision of continental Europeanism envisaged building on the already existing 'variable geometry' of European integration (notably the Council of Europe and the Organization for Security and Co-operation in Europe (OSCE)) to create a genuinely multipolar and pluralist vision of continental unity. Instead, the Wider European project was increasingly subsumed into a rampant Atlanticism and forced the countries in between the EU and Russia to choose between the two. The result was the Ukraine conflict and the new division of Europe.

Chapter 10 (Samir Amin) argues that among the 'Rest' only China is implementing a national project of modern industrial development in connection with the renovation of family agriculture. But outside China the other so-called emergent countries of the South (Brazil, Russia, India and China – BRIC) still walk only on one leg: they are opposed to the depredations of militarized globalization, but remain imprisoned in the straightjacket of neoliberalism. It is suggested to move away, as much as possible, from the 'liberal' recipe and the electoral masquerade associated with it and to set up a brand of new state capitalism with a social dimension (social, not socialist). That system would open the road to eventual advances toward a socialization of the management of the economy and therefore authentic new advances toward an invention of democracy responding to the challenges of a modern economy.

Finally, in the Conclusions (Piotr Dutkiewicz) there is an attempt to summarize different views presented in the chapters of the book and to plot the main scenarios of future developments of the world system and international economic relations. It is argued that the book advances three main sets of arguments. The first group of arguments based on evidence from three macro regions is focused on reasons for a successful/unsuccessful economic convergence (see chapters by Popov and Sundaram, Popov, Lin, Ghosh, Ocampo). The second major argument – related to state–market relations in the Rest – proposes that a 'new developmentalism' should go beyond the reductionist approach of two dominating economic schools – structural (where the state rules) and neoliberal (where the unconstrained market dominates) toward a blend of both in a so-called 'dual track approach' to secure accelerated growth (see chapters by Popov, Lin, Bresser-Pereira). The third group of arguments advances ideas on policy measures and processes to improve 'well-being of the Rest' (see chapters by Popov, Lin, Patnaik, Ocampo, Sakwa, Amin).

1. Convergence? More developing countries are catching up

Vladimir Popov and Jomo Kwame Sundaram*

Normally, the literature on convergence and divergence in the world economy looks at beta-convergence and sigma-convergence. The former (beta-convergence) focuses on the coefficient of per capita GDP in the regression equation for growth rates – if positive, it means poorer countries are growing more slowly than the rich, and divergence is taking place; a negative coefficient means that growth is higher in poorer countries, which are therefore converging with the rich countries. The latter (sigma-convergence) looks at the standard deviation of the average per capita income of different countries from the world average – if it is increasing, national per capita incomes are diverging from the world average, whereas a decrease signifies convergence (see Maurer, 1995 for a survey).

We propose a more nuanced, substantial and less statistical approach to show that while some developing countries are converging with the rich countries, most others are not, with many falling behind. We accept Amsden's (2011) definition of the 'Rest' and her distinction between different trajectories of development – independent (East and South Asia) and integrationist (Latin America). In 1500, the ratio of average per capita income in the West (Western Europe) and the Rest (all other countries) was approximately 1:1. By 1900, the ratio of average per capita incomes in the West (Western Europe and its former settler colonies in North America and Australasia) and the global South (developing countries) had increased to 6:1, and remained around that level for the next century. If China is excluded, the ratio of average per capita incomes in rich countries and poor countries has actually increased, but not as quickly as in the past (Wade, 2004) (Figures 1.1 and 1.2).

In the second half of the twentieth century, however, examples of successful catch-up development grew. Japan, Hong Kong, Singapore,

* The views expressed are those of the authors and not necessarily those of their respective organizations. We are grateful to Anis Chowdhury, Piotr Dutkiewicz and Alex Trepelkov for important comments and discussion. The usual disclaimers apply.

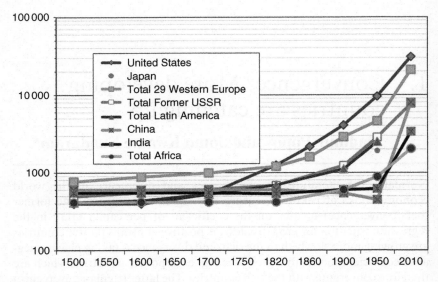

Source: Maddison Project (2013).

Figure 1.1   *Purchasing power parity gross domestic product (PPP GDP)*
               per capita in major countries and regions since 1500 (1990
               international Geary-Khamis dollars, log scale)

Taiwan and South Korea (in chronological order) were the only states/
territories that successfully caught up with the West to become developed
countries during 1950–90. In recent decades, growth has accelerated in
Southeast Asia (Sundaram et al., 1997) and China (Lin, 2012). Together
with the recent acceleration of growth in India, Bangladesh and some
other developing countries, this seems to signify a partial end to the
Great Divergence (Nayyar, 2013; WESS, 2010). It may well be that in the
twenty-first century, the world will experience a gradual global convergence
in income levels, with the gap between the North and the South narrowing
(Figures 1.1 and 1.2).

Other regions of the global South (especially sub-Saharan Africa, as well
as Eastern Europe and the former Soviet Union) have not been catching
up, with some even falling behind, especially in the 1980s and 1990s, during
the heyday of the Washington Consensus (Ocampo et al., 2007). But for
the first time in half a millennium, the *average* gap in per capita GDP has
stopped widening, and started to close for several major economies.

Measures of global income inequality also point to slowing economic
divergence in the second half of the twentieth century and even reversal of

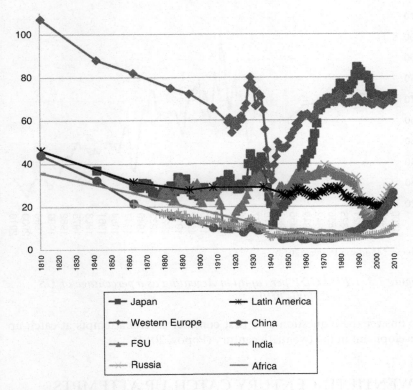

Note: FSU = Former Soviet Union.

Source: Maddison Project (2013).

Figure 1.2   PPP GDP per capita (in 1990 international Geary-Khamis dollars) as a percentage of US level

the trend with African and Asian decolonization after the Second World War. Inequalities among countries, if measured by weighting the average national incomes of countries by population size, clearly increased during 1820–1950, before falling thereafter. Even if China is excluded, the disparity between the global North and South did not rise significantly after 1950, as it had before. It remained stable during 1950–80, increased during 1980–2000 and fell afterwards (Milanovic, 2009).

Between-country disparities have started to decline since 2000, reversing the previous divergence in national income levels (WESS, 2014).

Why has the income gap between the West and the Rest, growing for nearly half a millennium, started to close? Is it temporary or enduring?

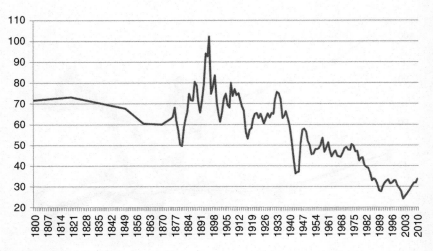

Source: Maddison Project (2013).

Figure 1.3   PPP GDP per capita in Argentina as a percentage of US level, 1800–2010

To answer these questions, we first consider several attempts at catch-up development in the twentieth century (Popov, 2014).

TWENTIETH-CENTURY CATCH-UP ATTEMPTS

There have been cases of losing rich country status, with the most prominent being Argentina in the twentieth century (Figure 1.3). But most countries that first industrialized in the eighteenth and nineteenth centuries (the West) have stayed rich, whereas the Rest stayed relatively poor, with per capita incomes below half the level of the West, until the mid-twentieth century.

From the 1930s to the 1960s, the USSR was the first major non-Western country to achieve successful catch-up development, narrowing its income gap with the West. However, in the 1970s and 1980s, the gap ceased to narrow, before widening dramatically in the early 1990s. Soviet catch-up development was clearly impressive until the 1970s. Russia had steadily fallen behind the West from the sixteenth to the nineteenth centuries, notwithstanding the much celebrated reforms of Peter the Great in the early eighteenth century, the elimination of serfdom in 1861 (Emancipation Act), as well as Witte's and Stolypin's reforms in the early twentieth century. However, for the first time in its history, Russia (USSR) started to

Source: Maddison Project (2013).

Figure 1.4   PPP GDP per capita in the USSR and Russia as a percentage of US level, 1820–2010

catch up with the West from the 1920s to the 1960s (Figure 1.4). In fact, until the 1960s, the USSR and Japan were the only two major countries that successfully closed their gaps with the West (Figure 1.2).

Although labor productivity growth rates in the 1930s were high (3 percent yearly), they were not exceptional unlike the higher rates observed in the 1950s (6 percent annually) (Figure 1.5) (Popov, 2007). Total factor productivity (TFP) growth rates increased from 0.6 percent annually in the 1930s to 2.8 percent in the 1950s before falling, even becoming negative, in the 1980s (Table 1.1). The 1950s was thus the 'golden period' of Soviet economic growth (Figure 1.6). Soviet growth in the 1950s was comparable to Japanese growth from the 1950s to the 1970s as well as Korean and Taiwanese growth during 1960–90; in Solovian growth accounting terms, rapid increases in labor productivity greatly offset declining capital productivity, so TFP increased (Table 1.1). But rapid Soviet economic growth was not sustained for even two decades (Figures 1.4 and 1.5), whereas it continued for three to four decades in East Asia, propelling Japan, South Korea and Taiwan into the ranks of developed countries.

Among the many reasons for the slowing Soviet growth rate from the 1960s to the 1980s, the most crucial appears to have been the 'computation problem' – the inability of a centrally planned economy to efficiently balance the supply and demand of millions of goods and services. This led to inadequate investments to replace retired fixed capital stock (Popov, 2007, 2014). As the task of renovating physical capital contradicted the short-term goal of fulfilling planned targets, Soviet planners preferred to

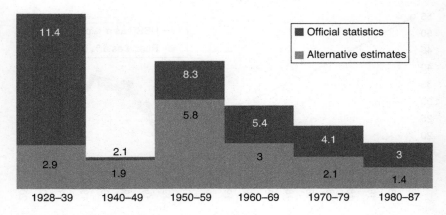

Source: Easterly and Fisher (1995).

Figure 1.5 *Annual labor productivity growth rates in the Soviet economy,*
1928–87 (%)

invest in new capacities instead of upgrading existing ones. Hence, after the massive investment of the 1930s during the Big Push, the highest productivity was achieved during the service life of the capital stock (averaging about 20 years) before the need for massive investment to replace retired stock emerged. Consequently, capital stock started to age rapidly, sharply reducing capital productivity and lowering labor productivity and the TFP growth rate. In retrospect, the relatively limited Chinese experience with central planning in the 1950s to 1970s before the transition to the market in the 1980s avoided such problems associated with the longer Soviet experience (1929–91). It is possible that a transition to a market economy in the Soviet Union would have been more successful if it had started in the 1960s (Popov, 2007).

Some countries in Latin America, Africa and the Middle East experienced growth spurts and seemed to be catching up with the West in the course of the second half of the twentieth century, but most of these growth spurts did not last. From the 1950s to the 1970s, many developing countries in Latin America and Africa experienced relatively fast growth, but most lost momentum after the debt crises of the early 1980s. Economists wrote about a 'lost decade' in Latin America (1980s) and longer stagnation in Africa (1980s, 1990s). The trajectory of Brazil (Figure 1.6), which experienced a half century of rapid growth before the 1980s, was arguably typical in this respect.

The first really successful catch-up in East Asia occurred after the Second World War – with five countries/territories having per capita

Table 1.1 Growth accounting for the USSR and Asian economies, 1928–87 (annual averages, %)

Country (period)	Output/worker	Capital/worker	Capital–output ratio	TPF growth (unit elasticity of substitution)	TPF growth assuming 0.4 elasticity of substitution
USSR (1928–39)	2.9	5.7	2.8	0.6	
USSR (1940–49)	1.9	1.5	-0.4	1.3	
USSR (1950–59)	5.8	7.4	1.6	2.8	1.1
USSR (1960–69)	3.0	5.4	2.4	0.8	1.1
USSR (1970–79)	2.1	5.0	2.9	0.1	1.2
USSR (1980–87)	1.4	4.0	2.6	-0.2	1.1
Japan (1950/57/65–1985/88/90)			2.3–3.2	1.7–2.5	
Korea (1950/60/65–1985/88/90)			2.8–3.7	1.7–2.8	
Taiwan (1950/53/65–1985/88/90)			2.6–3.1	1.9–2.4	

Source: Easterly and Fisher (1995).

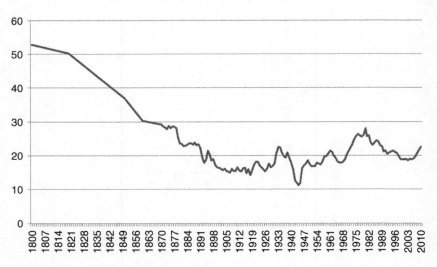

Source: Maddison Project (2013).

*Figure 1.6   PPP GDP per capita in Brazil as a percentage of US level,
            1800–2010*

incomes between 10 percent to 40 percent of the US level before the
Second World War, joining the rich countries' ranks in the second half of
the twentieth century – Japan, Hong Kong, Singapore, Taiwan and South
Korea in chronological order (Figure 1.7). The Hong Kong and Singapore
cases involve cities with populations of several million people, while the
other three are indisputable cases of successful catch-up development.

As with the Marshall Plan in Western Europe from the late 1940s, rapid
post-war growth in Japan, South Korea and Taiwan was helped by the
US interest in preventing the spread of communism in Asia. It provided
unprecedented aid as well as policy and fiscal space that played a crucial
role in accelerating economic growth and structural transformation in
these countries. With China accelerating growth and structural transformation in the 1950s, Malaysia, Thailand and Indonesia followed in the
1960s and 1970s, with Vietnam following later (Figure 1.8) with gradual
'Chinese-style' market-oriented reforms from the mid 1980s.

Such post-war growth accelerations were not unique to East Asia, including countries as varied as Botswana and Lesotho in sub-Saharan Africa,
India and Sri Lanka in South Asia, Israel, Oman and Tunisia in the Middle
East and North Africa (Figure 1.9). In Europe, rapid growth was observed
in Greece, Ireland, Montenegro, Portugal and Spain (Table 1.2). While no
developing countries outside East Asia have achieved per capita income of

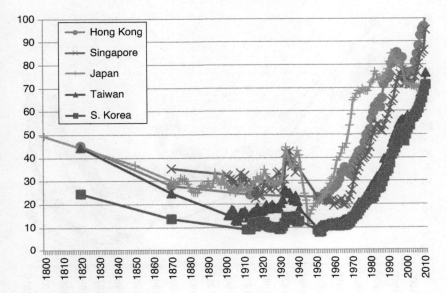

Source: Maddison Project (2013).

Figure 1.7 *PPP GDP per capita in countries/territories that took off after the Second World War (Japan, Taiwan, Hong Kong, Singapore, South Korea)*

over 50 percent of the US level, the gap in levels of economic development between the Rest and the West has stopped widening, and arguably been reversed, especially with the developed country slowdown following the 2008 financial crisis and the commodity price boom until 2014.

THE SOUTH AND THE WEST IN 2060

There are predictions that due to poor governance, corruption and lack of structural reforms, growth in emerging economies will slow down compared to the 2000–12 period when growth was untypically high (Åslund, 2013). But most predictions have been based on assumptions that particular growth-oriented policies will or will not be enacted.

Imagine, for a moment, a debate about future economic miracles in 1960: some would have bet on more free, democratic and entrepreneurial India and Latin America, while others would have envisioned the success of authoritarian (sometimes even communist), centralized and heavy-handed government interventionist East Asia. Today, the conventional

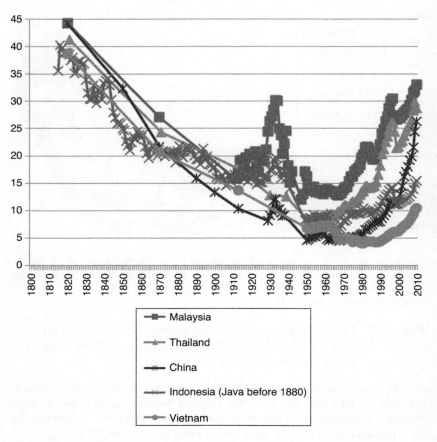

Source: Maddison Project (2013).

Figure 1.8   PPP GDP per capita in countries that took off in the 1960s and later (Southeast Asia, China)

wisdom seems to point to democratic countries encouraging individual freedoms and entrepreneurship, like Mexico and Brazil, Turkey and India, as those with future growth acceleration prospects, whereas currently authoritarian, rapidly growing regimes, like China and Vietnam, are thought to be doomed to experience growth slowdowns, if not recessions, in the near future. But conventional wisdom predictions today could prove to be wrong, as they did in the past.

If the growth rates of the recent half century (1960–2010) continue for another 50 years (2010–60), the world would look very different

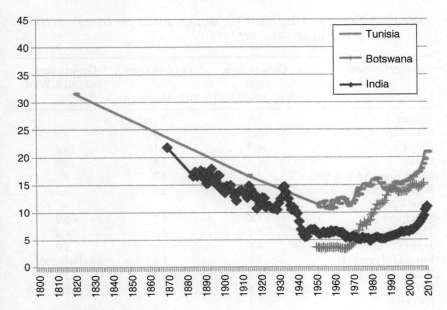

Source: Maddison Project (2013).

Figure 1.9   PPP GDP per capita in India, Tunisia, Botswana

(Figure 1.10) – China and Japan would have higher GDP per capita than the USA (if their population is five times larger, their total GDP will be six times higher than the US GDP). If other countries like India catch up with the West, Europe, Japan and the USA together would account for less than 20 percent of world output.

The rise of Asia, especially China, is usually discussed in geopolitical terms – new superpowers, multipolar versus unipolar world, changing global leadership – or in terms of increasing demand for global resources and contribution to global pollution and warming. But there are other, no less important, albeit less expected and less visible consequences of the rise of East and South Asia.

First, the rise of China, if it continues, would become a turning point for the world economy because for the first time in history, successful economic development on a major scale would be based on an indigenous, not a Western-type, economic model. Because China was so successful in catch-up development, it is no surprise that it has become extremely appealing to the developing world. The attractiveness of the recent Chinese economic growth experience could be compared with

Table 1.2   Fastest growing countries: average annual per capita real GDP growth rates, 1950–2013 (%)

Country (period)	Growth rate, 1950–2010 (Maddison)	Growth rate, 1960–2010 (Maddison)	Growth rate, 1960–2013 (WDI)
Taiwan	5.5	5.9	
S. Korea	5.5	5.9	6.0
China	4.9	5.1	6.6
Oman	4.7	4.8	6.5
Hong Kong SAR, China	4.5	4.7	4.2
Botswana (Maddison data until 2008)	4.5	5.1	5.7
Singapore	4.4	5.2	5.2
Thailand	4.2	4.4	4.4
Japan	4.1	3.5	3.2
Burma (Myanmar)	3.8	3.8	2.8 (1960–2004)
Spain	3.5	3.5	2.7
Greece	3.5	3.1	2.3
Portugal	3.3	3.2	3.0
Israel	3.3	2.9	3.0
Austria	3.2	2.7	2.6
Malaysia	3.2	3.8	3.8
Ireland	3.1	3.3	3.1 (1971–2013)
India	2.9	3.0	3.1
Indonesia	3.0	3.1	3.5
Tunisia	3.0	3.2	2.9
Montenegro	3.2 (1952–2010)	3.2	
Lesotho (until 2008)	2.9	2.9	3.1
Sri Lanka	2.5	2.9	3.4

Sources: Maddison Project (2013); World Development Indicators (WDI) database.

the popularity of the Soviet catch-up development model to the 'Third World' in the 1960s. Even though the Soviet model collapsed, the Chinese model has become heir to the Soviet model in this regard. While it is no longer a centrally planned economy, it is by no means the model of the private, liberal market economy recommended by the Washington Consensus.

For the last three decades, the rise of East Asia, and especially China more recently, has made some (state) interventionist or dirigiste model of catch-up development attractive. Not all developing countries have the same institutional capacities and capabilities as China – necessary

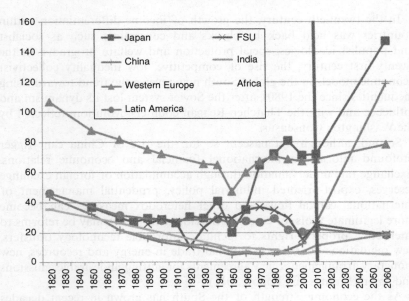

Note: FSU = Former Soviet Union.

Source: Maddison Project (2013).

Figure 1.10   PPP GDP per capita as a percentage of US level (2060 scenario, assuming continuation of 1960–2010 growth during 2010–60)

components of successful non-Western growth models. But many do, and those that do not may eventually be compelled by circumstances to strengthen institutional and learning capacities and capabilities.

Despite the considerable increase in income inequalities in China after 1985 (Gini coefficients rising),[1] the level of its inequalities may still be considered tolerable given the size of the country's population.[2]

[1]   Previously, the Chinese National Bureau of Statistics (NBS) conducted separate household surveys for rural and urban areas, so the Gini coefficients for the whole country were computed by researchers based on certain assumptions about rural–urban income disparities. By December 2012, the NBS had collected data for samples of 140 000 urban and rural households from 31 provinces, autonomous regions and municipalities. The NBS set up a new sample system and began to sample 400 000 households starting from 1 December 2012 (Zhao Qian, NBS reveals Gini coefficient methods. *Global Times*, 4 February 2013). According to this nationwide household survey, the Gini index in China was 47–49 percent in 2003–12.

[2]   It is important to take into account the size of the country – in terms of both territory and population. Three Chinese provinces (Guangdong, Shandong, Henan) have populations of over 95 million, another seven have over 50 million, that is, bigger than most states, so China should be compared with multistate regions, like the USA, India, European Union or

In the twentieth century, the growth of income differentiation within countries was held back by checks and constraints such as socialist and populist ideologies, social protection and welfare programs. In the twenty-first century, the rise of competitive, low inequality collectivist economic models in the global South may reverse the trend toward rising inequalities since the 1980s, after the Soviet system lost its dynamism and influence and with the Thatcher–Reagan counter-revolution, reflected by the Washington Consensus.

Second, although not nascent so far, the rise of China can trigger profound reforms to international financial and economic relations. Exchange rate undervaluation through accumulation of foreign exchange reserves, export-oriented industrial policy, prudential management of international capital flows and other heterodox measures can become more legitimate tools for catch-up development. There may be reforms to intellectual property rights to facilitate affordable technology transfers, new regulations for the international trade in energy and resources, new monetary arrangements, new agreements for cutting undesirable emissions and so on (Montes and Popov, 2011).

As the economic strength of the South has grown in recent decades (Figure 1.10), it has pushed and will push for changes in international economic relations more conducive to its catch-up development aspirations (Arrighi, 2007). The result may be more favorable conditions for catch-up development of all countries in the South and lower disparities between the world's 'rich' and 'poor.'

A new international economic order, the popular demand of the South in the 1970s, may be back on the agenda of North–South negotiations with the creation of new developing country institutions (BRICS' New Development Bank, Asian Infrastructure Investment Bank). Democratization of international economic relations – that is, adoption of rules-of-the-game giving greater voice and weight to the South together with acceleration of growth in the developing world – has the potential to make globalization 'good for the poor.'

If this interpretation of recent development trends is correct, the next region of successful catch-up development may well be South Asia and

Association of Southeast Asian Nations (ASEAN), rather than with particular states. In the EU 27, for instance, the coefficient of income inequality around 2005 was about 40 percent, with 23 percentage points coming from inter-country inequalities. In China (29 provinces), it was over 40 percent, with 24 percentage points due to inter-province disparities. In the USA, the inequality coefficient was similar (over 40 percent), but only six percentage points were due to income disparities among states (Milanovic, 2012). If China manages to reduce income inequalities among its provinces (and among the European Union countries) to a level close to the disparities among US states, overall inequality among citizens would fall significantly.

other regions willing to draw lessons from East Asian experiences as most appropriate to their own circumstances. The former Soviet Union, Latin America, sub-Saharan Africa and even the rest of Asia can eventually catch up and the global South would come closer to the West in terms of productivity and per capita income.

REFERENCES

Amsden, Alice (2011). *The Rise of 'The Rest'. Challenges to the West from Late-industrializing Economies*. New York: Oxford University Press.

Arrighi, Giovanni (2007). *Adam Smith in Beijing: Lineages of the Twenty-first Century*. London: Verso.

Åslund, Anders (2013). Why growth in emerging economies is likely to fall. Working Paper, Peterson Institute for International Economics, November, Washington, DC.

Easterly, William and Stanley Fisher (1995). The Soviet economic decline. *The World Bank Economic Review*, **9** (3), 341–71.

Lin, Justin (2012). The *Quest for Prosperity: How Developing Economies Can Take Off*. Princeton, NJ: Princeton University Press.

Maddison Project (2013). The Maddison Project. www.ggdc.net/maddison/maddison-project/home.htm (accessed 13 February 2017).

Maurer, Rainer (1995). OLS-estimation of conditional and unconditional sigma- and beta-convergence of per capita income: implications of Solow-Swan and Ramsey-Cass models. Kiel Working Paper No. 698, Kiel Institute for the World Economy.

Milanovic, Branko (2009). Global inequality recalculated: the effect of new 2005 PPP estimates on global inequality. MPRA Paper No. 16538, University Library of Munich, Munich.

Milanovic, Branko (2012). Does economic inequality set the limits to EU expansion? Paper presented at the Conference on Sovereign Insolvency, November, Opatija.

Montes, Manuel and Vladimir Popov (2011). Bridging the gap: a new world economic order for development. In Craig Calhoun and Georgi Derlugian (eds), *Aftermath. New Global Economic Order*. New York: SUNY Press, pp. 119–48.

Nayyar, Deepak (ed.) (2013). *Catch Up: Developing Countries in the World Economy*. New Delhi: Oxford University Press.

Ocampo, J.A., J.K. Sundaram and Rob Vos (2007). Explaining growth divergences. In J.A. Ocampo and J.K. Sundaram (eds), *Growth Divergences. Explaining Differences in Economic Performance*. Hyderabad: Orient Longman, pp. 10–33.

Popov, Vladimir (2007). Life cycle of the centrally planned economy: why Soviet growth rates peaked in the 1950s. In Saul Estrin, Grzegorz Kolodko and Milica Uvalic (eds), *Transition and Beyond*. Basingstoke: Palgrave Macmillan, pp. 35–57.

Popov, Vladimir (2014). *Mixed Fortunes: An Economic History of China, Russia and the West*. New York: Oxford University Press.

Sundaram, J.K., with Chen Yun Chung, Brian C. Folk, Irfan ul-Haque, Pasuk Phongpaichit, Batara Simatupang and Mayuri Tateishi (1997). *Southeast Asia's Misunderstood Miracle: Industrial Policy and Economic Development in Thailand, Malaysia and Indonesia*. Boulder: Westview.

Sundaram, J.K. and Vladimir Popov (2015). Income inequalities in perspective. ESS Document No. 46, International Labour Office, Geneva, and Initiative for Policy Dialogue (IPD), Columbia University, New York.
Wade, Robert H. (2004). Is globalization reducing poverty and inequality? *World Development*, **32** (4), 567–89.
WDI database (2010). World Bank, Washington, DC.
WESS (2010). *World Economic and Social Survey 2010. Retooling Global Development*. New York: United Nations.
WESS (2014). *World Economic and Social Survey 2014: Reducing Inequality for Sustainable Development*. New York: United Nations. www.un.org/en/development/desa/policy/wess/wess_archive/2014wess_overview_en.pdf (accessed 13 February 2017).

2. World hegemonies and global inequalities

Sahan Savas Karatasli, Sefika Kumral, Daniel Pasciuti and Beverly J. Silver

INTRODUCTION

The United Nations Development Programme (UNDP) devoted the theme of the 2013 *Human Development Report* to 'The Rise of the South,' arguing that 'never in history have the living conditions and prospects of so many people changed so dramatically and so fast' as they have in the past two decades (UNDP, 2013, p. 11). As Vladimir Popov notes (in this volume), 'for the first time in 500 years the average gap in per capita GDP has stopped widening and started to close for some major economies.'

Many have interpreted this trend as the sign of a 'great convergence.' Martin Wolf (2011) argued that 'the huge economic advantage over the rest of humanity' that 'the peoples of western Europe and their most successful former colonies achieved' – the 'Great Divergence' of the nineteenth and early twentieth centuries – 'is being reversed more quickly than it emerged.' Neo-modernization and 'flat-world' theories are reemerging with claims that 'globalization' is now leading to the long anticipated convergence or 'catching up' (Rostow, 1960) of the underdeveloped world with the wealth standards of the developed world (Firebaugh, 2000; Mahbubani, 2013; Sala-i-Martin, 2006; see also Milanovic, 2013).

There are contrarians who argue that we have seen analogous periods of declining inequality between countries over the past half-century, but these periods were short-lived and followed by sharp reversals. Most notably, in the 1970s there were high expectations that a large cluster of rapidly industrializing middle income countries – ranging from Brazil and Mexico to South Africa and Poland – were not only closing the gap in terms of levels of industrialization but were also catching up with the 'developed' countries in per capita income levels. But economic 'miracles' turned to 'mirages' with debt crises, International Monetary Fund (IMF)-imposed structural adjustment and the ensuring 'lost development decade' of the 1980s.

The short-lived nature of this catching up was consistent with world-systems and dependency theorists (Amin, 1974; Cardoso and Faletto, 1979; Chase-Dunn and Rubinson, 1977; Frank, 1967; Wallerstein, 1979) who pointed to systemic processes that ensured the reproduction of the overall global hierarchy of wealth – a core–periphery bimodal distribution for dependistas and a core–semiperiphery–periphery trimodal distribution for world-systemists. While from a world-systems perspective, it was possible (even expected) that individual small countries might move up (and down), the unequal overall hierarchy of per capita wealth on a global scale was expected to remain unchanged. As long as we were in a capitalist world-economy, widespread long-term upward mobility of countries was not conceivable. Empirical studies that focused on the pattern of global inequality over the course of the twentieth century bore out this theoretical prediction of a relatively stable trimodal distribution of world population with only rare (and demographically small) cases of upward (or downward) mobility across the three zones (Arrighi and Drangel, 1986; see also Arrighi et al., 1996, 2003; Babones, 2005; Korzeniewicz and Martin, 1994; Korzeniewicz and Moran, 1997; Wade, 2004).

Thus, the fundamental question we address in this chapter is whether the latest round of catching up – this time characterized by demographically large, low income countries (most notably China and India) that are narrowing the per capita income gap with middle income countries – will prove as ephemeral as it was in the 1970s – a prelude to another 'lost development decade' – or whether we are witnessing an epochal shift; and if the latter, should this epochal shift be understood as a 'great convergence' or as a fundamentally different type of transformation.

Needless to say, our question cannot be answered by a linear projection of trends from the last two or three decades. If we understand reproduction and transformation of the global hierarchy of wealth as something rooted in the systemic processes of global capitalism, then we need a historically grounded theoretical lens and *longue durée* empirical perspective that encompasses the time-space of historical capitalism, including the period leading up to the 'Great Divergence.'

Giovanni Arrighi's (1994 [2010]) *The Long Twentieth Century* provides us with a historically grounded theoretical lens with which to address this question. Arrighi reconstructs the history of capitalism as being composed of four overlapping long centuries or systemic cycles of accumulation: (1) a Genoese-Iberian cycle, stretching from the fifteenth through the early seventeenth centuries; (2) a Dutch cycle, stretching from the late sixteenth through the late eighteenth centuries; (3) a British cycle, stretching from the mid eighteenth through the early twentieth centuries; and (4) a US cycle, stretching from the late nineteenth century to the present. Each cycle is named after (and defined by) the particular complex of governmental and business agencies that led the world capitalist system, first toward material and then toward the financial expansions that jointly constitute the cycle.

Key elements of Arrighi's theory of systemic cycles of accumulation (SCAs) are relevant to the question posed in this chapter. System-wide financial expansions – such as we are witnessing today – have characterized the end of all previous systemic cycles of accumulation; they have been a sign that the limits of the previous material expansion have been reached and they are one of the mechanisms through which the conditions for a new material expansion emerges (Braudel, 1984). Historically, periods of financial expansion have been periods of world-hegemonic transition, in the course of which a new leadership emerged interstitially and over time reorganized the system. Especially important for the question at hand, each of these financial expansion periods has been characterized by a shift in the geographical center of world capital accumulation – from Southern Europe to Northern Europe in the second half of the sixteenth century, to the British Isles in the mid eighteenth century, and to North America in the late nineteenth and early twentieth centuries.

Notwithstanding the use of the term systemic *cycles* of accumulation in *The Long Twentieth Century,* Arrighi builds an evolutionary theory in which world capitalism undergoes a fundamental transformation from one systemic cycle to the next. Each new long century and each new hegemony (Dutch versus British versus US) was based on a fundamental reorganization of the global system rather than the result of the rise and decline of great powers within an invariant structure (Arrighi, 1994 [2010]; Arrighi and Silver, 1999).

As Arrighi (1994 [2010], p. 374) notes, the role played by financial expansions in creating successive shifts in the geographical center of capital accumulation (and in the restarting of each major new phase of capitalist development) can be found in embryonic form in *Capital*. Marx (1867 [1992], pp. 755–6) took note of a historical sequence whereby expansions of the financial system recurrently played a key role in the transfer of surplus capital from declining to rising geographical centers of capitalist trade and production. Marx observed a sequence that started with Venice, which 'in her decadence' lent large sums of money to Holland; followed by Holland, which lent out 'enormous amounts of capital, especially to its great rival England' when the former 'ceased to be the nation preponderant in commerce and industry'; and finally England, which was doing the same vis-à-vis the United States in Marx's own day.

The question for us becomes whether the current 'rise of the Rest' can be interpreted as the latest in a series of major shifts in the geographical center of capital accumulation and fundamental reorganizations of the world capitalist system. In order to answer this question, the next sections analyse the global distribution of wealth from 1500 to 2008. Consistent with Arrighi's theory of systemic cycles of accumulation, we find that the global hierarchy of wealth has been characterized by successive fundamental reorganizations. More specifically, we find that the global wealth distribution shifts from unimodal to bimodal during the Dutch-led financial expansion and transition to British-led world hegemony in the late eighteenth and early nineteenth centuries, and then from bimodal to trimodal during the British led financial expansion and transition to US world hegemony in the late nineteenth and early twentieth centuries. In the early twenty-first century, a quadrimodal distribution of global inequality is emerging.

Seen from this angle of vision, what we have been observing since the late 1990s – namely, the rise of China, India and a cluster of peripheral countries from the global South – may mark the dissolution of the relatively stable trimodal distribution of the twentieth century. In other words, we may be witnessing the fourth in a series of fundamental reorganizations of the global hierarchy of wealth. However, there is a fundamental difference between the current restructuring of the global hierarchy of wealth and the previous three in that it is the first time that the rising centers of capital accumulation are located outside the global North/West. Nevertheless, the current transformation in the pattern of global inequality is not occurring in the way expected by modernization theory. The distribution of wealth in the world-economy is not converging toward a unimodal distribution, nor is China and India or the rest of the non-core catching up with the per capita wealth and consumption standards of core countries.

THE CHANGING DISTRIBUTION OF GLOBAL WEALTH IN THE *LONGUE DURÉE*

The empirical analysis of the chapter builds upon and extends Arrighi and Drangel's (1986) method which was designed to assess the validity of Wallerstein's claim that the capitalist world-economy is characterized by a stable trimodal structure. Arrighi and Drangel (1986) suggested that the existence (or non-existence) of distinct zones of the capitalist world-economy can be empirically observed through an examination of smooth distributions of world population along a log gross national income (GNI) per capita hierarchy. In order to develop a *longue durée* analysis of the changing global wealth hierarchy, we revised their method using (1) Gaussian kernel densities (instead of smoothed histograms);

and (2) a revised version of Maddison's gross domestic product (GDP) and population estimates, where missing values are imputed using linear interpolation and extrapolation methods based on the growth rates of the nearest neighbor as used by Bourguignon and Morrisson (2002).

As Figure 2.1 shows, the global distribution of wealth was not stable over the *longue durée*. It was a unimodal distribution from the sixteenth century to the nineteenth century, it moved from a unimodal to a bimodal distribution in the early nineteenth century (during the transition from the Dutch to the British world hegemony), and from a bimodal to a tri-modal distribution in the late nineteenth century (during the transition from the British to US world hegemony). Furthermore, since the turn of the twenty-first century (during the crisis of the US world hegemony) the world-economy has been moving from a trimodal to a new quadrimodal structure. To understand these successive transformations, the next four sections examine the relationship between these successive transformations in the global hierarchy of wealth and systemic cycles of accumulation.

POLARIZATION WITHOUT GREAT DIVERGENCE: UNIMODAL DISTRIBUTION OF THE LONG SIXTEENTH CENTURY

From the sixteenth century to the eighteenth century, the world-economy had a clear unimodal distribution of wealth (Figure 2.1). The majority of the world population was stationed in the middle of the income distribution, constituting a singular mode. This unimodal distribution was a consequence of the low level of variation of wealth between different regions of the world in this early period of historical capitalism. While differentiation of wealth between different regions of the world was not high enough to disturb this unimodal structure until the nineteenth century, it was high enough to produce an emerging differentiation of wealth between world regions. Western Europe – that is, the Italian peninsula (Italy), the Low Lands (the Netherlands, Belgium) and the United Kingdom – was at the top of the wealth scale (with log GDP per capita values around 2.9–3.0 in 1500 and around 3.00–3.30 in 1700). The majority of the world population and most world regions – including countries like China, India, Ottoman Turkey and Russia – were stationed around 2.75 log GDP per capita from 1500 to 1700. At the bottom of the world hierarchy was a group of Latin American and sub-Saharan African regions/countries.[1]

---

[1] For more detailed figures showing the global distribution of wealth presented in Figure 2.1, see Karatasli (forthcoming).

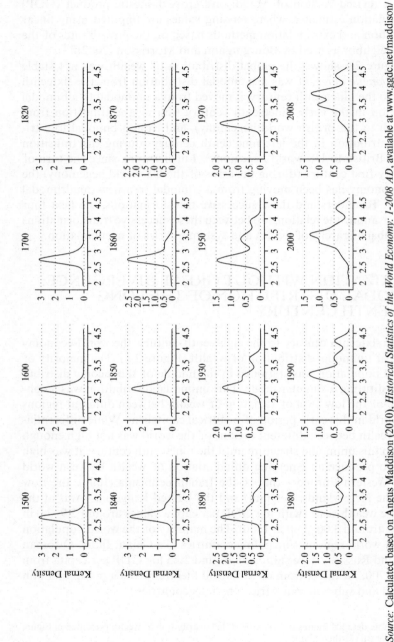

Source: Calculated based on Angus Maddison (2010), *Historical Statistics of the World Economy: 1-2008 AD*, available at www.ggdc.net/maddison/ Historical_Statistics/horizontal-file_02-2010.xls. For details on the data and methods used to produce Figure 2.1, see Karatasli (forthcoming).

Figure 2.1   Changing modes of wealth distribution in the world-economy, 1500–2008

28

Interestingly, from 1500 to 1700, upward and downward mobility at the right tail of the unimodal distribution resembled the dynamics of systemic cycles of capitalist accumulation as explained by Arrighi (1994 [2010]). Former centers of systemic cycles of accumulation (that is, the northern Italian city states) were at the top of this hierarchy in the fifteenth century, but they gradually declined. The center of the new systemic cycle of capitalist accumulation and the emerging hegemonic power of the capitalist world-economy of the era – the United Provinces/Holland – had the highest upward mobility from 1500 to 1700. The United Kingdom – center of the systemic cycle of accumulation and the world-hegemonic power of the long nineteenth century – was also gradually rising as the crisis of the Dutch hegemony started to unfold in the eighteenth century.

As Arrighi (1994 [2010]) observed, these transformations were linked to financial expansion processes initiated by declining centers of historical capitalism. From the mid-sixteenth century to the mid-seventeenth century, the financial expansion process was led by Genoese merchant-traders – who were the backbone of the Great Discoveries and the rise of the transatlantic trade by Iberian powers (that is, Spain and Portuguese) in the long sixteenth century. As the initiators of the financial expansion process gradually started to decline, the new recipients of global financial flows (that is, Dutch business-government complexes) started a new systemic cycle of accumulation on a global scale and experienced significant upward mobility.

At the lower end of this unimodal distribution, we see a group of African regions that were growing at the rate of the world average as well as some Latin American and Eastern European regions who were growing slightly faster than African regions. Considering that the capitalist world-economy had not yet incorporated African regions but only some Latin American and Eastern European regions (Hopkins and Wallerstein, 1982), it appears that in this early period of historical capitalism some peripheral regions of the capitalist world-economy (that is, American settler colonies) were doing relatively better than 'external areas' of the capitalist world-economy. More interestingly, we do not see significant downward mobility among East Asian colonies as a result of Portuguese expansion in the Indian Ocean or Dutch colonization of the Indonesian archipelago. These patterns are the opposite of the trends during the British systemic cycle of the long nineteenth century.

Asian economies did not experience significant downward mobility in this early period of historical capitalism because the Asia-centered world-economy was too large and too strong to be affected by activities of European merchants in this era. It would not be an exaggeration to suggest that European merchants only added new communities to the already diverse and heterogeneous merchant populations in Asia (Braudel, 1984). While European military intrusion in Asia was much higher during the Dutch than the Genoese-Iberian systemic cycles, it still was not high enough to disarticulate the Asia-centered world-economy. Hence, despite gradual polarization, a Great Divergence process did not take place in this era.

FIRST GREAT DIVERGENCE: FROM UNIMODAL TO BIMODAL DISTRIBUTION OF WEALTH

From the eighteenth century to the mid nineteenth century (during the transition from Dutch to British world hegemony), the world-economy gradually moved from a unimodal to a bimodal distribution (see Figure 2.1). This transition – analogous to Pomeranz's (2000) *Great Divergence* process – was a consequence of a major bifurcation in the global distribution of wealth. This first Great Divergence emerged due to the upward mobility of Western Europe, especially the United Kingdom and some of the settler colonies of the British Empire (including the United States, Canada, Australia, New Zealand), which rapidly moved from the lower end of the global distribution of wealth to its higher end. Together with higher growth rates in Europe, this upward mobility consti-tuted these 'Western' regions as a distinct cluster in the global distribution of wealth – widely labeled as the 'core.' The rest of the world constituted a second distinct 'peripheral' mode of the world-economy.

The effects of the transition from the Dutch to the British systemic cycle of accumulation on mobility at the higher end of the global wealth distribution were similar to the transition from the Genoese (Italian) to the Dutch systemic cycle of accumulation. In the 1700–1850 period, the leading center of the systemic cycle of capitalist accumulation and the declining world-hegemonic power (that is, United Provinces/Netherlands) initiated a financial expansion process and had lower growth rates on a logarithmic scale than most other core countries. Similar to its Dutch counterpart in the previous era, the British Empire – as the major recipient of global financial flows, the emerging center of the systemic cycle of accumulation, the ini-tiator of industrial capitalism, and the new world-hegemonic power of the long nineteenth century – was rising to the top of the global wealth hier-archy together with some of its settler colonies. One of these colonies, the United States, not only gained independence during this transition period, but would become the world hegemon in the next long century.

There are two interesting patterns regarding the mobility at the middle and the lower end of the global wealth distribution from 1700 to 1850.

First, the rise of the 'West' in 1700–1850 did not coincide with a simultaneous decline of the 'Rest' of the world as a whole. On the contrary, the majority of world regions remained in their relative positions from 1700–1850. This can partly be explained by the limited expansion of the capitalist world-economy in this period. After all, in the 1700–1850 era, the European-centered capitalist system – Wallerstein's capitalist world-economy (with a hyphen) – had not yet incorporated the China-centered world-system in East Asia, the Southeast Asian hinterland of this system, or sub-Saharan Africa (except for some areas on the Western African coast). In addition to the Americas (which had already been incorporated), the only new areas incorporated during the transition from the Dutch to the British systemic cycle were parts of the West African coast, Russia, the Ottoman Empire and the Indian subcontinent.

Second, unlike the previous 1500–1700 era, peripheral regions of the capitalist world-economy were no longer doing relatively better than the external areas of capitalism. On the contrary, the newly incorporated and peripheralized regions of the world-economy experienced a significant loss of wealth and economic power. The clearest example is the Indian subcontinent. The military, political and economic conquest of India took place during the second half of the eighteenth century (see Arrighi et al., 1999, p. 223). These newly incorporated and peripheralized regions of the Indian subcontinent – including India, Pakistan, Sri Lanka, Bangladesh and Nepal regions – experienced a significant downward mobility in the global distribution of wealth, which started the gradual disarticulation of the Asia-centered world-economy. This was how a bimodal distribution of wealth emerged in the midst of the Dutch-led financialization and the advance of industrial capitalism.

SECOND GREAT DIVERGENCE: FROM BIMODAL TO TRIMODAL DISTRIBUTION OF WEALTH

While the world-economy had a relatively stable bimodal distribution from the mid to the late nineteenth century (partly resembling the center-periphery structure as described by dependency theorists), at the turn of the twentieth century a trimodal distribution of global wealth emerged (resembling the core–semiperiphery–periphery structure postulated by world-systems theory). This transition from a bimodal to a trimodal distribution occurred due to a second bifurcation among non-core locations that took place during the crisis of British world hegemony beginning around the 1873/96 depression and the rise of the British-led financial expansion (see Figure 2.1). This second bifurcation divided the periphery into two distinct groups. The lower half (the new periphery of the long twentieth century) was mainly composed of sub-Saharan African regions and the South and East Asian regions/countries (the Indian subcontinent and China and its former hinterland). The upper half (the emergent semiperiphery) was mainly composed of countries in Southern Europe (Italy, Spain, Greece), Eastern Europe and Western Asia (including Russia and Ottoman Empire/Turkey) and Latin America.

During the transition from British to US world hegemony the ongoing rise of the core went hand in hand with a sharp economic decline of East Asia and South Asia. This rapid decline was a consequence of the British Empire's ability to subordinate and disarticulate the China-centered East Asian world-economy (Arrighi et al., 1999, p. 225) and the incorporation of East Asia into the British-centered capitalist system using its military might (Arrighi, 2007).

Hence, there is some truth in Andre Gunder Frank's claim that the Chinese decline started only after 1860, not before (Frank, 2015, pp. 3–8, 100). While the First Opium War of 1839–42 and the Nanjing Treaty of 1842 weakened the Chinese Empire, the real decline did not come until the Second Opium War of 1856–60, interlinked with social rebellions and another round of military conflicts. These struggles were decisive in undermining the traditional economic structures of the Qing dynasty, producing the rapid decline of China and disarticulating the China-centered East Asian world-economy in the last quarter of the nineteenth century (Arrighi, 2007, pp. 336–44; Frank, 2015, p. 100). Together with the imperial race for colonization of sub-Saharan Africa during the last quarter of the nineteenth century and the continued exploitation of the Indian subcontinent, the decline of the China-centered East Asian world-economy split the periphery into two zones, creating the peripheral and the semiperipheral regions of the twentieth century.

THIRD GREAT DIVERGENCE: FROM TRIMODAL TO QUADRIMODAL DISTRIBUTION OF WEALTH

The three-tiered global wealth structure emerged in the late nineteenth century, stabilized after the terminal crisis of the British world hegemony (the 1929 Great Depression) and remained relatively stable until the 1990s. Despite the expectations of modernization theorists and all developmentalist attempts, the gap between core, semiperipheral and peripheral locations did not disappear in the twentieth century. There was a strong stability in the trimodal structure (Arrighi and Drangel, 1986). While the semiperipheral mode came close to catching up to the core mode in the

1968–73 era, in the course of the next two decades, the trimodal distribution was restabilized when the world-hegemonic power and its allies started to restructure the global political-economy by switching from 'the development project' to 'the globalization project' (McMichael, 2012). In both the Reagan and Clinton eras, these transformations went hand in hand with financial expansion processes led by the world-hegemonic power.

Like all previous financial expansion periods, the US-led financial expansion fundamentally changed the global hierarchy of wealth. The relatively stable trimodal distribution started to dissolve by the late twentieth and early twenty-first century, producing a quadrimodal distribution of global wealth (see Figure 2.1). The transition from the trimodal to quadrimodal distribution has similarities as well as stark differences with previous transition periods. While the key similarity is the role played by the financial expansion process led by the declining centers of capitalism, the main difference is the geo-economic position of the recipients of global financial flows. Unlike the previous Genoese, Dutch or British financial expansion periods, this time it was not core or semiperipheral 'Western' regions/countries (such as the United Kingdom in the late eighteenth century or the United States in the late nineteenth century) which attracted global financial flows and managed to start a new system-wide expansion of trade and production but a cluster of peripheral East and South Asian countries, including those with massive populations such as China and India (see Palat, 2012). Similar to previous financial expansion periods, this led to a rapid upward mobility of the new centers of material expansion of trade and production in the late twentieth and early twenty-first centuries. Because of their unique geo-economic locations, their gigantic populations, and their South–South commerce and production networks, upward mobility of these regions resulted in the advance of a cluster of peripheral countries to the middle of the global income distribution.

This trend, however, does not indicate the upward mobility of the world periphery as a whole. Similar to analogous past periods, we witness another major bifurcation of the periphery. The upward mobility of some East and South Asian countries (for example, China, India, Thailand) and some African countries (for example, Botswana, Lesotho) went hand in hand with significant downward mobility – sometimes even in absolute log GDP per capita level – of sub-Saharan African countries (such as Zaire, Niger, Burundi, Central African Republic, Liberia, Somalia), some Central/South American countries (such as Haiti, Nicaragua) and some Middle Eastern countries (such as Iraq). Hence, it would be a mistake to conceive of this process as a great convergence. Rather than producing a unimodal distribution, this double movement of upward and downward mobility is transforming former peripheral and semiperipheral zones and producing a quadrimodal distribution with a four-tiered structure consisting of a lower periphery, an upper periphery, a new expanded semiperiphery and core regions. Contrary to the predictions of modernization theory, however, there is not much change in the size and composition of the core locations either (Karatasli, forthcoming). In sum, in the early twenty-first century, there is no 'catching up' with core locations but instead another reconfiguration of the hierarchy of wealth among non-core locations.

CONCLUSION

Seen from the theoretical angle of vision taken in this chapter, the current 'rise of the Rest' can be interpreted as the latest in a series of major reorganizations of the global hierarchy of wealth over the *longue durée* of historical capitalism. The relatively stable trimodal distribution of the twentieth century has broken down and, even if rising countries such as China and India experience serious slowdowns and crises – as will almost certainly be the case – we are unlikely to return to a stable trimodal pattern. Although such crises should put to rest neo-modernization projections of an impending unimodal distribution and 'catching-up' of the Rest with the global North/West, the transformation in the global hierarchy of wealth that has taken place in the early twenty-first century is far more fundamental (in demographic and wealth generation and so on) than the 'catching up' that occurred in the 1970s.

To put it within the context of Arrighi's theory of systemic cycles of accumulation, whereas the 'catching up' development of the 1970s was one of the many signs of the 'signal crisis' of US world hegemony, the more fundamental transformation of the early twenty-first century is one of the many signs that we have entered the 'terminal crisis' period of US world hegemony. In the 1980s and 1990s the United States (and the global North/West more generally) was able to reflate its power temporarily – and experience a belle époque – among other things by becoming the center of a major system-wide financial expansion. But financial expansions – as discussed above – have historically been among the main mechanisms through which new geographical centers of capital accumulation have emerged.

If this analysis is correct, then the crises we will be witnessing will not herald a return to a stable trimodal distribution of income, as happened in the 1980s and 1990s. At the same time, it is important to point out that we are not arguing that a stable quadrimodal distribution of global wealth has emerged. We have not entered a new period of world hegemony; rather, we have entered a (potentially long) period of hegemonic breakdown and systemic chaos. We may very well see significant turbulence in the global hierarchy of wealth interlinked with significant turbulence in the world-economic and political system as a whole. To paraphrase Antonio Gramsci (1971, pp. 275–6), 'the old is dying and the new cannot be born; in this inter-regnum a great variety of morbid symptoms appear.' The more the global North/West (and the United States in particular) struggle to maintain preeminent status in the wealth hierarchy, the more these morbid symptoms will multiply. Likewise, the longer that all countries seek to follow the eco-logically destructive Western development model, the more these morbid symptoms will multiply (see Arrighi and Silver, 1999, pp. 288–9).

The emergence of a stable new global order will require an even more profound social, political and economic reorganization of the world system than has been the case in past centuries. For the 'rise of the West' was premised on a model of capitalist accumulation that externalized the costs of reproduction of nature and of labor for the vast majority of the world's population. Accommodating the 'rise of the Rest' – that is, accom-modating all of humankind – will require an approach to development that prioritizes the protection of nature and human livelihoods over profits – in other words, a dramatically different model than the one that has prevailed over the *longue durée* of historical capitalism.

REFERENCES

Amin, Samir. 1974. *Accumulation on a World-Scale*. New York: Monthly Review Press.

Arrighi, Giovanni. 1994 [2010]. *The Long Twentieth Century: Money, Power, and the Origins of Our Times*. London: Verso.

Arrighi, Giovanni. 2007. *Adam Smith in Beijing: Lineages of the Twenty-First Century*. London: Verso.

Arrighi, Giovanni and Jessica Drangel. 1986. 'Stratification of the World-Economy: An Exploration of the Semiperipheral Zone'. *Review* **10**(1), 9–74.

Arrighi, Giovanni and Beverly Silver. 1999. *Chaos and Governance in the Modern World-System*. Minnesota: Minnesota University Press.

Arrighi, Giovanni, Roberto Patricio Korzeniewicz, David Consiglio and Timothy P. Moran. 1996. 'Modeling Zones of the World-Economy: A Polynomial Regression Analysis (1964–1994)'. Paper presented at the 1996 Annual Meeting of the American Sociological Association, New York City.

Arrighi, Giovanni, Iftikhar Ahmad and Miin-wen Shih. 1999. 'Western Hegemonies in World-Historical Perspective'. In Giovanni Arrighi and Beverly Silver (eds), *Chaos and Governance in the Modern World-System*. Minnesota: Minnesota University Press, pp. 217–70.

Arrighi, Giovanni, Beverly Silver and Benjamin Brewer. 2003. 'Industrial

Convergence and the Persistence of the North–South Divide: A Rejoinder'. *Studies in Comparative International Development* **38**(1), 3–31.

Babones, Salvatore J. 2005. 'The Country-Level Income Structure of the World-Economy'. *Journal of World-Systems Research* **11**(1), 29–55.

Bourguignon, François and Christian Morrisson. 2002. 'Inequality Among World Citizens: 1820–1992'. *American Economic Review* **94**(2), 727–44.

Braudel, Fernand. 1984. *Civilization and Capitalism, Fifteenth–Eighteenth Century. Volume 3, The Perspective of the World*. New York: Harper and Row.

Cardoso, Fernando H. and Enzo Faletto. 1979. *Dependency and Development in Latin America*. Berkeley: University of Berkeley Press.

Chase-Dunn, Christopher and Richard Rubinson, 1977. 'Toward a Structural Perspective on the World-System'. *Politics and Society* **7**(4), 453–76.

Firebaugh, Glenn. 2000. 'The Trend in Between-Nation Income Inequality'. *Annual Review of Sociology* **26**, 333–4.

Frank, Andre Gunder. 1967. *Capitalism and Underdevelopment in Latin America: Historical Studies of Chile and Brazil*. New York: Monthly Review Press.

Frank, Andre Gunder (author) and Robert A. Denemark (ed.). 2015. *ReOrienting the 19th Century: Global Economy in the Continuing Asian Age*. Boulder, CO: Paradigm.

Gramsci, Antonio. 1971. *Selections from the Prison Notebooks*. New York: International Publishers.

Hopkins, Terence K. and Immanuel Wallerstein. 1982. *World-Systems Analysis: Theory and Methodology*, Vol. 1. Beverly Hills, CA: Sage.

Karatasli, Sahan Savas. Forthcoming. 'The Capitalist World-Economy in the *Longue Durée*: Changing Modes of the Global Distribution of Wealth, 1500–2008'. *Sociology of Development*.

Korzeniewicz, Roberto Patricio and William G. Martin. 1994. 'The Global Distribution of Commodity Chains'. In Gary Gereffi and Miguel Korzeniewicz (eds), *Commodity Chains and Global Capitalism*. Westport, CT: Praeger, pp. 67–91.

Korzeniewicz, Roberto Patricio and Timothy P. Moran. 1997. 'World-Economic Trends in the Distribution of Income, 1965–1992'. *American Journal of Sociology* **102**(4), 1000–1039.

Mahbubani, Kishore. 2013. *The Great Convergence: Asia: The West, and the Logic of One World*. New York: Public Affairs.

Marx, Karl. 1867 [1992]. *Capital: A Critique of Political Economy*. Trans. Samuel Moore and Edward Aveling. Vol. I. New York: International Publishers.

McMichael, Philip. 2012. *Development and Social Change: A Global Perspective*. Beverly Hills, CA: Sage.

Milanovic, Branko. 2013. 'Global Income Inequality in Numbers: In History and Now'. *Global Policy* **4**(2), 198–208.

Palat, Ravi Arvind. 2012. 'Much Ado about Nothing? World-Historical Implications of the Re-emergence of China and India'. *International Critical Thought* **2**(2), 139–55.

Pomeranz, Kenneth. 2000. *The Great Divergence: China, Europe, and the Making of the Modern World Economy*. Princeton, NJ: Princeton University Press.

Rostow, Walt W. 1960. *The Stages of Economic Growth: A Non-Communist Manifesto*. Cambridge: Cambridge University Press.

Sala-i-Martin, Xavier. 2006. 'World Distribution of Income: Falling Poverty and Convergence, Period'. *Quarterly Journal of Economics* **121**(2), 351–97.

UNDP. 2013. *Human Development Report 2013. The Rise of the South: Human Progress in a Diverse World*. New York.

Wade, Robert H. 2004. 'Is Globalization Reducing Poverty and Inequality?'. *World Development* **32**(4), 567–89.

Wallerstein, Immanuel. 1979. *The Capitalist World-Economy.* New York: Cambridge University Press.

Wolf, Martin. 2011. 'In the Grip of a Great Convergence', *Financial Times*, 4 January. https://next.ft.com/content/072c87e6-1841-11e0-88c9-00144feab49a (accessed 15 February 2017).

3. Why growth rates differ

Vladimir Popov

The question why some countries are growing faster than others is the central one in economics. It is in fact the old question about the nature and the causes of the wealth of nations (Smith, 1776). In a retrospective view of economic growth this question is often formulated as 'why the West got rich before the Rest?' and 'why some developing countries are catching up with the West, but others do not?' Unfortunately, there is no consensus among economists about what exact policies are needed for engineering high growth (Popov, 2011).

Many agree that the crucial factor of economic growth in the long term is institutions (Rodrik, 2004; Rodrik et al., 2002), but there is less agreement on what determines the institutional strength. This chapter uses objective measures of the institutional capacity (shadow economy and murder rate) to trace the trajectories of institutional developments in the Global South and discusses the hypotheses to explain these trajectories.

GROWTH, POLICIES AND INSTITUTIONS

It is said that failure is always an orphan, whereas success has many parents. No wonder, both neo-classical and structuralist economists claim that economic success stories in the Global South prove what they were saying all along. It is not difficult to find many contradictory statements in the literature about the reasons for economic success: economic liberalization and free trade are said to be the foundations of rapid growth in some countries, whereas successes of other countries are credited to industrial policy and protectionism; foreign direct investment is normally considered as a factor contributing to growth, but it is pointed out that it did not play any significant role in the developmental success of Japan, South Korea and pre-1990s China. Privatization of state enterprises, free trade, liberalization of the financial system, democratic political institutions – all these factors, just to name a few, are usually believed to be pre-requisites of successful development, but it is easy to point out success stories that are not associated with these factors.[1] It is debated whether foreign aid boosts growth or merely crowds out domestic savings and investment (Channing et al., 2010; United Nations, 2003).

In the 1970s the breathtaking economic success of Japan that transformed itself into a developed country in just two postwar decades was explained by 'Japan incorporated' structure of the economy – special relations between (a) the government and companies (the omni-powerful Ministry of International Trade and Industry – MITI); (b) between banks and non-financial companies (bank-based financial system); and (c) between companies and workers (lifetime employment). After the stagnation of the 1990s, and especially after the 1997 Asian financial crisis that affected Japan as well, these same factors were largely labeled clear manifestations of 'crony capitalism' that should be held responsible for the stagnation (Popov, 2008).

The analysis of policies that contributed most to poverty reduction and the achievement of other Millennium Development Goals in 2000–15 also suggests that there is no single strategy that leads to success under all conditions and at all development stages (WESS, 2015).

Reforms that are needed to achieve success are different for countries with different backgrounds and at different stages of development (Polterovich and Popov, 2005, 2006). Manufacturing growth is like cooking a good dish – all the needed ingredients should be in the right proportion; if only one is under- or over-represented, the 'chemistry of growth' will not happen. Fast economic growth can materialize in practice only if several necessary conditions are met at the same time. Rapid growth is a complicated process that requires a number of crucial inputs – infrastructure, human capital, even land distribution in agrarian countries, strong state institutions, economic stimuli, among other things. Once one of these crucial necessary ingredients is missing, the growth just does not take off. Rodrik et al. (2005) talk about 'binding constraints' that hold back economic growth; finding these constraints is the task of 'growth diagnostics.' In some cases, these constraints are associated with lack of market liberalization, in others, with lack of state capacity or human capital or infrastructure. Why did economic liberalization work in Central Europe but not in sub-Saharan Africa or Latin America? The answer, according to the approach outlined, is that in

---

[1] Often the same international organizations issued reports that advocated different policies for growth. For instance, *The East Asian Miracle* report of the World Bank (1993) acknowledged the role of the state and industrial policies in rapid growth, but it was argued in the World Development Report of 1996 (p. 142) that consistent policies, combining liberalization of markets, trade, and new business entry with reasonable price stability, can achieve a great deal even in countries lacking clear property rights and strong market institutions. The next World Development Report (1997) was entitled *The State in the Changing World* and emphasized the crucial importance of state institutions for growth.

Central Europe the missing ingredient was economic liberalization, whereas in sub-Saharan Africa and Latin America there was a lack of state capacity, not a lack of market liberalization. Why did liberalization work in China and Central Europe and not in the Commonwealth of Independent States (CIS)? Because in the CIS it was carried out in such a way as to undermine state capacity – the precious heritage of the socialist past – whereas in Central Europe, and even more so in China, state capacity did not decline substantially during transition (Popov, 2014a).

It is difficult therefore, if not impossible, to find universal recipes for rapid growth. However, there is a different way to approach the question – to look not at policies enacted in fast growing countries ('good' policies vary depending on initial conditions and stages of development) but at the institutions that were conducive to adopting these policies or at least made them possible. Here we consider only state institutions or, to be more precise, state institutional capacity defined as the ability of the state to enforce rules and regulations. Subjective measures of state capacity – indices of government effectiveness, rule of law, corruptions and so on – have a number of shortcomings (Popov, 2011), so I suggest objective indicators, such as crime rate, murder rate,[2] the share of the shadow economy, to reflect the ability of the state to enforce its monopoly on violence and monopoly on taxation.

The general rule is that developed countries, East Asia, South Asia and Middle East and North Africa (MENA) countries have murder rates of 1–10 murders per 100 000 inhabitants and a shadow economy of less than 30 percent of gross domestic product (GDP), whereas in sub-Saharan Africa, Latin America and some former Soviet Union republics (Baltics, Belarus, Kazakhstan, Moldova, Russia, Ukraine) the murder rate is higher by an order of magnitude (10–100 murders per 100 000 inhabitants) and the shadow economy is way over 30 percent of GDP. Economic growth in large regions of the Global South correlates strongly with the murder rate and the shadow economy (negative correlation – the higher the murder rate and the shadow economy, the lower is growth). East Asia is ahead of other regions in terms of growth, followed by South Asia and MENA, while Latin America, sub-Saharan Africa and the Former Soviet Union (FSU) are falling behind.

In fact, the murder rate and the share of the shadow economy – the objective indicators of the institutional capacity of the state – turn out to be the best institutional predictors of the long-term growth rates of GDP per capita. In regressions for over 50 years (1960–2013) for 80 countries for

---

[2]   Crimes, especially non-violent, are registered better in developed countries than in developing countries. Here I use the murder rate – in most countries grave crimes, like murders, are registered most accurately.

which data are available, up to 40 percent of variations in GDP per capita growth are explained by the level of development (GDP per capita) and institutional indicators (murder rate and share of the shadow economy).[3] These regressions are quite robust and hold for different sub-periods (1960–75, 1975–2000, 2000–13). Among variables that are not directly related to growth, such as investment rate, population growth rates and so on, state institutional capacity turns out to be the single most important predictor of growth The negative relationship between growth rate and state institutional weakness as measured by the murder rate and share of the shadow economy are clearly shown in Figures 3.1 and 3.2.

The usual objection to these regressions is that institutional capacity variables are endogenous, that is, not only do they influence growth but they are influenced by growth themselves. The data for the murder rate and the shadow economy are for the years 2002 and 2005, respectively – the very end of the investigated period of economic growth (1960–2013), which may be a problem since the cause should of course precede the effect in time. However, the data on murders and the shadow economy for the earlier period are largely missing[4] and it is possible to run reasonable cross-country regressions (40 observations) only for the very recent short period. The results for growth in the 2000–13 period with data on the shadow economy and murders for the 1990s are very strong,[5] but the period is too short to proxy long-term growth.

[3] $y = -0.0003^{***} \ Ycap75 - 0.03^{*}MURDERS - 0.14^{***}SHADOW + 5.32^{***}$
          (–4.95)   (1.67)   (–4.82)   (8.55)
$N = 80$, $R^2 = 0.38$, robust standard errors, T-statistics in parentheses.

$y = 0.003^{***}POPDENS - 0.0002^{***} \ Ycap75 - 0.023 \ MURDERS - 0.067^{***}SHADOW$
          (4.08)   (–4.33)   (–1.62)   (–40)
$+ 5.04^{***}$
(7.67)
$N = 80$, $R^2 = 0.40$, robust standard errors, T-statistics in parentheses, where: y is annual average growth rates of per capita GDP in 1960–2013 (%); POPDENS is number of residents per 1 square km in 2000; Ycap75 is per capita PPP GDP in 1975 in dollars; MURDERS is number of murders per 100 000 inhabitants in 2002; and SHADOW is share of the shadow economy in GDP in 2005 (%).
Data on growth, population density and PPP GDP per capita are from the World Bank World Development Indicators, data on murders are from the World Health Organization (WHO), data on the shadow economy are from Schneider (2007) (measures of the shadow economy are derived from divergence between output dynamics and electricity consumption, demand for real cash balances and so on).
[4] For 20–30 observations, these regressions hold for the 1975–2013 period with data on the shadow economy and murders for the middle of the growth period, that is, the 1990s.
[5] $y = 6.58^{***} \log Ycap1999 - 0.040^{**} \ MURDERS - 0.042^{***}SHADOW + 30.71^{***}$
          (5.26)   (–1.99)   (–2.03)   (5.48)
$N = 43$, $R^2 = 0.64$, robust standard errors, T-statistics in parentheses, where: y is the annual average growth rates of per capita GDP in 2000–13 (%); and murders and shadow economy estimates are for the 1990s (data on murders are from the WHO, on the shadow economy from Friedman et al., 2000).

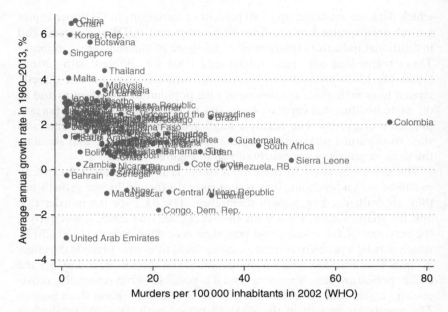

Sources: World Bank World Development Indicators; World Health Organization.

*Figure 3.1   Murder rate in 2002 per 100 000 inhabitants and average
            annual per capita GDP growth rates in 1960–2013 (%)*

The standard way to deal with the endogeneity is to look for instrumental
variables, but it is virtually impossible to find such variables for institutions
that are not correlated with growth. It can be argued though that murder
rates did not change much in the last half century, and in this case the
endogeneity argument does not hold: the murder rate is not influenced by
economic growth or influenced so little that changes during half a century
are not significant. Partial support for this argument is provided by data
in Figure 3.3 – in most countries the murder rate did not change much in
1960–2013. Exceptions are countries/territories affected by turmoil, wars
and/or transition from communism to capitalism (Northern Ireland in
the 1960s, Cyprus in the 1970s, Russia and former Soviet republics in the
1990s – none of these experienced fast growth).

The crucial question, then, is what determines the institutional capacity
of the state, if not economic growth? Why do some countries have strong
institutional capacity for many decades and enjoy rapid growth, whereas
others are locked in a trap with poor institutions and low growth?

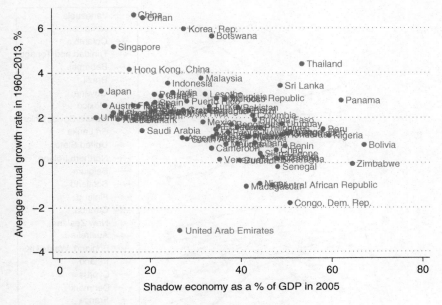

Sources: World Bank World Development Indicators; Schneider (2007).

Figure 3.2   Shadow economy in 2005 and annual average growth rates of per capita GDP in 1960–2013 (%)

GENESIS OF INSTITUTIONS

Most of the participants of the recent debate about the major factors of economic growth (geography versus institutions versus international trade) seem to have concluded that institutions trump all other factors (Rodrik et al., 2002). In an article with the self-explanatory title, 'Institutions Rule', the authors examine the impact of three basic factors on growth – geography (proxied by the distance to the equator and regional dummies), trade openness (the share of trade in GDP) and institutions. The difficulty, of course, is that all three factors are interlinked and institutions and trade openness not only influence growth but also depend on growth themselves. To properly estimate the contribution of each factor, the authors measure institutions using the settlers' mortality rate (Acemoglu et al., 2001), and measure the share of trade in GDP with the predicted share of trade (from gravity models). Then, after giving geographical variables a 'fair chance' to compete with instrumental variables of institutions and

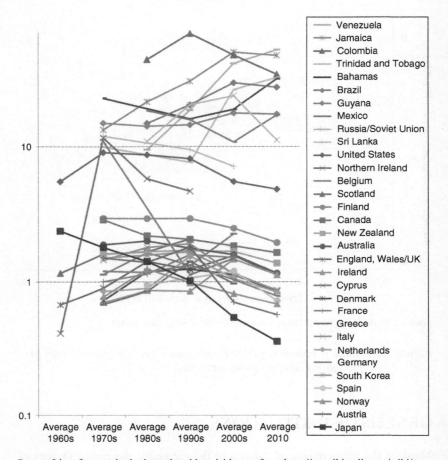

Source: List of countries by intentional homicide rate from http://en.wikipedia.org/wiki/
List_of_countries_by_intentional_homicide_rate. Data are taken from different sources
(mostly national data provided to the World Health Organization) and sometimes are not
strictly comparable.

Figure 3.3   *Average murder rates in 1960–2013 by decades, per 100 000
                inhabitants, log scale (countries for which data are available
                for three and more decades)*

trade openness, they conclude that 'institutions rule,' that is, the impact
of institutions is most crucial. Institutions are largely, but not totally,
determined by geography, and in turn they determine trade openness and
growth. The direct impact of geography on growth (apart from the impact

through institutions) turns out to be insignificant. In short, institutions trump geography and institutional capacity is not always determined by geography.

The difference from the straightforward geographical determinism approach is obvious, but there is an important difference from the approach used by Acemoglu et al. (2001) as well. Rodrik et al. (2002) believe that geography, particularly settlers' mortality rates, is a good predictor of institutional quality, but not the major cause of it. The genesis of institutions is a complex process with many determinants, and finding an appropriate econometric instrument is not the same as finding the proper explanation. Rodrik (2004) explains the difference using the following example: the variation in GDP per capita in countries that were never colonies is no less substantial than among colonized countries – here, Ethiopia and Afghanistan are at one end of the spectrum and Japan is at the other with Turkey and Thailand somewhere in between. What accounts for the different quality of institutions in this non-colonized part of the world?

There are two major schools of thought that offer different answers to these questions (see Popov, 2014a for description and references); one recognizes the key role of institutions, the other does not. One (evolutionary or Western) school hypothesizes that in the sixteenth century and afterwards countries we now call developed, or the West, acquired some features and institutions that were absent in more traditional societies (Landes, 1998; Mokyr, 2002 – to name just a couple of contemporary authors). These features range from abolition of serfdom and Protestant ethics to protection of property rights and free universities.

Another school (Oriental) questions the logic of evolution triggered by social forces themselves (Diamond, 1997; Pomeranz, 2000; Wong, 1997 – to give some contemporary examples) and pays special attention to seemingly minor historical events – fortunate and unfortunate, but mostly accidental – that pre-determined the development of countries and continents for centuries to come. In this view, explain the editors of the book that examines important unrealized counterfactuals in human history,

> Western dominance was the by-product of natural forces that reflect no credit on Western civilization: geographical accidents such as location of mountains and coastlines, geological accidents such as the ready availability of coal or gold or arable land, climatological accidents such as the timing of the ice ages or the direction of the ocean currents, and biological accidents (not always so accidental) that affect the susceptibility of various population groups to lethal diseases. (Tetlock et al., 2009, p. 9)

In recent decades the rise of Asia gave additional credibility to theories that reject the superiority of the Western economic model and the inevitability of the Western success. 'As Japan, the Asian Tigers and China developed into major economic powers,' writes Ian Morris,

> more and more scholars concluded that theories explaining West's success through long-term cultural, environmental, or racial causes simply could not be right. The big story in world history, they began suggesting, was not the long-term, inexorable rise of the West; it was the tale of a multipolar world, which the West had only recently, temporarily, and perhaps even accidently come to dominate. (Morris, 2013, p. 2)

The problem with these explanations is that there were many countries before the sixteenth century possessing social structures with many of the same features credited with, or conducive to, growth acceleration by the Western school and with many minor accidental events said to promote growth by the supporters of the Oriental school. But these countries never experienced productivity growth comparable to that started in Britain and the Netherlands in the sixteenth century and later in the rest of Europe (0.2–0.3 percent a year in 1500–1800 and 1 percent and more a year afterwards).

A different interpretation accepted in this chapter is that dismantling traditional collectivist institutions in Western countries was associated with increased income inequality and even decreased life expectancy, but allowed the redistribution of income in favor of savings and investment at the expense of consumption (Popov, 2014a). The elimination of collectivist (community) institutions was a risky experiment that put masses of the population below the subsistence minimum and caused a reduction or slowdown of growth in the population – the foundation of the military might (number of people – number of soldiers) in the Malthusian growth regime.

Early attempts to ensure the priority of the rights of the individual over the rights of the community at the expense of collective interests and low inequality (Greece, Rome, Byzantine) led to the impoverishment of the masses, higher mortality and foreign conquest. Only in Northwest Europe in the sixteenth to the eighteenth centuries did this policy somehow succeed for the first time in history.

It is not the abundance of competition or entrepreneurship or ideas for technological innovations that allowed the West to accelerate the growth rates of productivity by an order of magnitude, it is first and foremost the abundance of savings and investment that resulted from growing income inequalities and that allowed an increase in the capital/labor ratio to cast in metal the ideas for new products and technologies. To put it differently, the West became rich not due to its inventiveness and entrepreneurial spirit but due to cruel and merciless dismantling of the community that previously provided social guarantees to the poorest.

When the same pattern was applied to developing countries (through colonialism – Latin America, sub-Saharan Africa, or voluntary Westernization in an attempt to catch up – Russian Empire), it resulted in the destruction of traditional institutions, an increase in income inequality and the worsening of starting positions for catch-up development. This group of countries replicated the Western exit from the Malthusian trap – they experienced an immediate increase in income differentiation, a rise in savings and investment and in the growth of productivity, but at the price of rising social inequality and deterioration of institutional capacities.

Other developing countries (East Asia, South Asia, MENA) were less affected by colonialism and managed to retain their traditional institutions. This delayed the transition to modern economic growth (Kuznets, 1966) until the mid twentieth century, but maintained a good starting position for economic growth – low inequality and strong institutions. Eventually, slow technical progress allowed these countries to find another (and less painful) exit from the Malthusian trap – increased income allowed an increase in the share of investment in GDP without a major increase in income inequality, and without worsening institutional capacity and a decrease in life expectancy.

More Westernized countries of the Global South (Latin America and the Russian Empire) raised their savings-investment rate and exited the Malthusian trap earlier than the others, in the eighteenth century, but at the price of undermining necessary conditions for future growth – low inequalities and strong institutions. So Latin America and Russia experienced some acceleration of growth afterwards, but it was not enough to catch up with the West. Colonization of sub-Saharan Africa (except for South Africa), unlike colonization of Latin America and Westernization of Russia, did not result in any considerable transfer of technology and human capital, but only increased inequalities and undermined institutions. So sub-Saharan Africa countries were disadvantaged on all counts and had the worst growth record in the world. On the contrary, most of the less Westernized countries of East and South Asia and MENA managed to preserve low inequality and efficient collectivist institutions. Their savings-investment ratios stayed at a level below 10 percent until the mid twentieth century, so they did not grow before then, but once saving started to increase gradually, they had the preconditions for fast growth. Some became economic miracles, rapidly catching up with the West (East Asia), others have speeded up their development in recent decades (South Asia), while others (MENA countries) are probably best positioned to accelerate their economic growth in the future.

The general model of global divergence is presented in Figure 3.4 (Popov, 2014a). Like all schemes this one is a simplification: it does not capture the

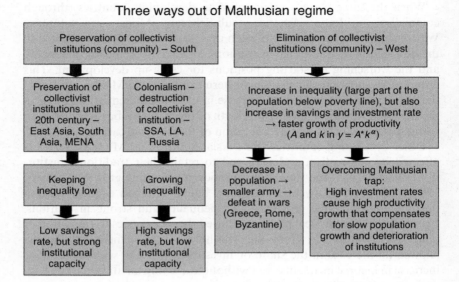

Figure 3.4   Explanation of the global divergence in growth since the 1500s

diversity of all circumstances, but traces the main factors responsible for changes. Today there are two major groups of developing countries: one (East and South Asia, MENA) has relatively low inequalities, strong state institutions (low murder rate and share of the shadow economy) and high savings and investment rate; the other (Latin America, sub-Saharan Africa, Russia and some former Soviet republics) has high inequalities, weak state institutions (high murder rate and shadow economy) and low savings and investment rate. Quite predictably the first group grows faster than the second.

The important examples of these two groups of countries are China and Russia. Institutional trajectories of the two states diverged in the seventeenth century, if not before then. Up until the Opium Wars (mid-nineteenth century) Chinese low inequalities and collectivist institutions were more conducive to the preservation of state capacity than Russian attempts to replace existing institutions by allegedly more advanced institutions imported from abroad from at least the seventeenth century. Russia had already been Westernized before 1917, and collectivist institutions introduced in Russia by the 1917 Revolution had already been largely alien to previous long-term institutional development. On the contrary, China aborted the unsuccessful Westernization attempt (1840s to 1949) and returned to collectivist (Asian values) institutions. What was a passing episode and deviation from the trend in Russia (1917–91) was a return to mainstream development and the restoration of a long-term trend in China (1949–79). Hence, economic liberalization from 1979 onwards in China, even though accompanied by growing income inequality and crime and murder rates, did not result in institutional collapse.

Like Russia in 1917, China re-established collectivist institutions in 1949 as a response to the failure of Westernization. Unlike Russia after 1991, since 1979 China has managed to preserve 'Asian values' institutions that are based on the priority of community interests over the interests of the individual (Popov, 2014a).

CONCLUSIONS

If the hypothesis about two institutional trajectories in the Global South is correct, we may see in the twenty-first century the successful catch-up development of East and South Asia and MENA countries, whereas Latin America, Russia and sub-Saharan Africa may be falling behind for some time. However, it may well be that states transit from one institutional trajectory to another – countries with low inequalities and strong institutions can join the opposite group and vice versa. There are few historical junctions where there is a chance to move to a different trajectory of institutional development and it may be that we are currently going through one of these junctions.

In most countries there has been an increase in income and wealth inequalities since the 1980s – a reversal of the trend of 50 or more proceeding years (Sundaram and Popov, 2015). In the 1970s to 1980s world socialism lost its dynamism and so was no longer a viable alternative to capitalism, which reduced stimuli for maintaining the welfare state and social programs in Western countries. The fall of the Berlin Wall, the collapse of the USSR and the conversion of Eastern Europe and former Soviet republics to capitalism added an additional push to the trends for growing income inequalities due to both the disappearance of the 'socialist counterbalance' for Western capitalism and rise in inequalities in the transition countries of Eastern Europe and the former Soviet Union.

The continuation of these trends could result in social upheavals in countries where social tensions rise due to growing inequalities. As large masses of the population will become disadvantaged due to increased inequalities, there may also be a rise of nationalism as rightist political groups will blame all the disasters and misfortunes on globalization (Popov, 2016). This may lead to conflicts, if not wars, between countries, with the collapse of international trade and capital flows, as in the 1930s.

The world can once again go over the familiar twentieth-century historical track and there may be a pause in or even a reversal of globalization, as in the Great Depression, when the outburst of protectionism led to the decline of international trade and capital movements. This is the worst scenario: the world degrading into social and national conflicts.

But there may be countries carrying out successful policies of limiting inequalities that could become more competitive, driving other countries 'out of business.' There has already been a decline in inequalities in some Latin American (Argentina, Bolivia, Brazil, Chile, Mexico, Peru) and East Asian countries (Malaysia, Thailand, Philippines) in recent decades. Also, a number of former communist countries, including Russia, which experienced a dramatic rise in income and wealth inequalities and a deterioration of state institutions in the 1990s, regained institutional strength rather quickly in the 2000s to 2010s. Increases in inequalities stopped, crime and murder rates and mortality rates fell markedly. It turned out that institutional developments proceed with a high degree of inertia, so short-term changes in institutional capacity (in the lifetime of a generation) caused by extraordinary circumstances may be reversed relatively quickly (Popov, 2017).

Even small socially oriented states, if they are successful, may create an efficient counterbalance to the tendency of unconstrained capitalism to cut welfare programs and increase inequalities. They may substantially limit the functioning of the market mechanisms through direct regulations and high progressive taxation to reduce bubbles and windfall profits. The crucial way of lowering inequalities is through public and collective property, so state enterprises, non-profit institutions, labor-managed enterprises and coops, operating not for profit but for public good, could become more common. New grassroots socialism growing from below might become more competitive than capitalist societies (Popov, 2014b). Such an optimistic scenario implies that social upheavals within countries and national conflicts between countries could be largely avoided.

REFERENCES

Acemoglu, D., S. Johnson and J.A. Robinson (2001). The Colonial Origins of Comparative Development: An Empirical Investigation. *American Economic Review*, **91** (5), 1369–401.

Channing, A., S. Jones and F. Tarp (2010). Aid, Growth, and Development: Have We Come Full Circle? *Journal of Globalization and Development*, **1** (2), Berkeley Electronic Press.

Diamond, J. (1997). *Guns, Germs and Steel: The Fate of Human Societies*. New York: W.W. Norton.

Friedman, E., S. Johnson, D. Kaufmann and P. Zoido-Lobatón (2000). Dodging the Grabbing Hand: The Determinants of Unofficial Activity in 69 Countries. *Journal of Public Economics*, **76**, June, 459–93.

Kuznets, S. (1966). *Modern Economic Growth: Rate, Structure and Spread.* New Haven, CT: Yale University Press.

Landes, D. (1998). *Wealth and Poverty of Nations. Why are Some So Rich and Others So Poor?* New York: W.W. Norton.

Mokyr, J. (2002). *The Gifts of Athena: Historical Origins of the Knowledge Economy.* Princeton, NJ: Princeton University Press.

Morris, I. (2013). *The Measure of Civilization. How Social Development Decides the Fate of Nations.* Princeton, NJ: Princeton University Press.

Polterovich, V. and V. Popov (2005). Appropriate Economic Policies at Different Stages of Development. New Economic School, Moscow. www.nes.ru/english/research/pdf/2005/PopovPolterovich.pdf (accessed 13 February 2017).

Polterovich, V. and V. Popov (2006). Stages of Development, Economic Policies and New World Economic Order. Paper presented at the Seventh Annual Global Development Conference, January, St Petersburg, Russia. http://http-server.carleton.ca/~vpopov/documents/NewWorldEconomicOrder.pdf (accessed 13 February 2017).

Pomeranz, K. (2000). *The Great Divergence: Europe, China, and the Making of the Modern World Economy.* Princeton, NJ: Princeton University Press.

Popov, V. (2008). Lessons from the Transition Economies. Putting the Success Stories of the Postcommunist World into a Broader Perspective. UNU/WIDER Research Paper No. 2009/15, Helsinki.

Popov, V. (2011). Developing New Measurements of State Institutional Capacity. PONARS Eurasia Policy Memo No. 158, May. MPRA Paper 32389, August.

Popov, V. (2014a). *Mixed Fortunes: An Economic History of China, Russia and the West.* New York: Oxford University Press.

Popov, V. (2014b). Socialism is Dead, Long Live Socialism! MPRA Paper No. 54294, March.

Popov, V. (2016). Is Globalization Coming to an End Due to Rise of Income Inequalities? MPRA Paper No. 73094, August.

Popov, V. (2017). Big Changes in Transition Countries: Lessons for Development Economics. WIDER.

Rodrik, D. (2004). Getting Institutions Right. CESifo. *Journal for Institutional Comparisons*, **2** (4), Summer.

Rodrik, D., A. Subramanian and F. Trebbi (2002). Institutions Rule: The Primacy of Institutions Over Geography and Integration in Economic Development, October. http://ksghome.harvard.edu/~.drodrik.academic.ksg/institutionsrule,%205.0.pdf (accessed 13 February 2017).

Rodrik, D., R. Hausmann and A. Velasco (2005). Growth Diagnostics. http://ksghome.harvard.edu/~drodrik/barcelonafinalmarch2005.pdf (accessed 13 February 2017).

Schneider, F. (2007). Shadow Economies and Corruption All Over the World: New Estimates for 145 Countries. *Economics.* Open Access, Open Assessment E-Journal, No. 2007-9, 24 July.

Smith, A. (1776). *An Inquiry into the Nature and Causes of the Wealth of Nations* (1st edn). London: W. Strahan.

Sundaram, J.K. and V. Popov (2015). Income Inequalities in Perspective. ESS Document No. 46, International Labour Office, Geneva, and Initiative for Policy Dialogue (IPD), Columbia University, New York.

Tetlock, P.E., R.N. Lebow and G. Parker (eds) (2009). *Unmaking of the West. 'What if' Scenarios that Rewrite the World History*. Ann Arbor, MI: University of Michigan Press.

United Nations (2003). *Monterrey Consensus on Financing for Development*. New York.

WDR (1996). *World Development Report 1996: From Plan to Market*. Washington, DC: World Bank.

WDR (1997). *World Development Report 1997: The State in a Changing World*. Washington, DC: World Bank.

WESS (2015). *World Economic and Social Survey 2015. MDG Lessons for Post-2015*. New York: United Nations.

Wong, R.B. (1997). *China Transformed: Historical Change and the Limits of the European Experience*. Ithaca, NY: Cornell University Press.

World Bank (1993). *The East Asian Miracle: Economic Growth and Public Policy*. Washington, DC.

4. Lessons from China and East Asia's catch up: the new structural economics perspective

Justin Yifu Lin

INTRODUCTION

Most countries in the world were stagnant, agrarian and poor in pre-modern times. The difference between per capita income across countries was small. The rapid increase in wealth and national power in the West occurred only after the industrial revolution in the eighteenth century (Kuznets, 1966), leading to a great divergence in the world.

Consequently, many developing countries became colonies or semi-colonies of the Western powers by the nineteenth century.

After World War II (WWII), most developing countries gained political independence from colonial powers and started their modernization drive. As shown in the upper panel of Figure 4.1, a few East Asian economies, such as Japan, Korea, Taiwan, Hong Kong and Singapore, were able to grow dynamically, becoming newly industrialized economies by the 1970s and high-income economies today.[1] China's growth performance after the transition from a socialist planned economy to a market economy in the late 1970s was most spectacular (Lin, 2012). The average annual gross domestic product (GDP) growth rate reached 9.9 percent in the period from 1979 to 2008. The per capita GDP, measured in purchasing power parity as a percentage of the US, increased from 5.5 percent in 1979 to 21.6 percent in 2008. With such an extraordinary growth performance, more than 600 million people in China got out of poverty in this period. However, most developing countries failed to catch up in spite of efforts

---

[1] By 2008, only two low-income economies, Korea and Taiwan, had grown to be high-income economies. Only 13 middle-income economies had become high-income economies. Among those 13 economies, eight were European economies from Western Europe, their income gaps were small to begin with, or oil-exporting countries, the other five were Japan and the four East Asian Tigers, Korea, Taiwan, Hong Kong and Singapore (Agenor et al., 2012; Lin and Rosenblatt, 2012).

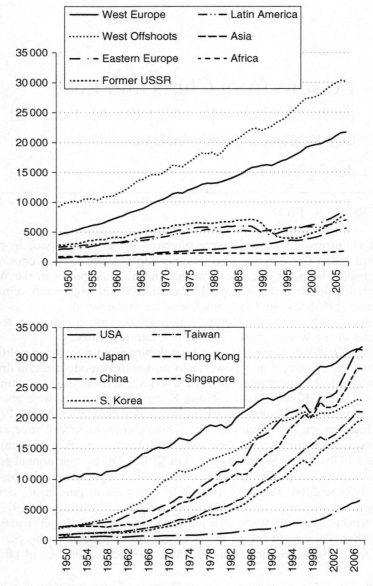

Note: In 1900 Geary-Khamis dollars.

Source: Maddison (2010).

Figure 4.1   Gross domestic product per capita, 1950–2008

over more than half a century. The lower panel of Figure 4.1 shows that the gaps of per capita GDP between the developed regions and the regions lagging behind have diverged further since WWII (Pritchett, 1997).

Economic development in a country, as represented by the increase of per capita GDP, is driven by increased labor productivity as a result of continuous technological innovations in the existing industries and industrial upgrading to new, higher value-added industries (Kuznets, 1966). Since the industrial revolution in the eighteenth century, the advanced countries in the West together with their technologies and industries have been on the global frontier. The technological innovation and industrial upgrading in these countries rely primarily on costly and risky research and development (R&D). The GDP growth rate in the developed countries has reached about 3 percent per year on average in the past century (Maddison, 2006). A developing country has the advantage of backwardness in technological innovation and industrial upgrading as it can borrow matured technologies and industries from the advanced countries for technological innovation and industrial upgrading. A developing country can potentially grow faster than the advanced countries and achieve convergence (Gerschenkron, 1962), as China and the East Asian economies have demonstrated. It is puzzling why, other than China and a few East Asian economies, most developing countries in the rest of the world have not tapped into this potential to achieve convergence. What was special about the East Asian economies? Can their success be replicated in other developing countries?

As Keynes said, 'it is ideas . . . which are dangerous for good or evil' (1935 [1964]). This chapter argues that development policies shaped by ideas embodied in dysfunctional developing thinking were responsible for the failure of the Rest to catch up with the West. The chapter is organized as follows. The next section provides a critique of two previous waves of prevailing development thinking, structuralism and neoliberalism, examining their failures in guiding developing countries to catch up with the West. The new structural economics is then introduced as an alternative to previous thinking, drawing from the success of China and East Asia, followed by a discussion on why East Asian economies are so special. Some concluding remarks complete the chapter.

RETHINKING ECONOMIC DEVELOPMENT

The failure of the 'Rest' to catch up with the West challenges the economics community to rethink the existing development theories. Development economics became a subfield of modern economics after WWII to guide the reconstruction of war-ravaged countries and the nation-building of newly independent former colonies. The first wave of development thinking was structuralism (Prebisch, 1950; Rosenstein-Rodan, 1943; Singer, 1950). There may be a natural tendency in human nature to try to imitate success. The dominance of the West that emerged from the industrial revolution was based on advanced manufacturing industries. The countries in the rest of the world, however, were still based on natural resource-intensive agriculture and mining, and these were seen as 'backward' rather than advanced sectors. Structuralism advised the developing countries in the rest of the world to adopt an import substitution strategy with direct state intervention to create institutions, including financial repression, distortion of prices and administrative allocation of resources, to mobilize capital to develop capital-intensive, large-scale manufacturing industries similar to those in the West (Lin, 2009).

Structuralism rejected the notion that the invisible hand of the free market could guide the process of development. The term 'structuralism' itself comes from the notion that structural rigidities are present in most economies, and in particular in countries at low levels of development. The idea behind structuralism was that structural rigidities in developing countries would prevent the process of industrialization, and 'self-sustained' growth could not become a reality without more interventionist government policies.

The underlying logic of state interventions in structuralism was convincing. All socialist countries as well as most newly independent capitalist countries followed the state-led, import substitution strategy advocated by structuralism post-WWII (Chenery, 1961). But countries that adopted this strategy typically fell into a pattern of rapid growth driven by large-scale investments, followed by long periods of stagnation and frequent crises (Lin, 2009). The overall results were universal development failure (Krueger and Tuncer, 1982; Lal, 1994; Pack and Saggi, 2006).

The failures of the structuralist approach led to the second wave of development thinking – neoliberalism, encapsulated in the Washington Consensus policy package.[2] The original ten tenets of the Washington Consensus were: (i) fiscal discipline; (ii) reordering public expenditure priorities; (iii) tax reform (broad base with moderate rates); (iv) liberalizing interest rates; (v) competitive (not overvalued) exchange rates; (vi) trade liberalization; (vii) liberalization of inward foreign direct investment; (viii) privatization; (ix) deregulation; and (x) property rights (for the informal sector). In many ways, the Washington Consensus was a reaction to the complex web of distortions that had to be created to try to

---

[2] See Williamson (1990, 2004).

support comparative advantage defying import substitution. In fact, each of the ten items on the list responded to a particular distortion perceived to exist – particularly in Latin American countries.[3] For example, there was the perception that debt-financed overinvestment in low productivity activities had created fiscal sustainability problems and wasteful public expenditure patterns. There was the perception that complex tax breaks had led to an inefficient tax system with low revenue mobilization. There was the perception that interest rate caps led to financial repression and low levels of financial intermediation, and that protectionism led to over-valued exchange rates. The Consensus critiqued public enterprises that had become inefficient and created a high cost for public services (as well as a fiscal drain). The Consensus also noted that restrictions on foreign direct investment had limited the potential for investment, and that a lack of property rights had locked out many poor people from access to formal credit markets.

The Washington Consensus was also a direct denial of the pervasive export pessimism that permeated the import substitution industrialization strategy. The focus was on liberalizing markets and balancing budgets – given that the end of the import substitution era coincided with sovereign debt defaults in a variety of developing countries. In the international development institutions, the Consensus became associated with structural adjustment lending in which multilateral development institutions provided financial support conditional on market-oriented reforms.

In the end, the Washington Consensus advised developing countries in the Rest to adopt the 'idealized' institutions of the West, that is, establishing a strong system of property rights, opening the economy to trade, privatizing state-owned enterprises and establishing broadly free markets through deregulation, moving from trying to copy industries to trying to copy the idealized market institutions of the West.[4] Again, the logic seemed sound. But growth rates of developing countries were lower and economic crises more frequent under Washington Consensus policies in the 1980s and 1990s than under the structuralist policies of the 1960s and 1970s. Some economists referred to this period as the 'lost decades' for developing countries (Easterly, 2001).

---

[3]   The original formulation was inspired by a meeting of high-level Latin American policy makers in Washington.

[4]   In fact, not all those policies recommended by the Washington Consensus were rigorously followed in the high-income countries. In the 1990s during the heyday of the Washington Consensus, many policy advisors for the high-income countries advised the developing countries to 'do as we say but not as we do.'

THE NEW STRUCTURAL ECONOMICS AS THE THIRD WAVE OF DEVELOPMENT THINKING

The few East Asian economies that successfully accelerated their growth post-WWII and converged to the West did not follow the approaches proposed by the dominant structuralist or neoliberal thinking. In the 1950s and 1960s, Japan and the four Asian tigers – Korea, Taiwan, Singapore and Hong Kong – were quietly catching up with developed countries. These newly industrializing economies grew rapidly from the 1950s to the 1970s by following an export-oriented development strategy based initially on labor-intensive, small-scale industries and gradually climbing the industrial ladder to larger, more capital-intensive industries (Amsden,1989; Chang, 2003; Lin, 2009; Wade, 1990), contradicting the prevailing structuralism, which advocated import substitution to build up large, heavy industries immediately.

In the 1980s and 1990s, under the sway of the Washington Consensus, economists branded planned economies as less efficient than market economies, calling for their transformation into market economies by use of shock therapy: removing all economic distortions by ending government interventions and by leaping in a single bound from a planned economy to a market economy. The mainstream idea at that time was that separating the transition into two or three steps, as China was doing, would only lead to failure. China's dual-track reform continued to protect and subsidize nonviable state-owned firms in the old prioritized capital-intensive industries while liberalizing the market for labor-intensive industries, which had been repressed. Many economists predicted rampant rent-seeking and deteriorating resource allocation (Murphy et al., 1992; Sachs et al., 2000). In reality, however, economies that experienced stability and rapid growth in the transition, like Cambodia, China, Vietnam and Mauritius, all followed the gradual, dual-track reform approach.

The few successful economies have the following in common: they were a market economy or transiting to a market economy, as emphasized by neoliberalism, while their governments also intervened actively in the economy, as emphasized by structuralism.

Policies based on structuralism and neoliberalism failed to achieve their intended goals of helping developing countries in the Rest converge with the West and they also failed to explain the rare economic development successes. These failures suggest the need for a third wave of development thinking.

When I started to promote the new structural economics as the third wave of development thinking (Lin, 2011), I called for a return to Adam Smith, but not to *The Wealth of Nations*, a short-hand way of referring to the ideas advocated by Smith based on his research findings, but to Smith's methodology exemplified in the full title, *An Inquiry into the Nature and Causes of the Wealth of Nations*. I proposed following Smith, analysing: What is the nature of economic development, and what are its causes?

As discussed in the introduction, rapid, sustained economic growth is a modern phenomenon, emerging in the West only in the eighteenth century. Before then, average annual growth of per capita income in Western Europe was just 0.05 percent; at that rate it would take an economy 1400 years to double per capita income. From the eighteenth century to the mid nineteenth century, annual growth in per capita income in Western European countries accelerated to 1 percent, enabling per capita income to double in just 70 years. From the mid nineteenth century to the present, per capita income growth accelerated to 2 percent a year, shrinking the doubling time to 35 years (Maddison, 2006). The impetus for accelerating growth was the industrial revolution of the mid eighteenth century: continuous technological innovations and industrial upgrading made possible the acceleration of labor productivity and income growth that boosted per capita income.[5]

In other words, modern economic growth is a process of continuous technological innovation, which raises labor productivity, and industrial upgrading, which moves an economy from low value-added industries to higher value-added ones. But taking advantage of the potential of technologies and new industries requires well-functioning hard infrastructure to provide power, raw materials and various inputs from domestic and foreign sources in order to sell products to large domestic and foreign markets. As the scale of trade increases, market exchanges are at arm's length, thus requiring contracts and contract-enforcing legal systems. And as the scale and risk of investment increase with the upgrading of technology and industries, the financial structure has to adapt too. Thus, as argued by Marx in his voluminous writings, the entire soft infrastructure of institutions needs to improve accordingly (Harrison and Rodriguez-Clare, 2010; Kuznets, 1966; Lin, 1989; Lin and Nugent, 1995).

Therefore, while modern economic growth appears to be a process of ever increasing per capita income driven by rising labor productivity, it is actually a process of continuous structural changes in technologies, industries, and hard and soft infrastructure. The new structural economics uses a

---

[5] The industrial revolution was still in its infancy when Adam Smith was writing *An Inquiry into the Nature and Causes of the Wealth of Nations*. Consequently, Smith paid little attention to technology innovation and industrial upgrading; rather, he focused on trade and specialization in given technologies and industries. Technological innovation is one of the main themes in Marxism, but it did not become a focus of mainstream economics until the notion of creative destruction made popular by Schumpeter (1942).

neoclassical approach to study why different countries have different structures in technologies, industries, soft and hard infrastructures, and what
causes the structure in a country to change (Lin, 2011). By convention,
such studies should be referred to as 'structural economics.' It is called
'new' structural economics to distinguish it from structuralism, the first
wave of development thinking.

The new structural economics proposes that a country's economic structure at any specific time is endogenous to its given factor endowments,
that is, the amounts of capital, labor and natural resources at that time.
Countries at different development stages differ in the relative abundance
of factor endowments. In developing countries, capital is generally relatively scarce, while labor and natural resources are relatively abundant. In
developed countries, capital is relatively abundant, while labor is relatively
scarce. Though an economy's factor endowments are given at any particular time, they can change over time. The new structural economics posits
an economy's factor endowments as the starting point for development
analysis for two reasons. First, they are an economy's total budget at that
time; and second, the structure of endowments determines the relative
prices of factors: prices of relatively abundant factors are low, while prices
of relatively scarce factors are high.

The relative factor prices determine a country's comparative advantages. Thus, a prerequisite to achieving competitive advantage is for a
country to develop its industries according to its comparative advantages
(Porter, 1990). For example, countries with relatively abundant labor and
relatively scarce capital would have a comparative advantage in labor-
intensive industries because factor costs of production will be lower than
in countries with relatively scarce and more expensive labor.

In developed countries, income and labor productivity are high because
their industries and technologies are capital intensive, which in turn is
because of the countries' relative capital abundance. If a developing
country wants to catch up with the income and industrial structure of
developed countries, it first needs to increase the relative abundance of
capital in its factor endowment structure to the level found in advanced
countries. The ultimate goal of economic development is to raise a country's income, the intermediate goal is to develop capital-intensive industries, and the immediate goal should be to accumulate capital quickly, so
that the country's comparative advantage changes to more capital-intensive industries. In other words, boosting a country's income requires industrial upgrading, and industrial upgrading requires changing a country's
endowment structure (Ju et al., 2015).

How can a country accumulate capital quickly? Capital comes from
saving economic surpluses. If a country's industries are all consistent with

its comparative advantages, as determined by its endowment structure, the country will be competitive in both domestic and international markets and generate the largest possible surplus. If all investments are made in industries that are consistent with the comparative advantages determined by a country's endowment structure, the returns to investment will be maximized and the propensity to save will be at its highest. With the largest possible surplus and the highest incentives to save, capital will be accumulated in the fastest way possible. The changes in endowment structure and comparative advantages pave the way for upgrading industrial structure and the accompanying improvements in hard and soft industrial infrastructure. In upgrading industrial structure, developing countries can benefit from the advantage of backwardness.

But comparative advantage is an economic concept. How is it translated into the choices of technologies and industries made by entrepreneurs? Entrepreneurs care about profits. They will invest in industries in which a country has a comparative advantage if relative factor prices reflect the relative scarcities of factors in the country's endowments (Lin, 2009; Lin and Chang, 2009). If capital is relatively scarce, the price of capital will be relatively high; if labor is relatively scarce, the price of labor (wages) will be relatively high. Under an undistorted price system, profit-maximizing entrepreneurs will use a relatively inexpensive factor to substitute for a relatively expensive factor in their choice of production technologies, investing in industries that require more of a relatively inexpensive factor and less of a relatively expensive factor. A price system with these characteristics can arise only in a competitive market. And that is why successful economies are either market economies or on their way to becoming one.

If markets are so important, what is the government's role in economic development? Economic development is a process of structural change with continuous technological innovations, industrial upgrading, and improvement in infrastructure and institutions. When the factor endowment structure changes, economies need first movers that are willing to enter new industries that are consistent with changing comparative advantages and that are eager to use the new technologies. The risks for first movers are high. If they fail, they bear all the losses, and if they succeed, other firms will immediately follow them into the industry. The resulting competition will eliminate any monopoly profits (Aghion, 2009; Romer, 1990). There is an asymmetry between the losses of failures and the gains of successes for the first movers (Hausmann and Rodrik, 2003).

No matter whether the first movers succeed or fail, they provide society with useful information. The government should encourage first movers and compensate them for the information externality they generate. Otherwise, there will be little incentive for firms to be first movers in technological innovation and industrial upgrading (Harrison and Rodriguez-Clare, 2010; Lin, 2009; Lin and Monga, 2011; Rodrik, 2004). In addition, the success or failure of first movers also depends on whether improved hard and soft infrastructure match the needs of the new industries. Improving infrastructure and institutions is beyond the capacities of individual firms. Therefore, as argued by the structuralists, the government needs to play an enabling role to facilitate the industrial upgrading. The government may either coordinate firms' efforts to improve infrastructure and institutions or provide those improvements itself. By spontaneous market forces alone without the government playing a facilitating role, the structural change will not happen at all or will happen very slowly.

The new structural economics helps in understanding why structuralism and neoliberalism did not work. Structuralism failed to recognize the endogeneity of economic structure to endowment structure and sources of market failures. The import substitution catch-up strategy required governments to give priority to capital- and technology-intensive industries, thus defying developing countries' comparative advantages. Firms in those industries were not viable in open and competitive markets. Entrepreneurs would not voluntarily invest in those industries, which were doomed to fail in competitive markets, without government protection and subsidies and help in mobilizing required capital for investment. Structuralism mistakenly regarded market failures arising from structural rigidities as the cause of developing countries' inability to develop advanced, capital-intensive industries and called on the government to protect and subsidize nonviable firms in comparative advantage-defying industries. It is the violation of comparative advantage causing the failure of structuralism despite the government playing a facilitating role in structural transformation.

The new structural economics also helps in understanding why neoliberalism did not work. Washington Consensus policy failed to recognize the endogeneity of government interventions caused by structuralism and the need for the government to facilitate structural change. In developing countries, market distortions were endogenous to the government's need to protect and subsidize nonviable firms that had been promoted by the government's previous import substitution strategies. Eliminating protections and subsidies abruptly would doom nonviable firms, resulting in large-scale unemployment, social and political unrest, and slow economic growth. To avoid those consequences and to continue to prop up nonviable capital-intensive industries that were still considered the cornerstone of modernization and national defense, governments often continued to protect them through new and less visible means after removing previous protections and subsidies in line with the precepts of the Washington Consensus. While the new protections and subsidies were necessitated by avoiding the collapse of nonviable firms in the old comparative advantage-defying industries, they are usually less efficient than the old ones, especially in the transition economies of the former Soviet Union and Eastern Europe (World Bank, 2002). In addition, neoliberalism threw the baby out with the bath water, vehemently opposing any role for governments in facilitating structural change. Chile was a typical example. A model student of Washington Consensus reform, Chile diligently implemented the Washington Consensus reforms in the 1980s and then removed all government protections, subsidies and interventions to facilitate industrial upgrading in spite of the previous success of the Chilean government's support to diversify the economy from mining to commercial agriculture and salmon farming. Chile ranks high among developing countries on the World Bank's Doing Business Index, based on indicators of the ease of doing business and investing. However, Chile has not seen dynamic structural change for more than 30 years after implementing the Washington Consensus reform, and as a result, unemployment is high, income gaps have widened, and Chile remains mired in 'the middle-income trap.'

The new structural economics also justifies the gradual, dual-track approach to reform that conventional economic thought labeled the wrong approach to transition. Dual-tracking calls for maintaining stability during the transition and stimulating dynamic and sustainable economic growth by continuing transitory protection of the nonviable firms in the old priority sectors while removing restrictions to entry and facilitating the development of previously repressed industries that are consistent with the country's comparative advantages. The dynamic growth of sectors consistent with comparative advantages helps the economy rapidly accumulate capital and changes the factor endowment structure. That makes some formerly nonviable firms in capital-intensive industries viable and creates jobs for workers who were unemployed because of the shutdown of nonviable firms. Once firms in the new sectors are viable, the transitory protection and subsidies can be eliminated, bringing the transition to a market economy to a smooth end (Lau et al., 2000; Lin, 2009, 2012; Naughton, 1995; Subramanian and Roy, 2003).

WHY EAST ASIAN ECONOMIES ARE SO SPECIAL

East Asian economies have been rather special in terms of their development and transition performance since World War II. Under similar prevailing thinking about development in the 1950s and 1960s and about transition in the 1980s and 1990s, why have the East Asian governments behaved so differently and achieved such miraculous economic success?

As discussed, China, Vietnam and other East Asian economies adopted a dual-track, gradual approach in their transition from centrally planned economies to market economies, which violated the basic tenets of the Washington Consensus and shock therapy. In terms of development policies in Korea and Taiwan, both governments initially adopted a policy mix – including financial repression, overvalued exchange rates, deficit budgets and neglect of the agricultural sector – to support the development of labor-intensive primary manufacturing industries to substitute the imports of manufactured household products – referred to as 'primary import substitution.' The policy package was typical in countries that adopted a structuralist import substitution strategy. What differentiated Korea and Taiwan from other developing countries were two factors, as discussed by Ranis and Mahmood (1992). First, after they succeeded in primary import substitution, they relied on their abundant labor resources and turned to primary export substitution: they changed their export mix from primarily land-intensive agricultural products to labor-intensive manufactured products instead of jumping to secondary import substitution – that is, attempting to develop big, heavy industries to substitute imports of capital-intensive machinery and equipment – as many other developing countries did. They did not move to the 'secondary import cum export substitution' phase until labor shortages occurred, real wages increased and the comparative advantages in labor-intensive industries were lost in the international market. Second, repression in the financial sector and overvaluation of the exchange rate were rather mild. The real interest rate was kept positive at all times and the difference between the exchange rate on the black market and the official market was small. Therefore, the government's policy mix was close to what the new structural economics advocated: providing information and overcoming the issues of coordination and externality in the process of industrial upgrading by a facilitating state. The industrial upgrading in Taiwan and South Korea has basically followed their comparative advantages in each stage of economic development. Similarly, in post-war Japan, the main industries upgraded from labor-intensive to capital-intensive industries in sequence – textile, simple machine tools, steel, shipbuilding, electronics, automobiles and computers – according to changes in comparative advantages (Ito, 1998; Shinohara, 1982). Singapore and Hong Kong also followed a similar pattern in economic development (World Bank, 1993).

It was not, however, the intentional choice of the government in Japan and other East Asian economies to do so. Under the influence of prevailing development thinking in the 1950s and 1960s, governments in East Asia also had a strong desire for the development of advanced capital-intensive industries – just like governments in other developing countries at that time. Their economies were, however, relatively small in population size and their natural resource endowments were extremely poor, which greatly constrained their ability to mobilize enough resources to subsidize the nonviable enterprises in the capital-intensive industries in the early stage of development (Lin et al., 1994; Ranis and Mahmood, 1992).

For example, in the early 1950s, Taiwan was influenced by the fashionable post-war development thinking and tried to protect and subsidize the development of heavy industries by using quantitative restrictions, tariff barriers and subsidized credits via strict regulation of banks and other financial intermediaries. The attempt, however, caused severe budget deficits and high inflation. The government in Taiwan had to give up the attempt and devalued its currency, liberalized trade and raised the real interest rate to encourage savings and contain inflation (Tsiang, 1984). Without preferential protection and subsidization, industrial upgrading in Taiwan closely followed the changes in its comparative advantages.

Similarly, the South Korean government, under the leadership of President Park Chung Hee, adopted an ambitious heavy and chemical industry drive in 1973. It was adopted, however, only after obtaining rapid economic growth by developing and exporting labor-intensive textiles, plywood, wigs and other light-industrial products for more than a decade in the 1960s. Therefore, the drive partially reflected the necessity arising from the demand for upgrading the industries. It was, however, too ambitious – causing the inflation rate, measured by the consumer price index, to jump from 3.1 percent in 1972 to 24.3 percent in 1973, 25.3 percent in 1974 and maintained in two digits throughout the rest of the 1970s. By late 1978 and early 1979, President Park was increasingly concerned with stabilization and social welfare and, after his assassination in October 1979, the South Korean government – like the Taiwanese government in the 1950s – held back its support to heavy and chemical industries (Stern et al., 1995).

A structuralist strategy is very inefficient. How long such a strategy can be maintained depends on the level of resources the government can mobilize to subsidize the nonviable enterprises and support the investment in the prioritized industries. Resource mobilization is constrained by the natural resource endowment and population size. Contrasting with the case of 'resource curse' in many parts of the developing world (Diamond, 1997; Pomeranz, 2000; Sachs and Warner, 2001), the East Asian economies were lucky in the sense that their governments needed to be pragmatic in their policies and unintentionally followed a development path implied in the new structural economics – even though their governments had strong motivations for nation-building and were influenced by the same prevailing development thinking.[6]

---

[6] An example is China's great leap forward in 1958–60, which aimed to use China's vast

In fact, the pragmatism has been the spirit of East Asia's traditional culture. China's Confucianism – which has a strong impact in East Asia – is pragmatic in nature, probably also owing to the resource constraints arising from high population density. The core of Confucianism is *zhongyong*, the golden mean, which advises people to maintain balance, avoid extremes and achieve harmony with the outside, changing world. The political philosophy and policy principles promoted by the communist leadership of Mao Zedong, Deng Xiaoping, Jiang Zemin and Hu Jingtao are, respectively, *shishiqiushi* (finding truth from the facts), *jiefangsixiang* (freeing one's mind from dogmatism), *yushijujin* (adapting to the changing environment) and *hexie* (harmony) – all reflective of the traditional Chinese culture of *zhongyong*. When Deng Xiaoping started his reforms in 1979 – in addition to his philosophy of freeing one's mind from the dogmatism of the left and the right – the adoption of a gradual, piecemeal approach could have also reflected the political constraints he faced. Deng was one of the first in the generation of political leaders to start the socialist revolution and become involved in introducing a planned economy to China. In an Asian society, the power of a leader is based mainly on the personal prestige that the leader receives from the people, rather than on the office they hold,[7] and it is hard for a leader to renounce policies that they have pursued in the past for fear of losing prestige in the minds of the people.[8] Therefore, when Deng replaced Mao as China's supreme leader after the death of Mao in 1976, it was natural for Deng not to denounce and discard the old system totally but to carry out piecemeal tinkering, Pareto-improving changes to the old system. Similarly, the reforms in Vietnam and other East Asian economies were initiated by the first-generation revolutionaries who had brought socialism and planned economies to their countries.

population to rapidly transform the country from a primarily agrarian economy dominated by peasant farmers to a modern, industrialized society. The result was a great famine in 1959–61, which caused 30 million extra deaths (Lin, 1990; Lin and Yang, 2000).

[7]   In his final years, Deng's only formal title was an honorary chairman of China's Bridge Society. He was, however, the de facto supreme leader until his death.

[8]   In China a leader's prestige is accumulated through the merits of his or her contributions to the people and the nation during their career and people's trust in his or her wisdom to provide good guidance for the nation's future. If a political leader openly admits that he or she made a mistake in a major policy in the past, people may lose confidence in their wisdom and the leader's prestige will be adversely affected.

CONCLUDING REMARKS

Modern economic growth originating in the West is characterized by a continuous structural transformation in technology, industry, and hard and soft infrastructure. As Gerschenkron (1962) postulates, developing countries in the Rest have an advantage of backwardness in economic development as they can borrow from a large backlog of technological innovations from the West and can adopt the latest technology without facing resistance from users of old technologies. If a developing country uses that advantage well, they will have faster technological innovation, industrial upgrading and economic growth than advanced countries and converge to the West in one or two generations.

The precondition for a developing country to use the advantage of backwardness is to follow the comparative advantage determined by its own factor endowment in the industrial upgrading and technological innovation in a market economy with a facilitating state, as practiced in the East Asian economies and elaborated in the new structural economics. Regrettably, under the drive of nation-building and the influence of prevailing structuralism, the governments in most developing countries adopted an import substitution strategy to develop the advanced industries prevailing in the West. To implement the strategy, their governments introduced all kinds of interventions and distortions to protect/subsidize the nonviable firms in the priority industries. Their economies became uncompetitive, growth was unsustainable and crises hit frequently. Instead of advantage, the backwardness became disadvantage in achieving rapid, sustained growth.

As the distortions and interventions are endogenous to the needs of protecting nonviable firms in the priority industries under the structuralist import substitution strategy, a pragmatic, dual-track, gradual approach to transition to a market economy, as followed in China, Vietnam and a few other economies, would be the appropriate way to achieve stability and dynamic growth in the transition process. However, under the influence of prevailing neoliberalism, most countries adopted the shock therapy in an attempt to eliminate the distortions and interventions simultaneously and immediately, causing a transition collapse followed by stagnation and frequent crises.

China and the East Asian economies were lucky not to follow the inappropriate prevailing thinking in their development and transition policies due to the constraints of poor resources and the inherent pragmatism in their culture. However, their success reveals the nature and causes of a developing country's attempt to catch up with the West. The new structural economics offers theories to explain the successes of the East Asian economies and the failures of the Rest. It is hoped that the ideas embodied in the new structural economics will assist the Rest to catch up with the West as successfully as the East Asian economies.

REFERENCES

Agenor, P.R., O. Canuto and M. Jelenic. 2012. 'Avoiding Middle-income Growth Traps'. *Economic Premise*, No. 98, World Bank.

Aghion, P. 2009. 'Some Thoughts on Industrial Policy and Growth'. Document de Travail 2009-09. Observatoire Français des conjonctures économiques, Sciences Po, Paris.

Amsden, A.H. 1989. *Asia's Next Giant*. New York and Oxford: Oxford University Press.

Chang, H.-J. 2003. *Kicking Away the Ladder: Development Strategy in Historical Perspective*. London: Anthem Press.

Chenery, H.B. 1961. 'Comparative Advantage and Development Policy'. *American Economic Review* **51** (1), 18–51.

Diamond, J.M. (1997). *Guns, Germs, and Steel: The Fates of Human Societies*. New York: W.W. Norton.

Easterly, W. 2001, 'The Lost Decades: Explaining Developing Countries' Stagnation in Spite of Policy Reform 1980–1998'. *Journal of Economic Growth* **6** (2), 135–57.

Gerschenkron, A. 1962. *Economic Backwardness in Historical Perspective: A Book of Essays*. Cambridge, MA: Belknap Press of Harvard University Press.

Harrison, A. and A. Rodríguez-Clare. 2010. 'Trade, Foreign Investment, and Industrial Policy for Developing Countries'. In D. Rodrik (ed.), *Handbook of Economic Growth*, Vol. 5. Amsterdam: North Holland, pp. 4039–213.

Hausmann, R. and D. Rodrik. 2003. 'Economic Development as Self-discovery'. *Journal of Development Economics* **72** (December), 603–33.

Ito, T. 1998. 'Japanese Economic Development: Are its Features Idiosyncratic or Universal?'. In J.Y. Lin (ed.), *Contemporary Economic Issues. Volume 1: Regional Experience and System Reform*, Proceedings of the 11th World Congress of the International Economic Association, Tunis, IEA Conference No. 121, London and New York: Macmillan and St Martin's Press, pp. 18–37.

Ju, J., J.Y. Lin and Y. Wang. 2015. 'Endowment Structures, Industrial Dynamics, and Economic Growth'. *Journal of Monetary Policy* **76**, 244–63.

Keynes, J.M. 1935 [1964]. *The General Theory of Employment, Interest and Money*. New York: Harcourt, Brace and World.

Krueger, A. and B. Tuncer. 1982. 'An Empirical Test of the Infant Industry Argument'. *American Economic Review* **72** (5), 1142–52.

Kuznets, S. 1966. *Modern Economic Growth: Rate, Structure and Spread*. New Haven, CT: Yale University Press.

Lal, D. 1994. *Against Dirigisme: The Case for Unshackling Economic Markets*. San Francisco, CA: International Center for Economic Growth, ICS Press.

Lau, L.J., Y. Qian and G. Roland. 2000, 'Reform Without Losers: An Interpretation of China's Dual-track Approach to Transition'. *Journal of Political Economy* **108** (1), 120–43.

Lin, J.Y. 1989, 'An Economic Theory of Institutional Change: Induced and Imposed Change'. *Cato Journal* **9**, September, 1–33.

Lin, J.Y. 1990. 'Collectivization and China's Agricultural Crisis in 1959–1961'. *Journal of Political Economy* **98** (6), 1228–52.

Lin, J.Y. 2009. *Economic Development and Transition: Thought, Strategy and Viability.* (Marshall Lectures), Cambridge: Cambridge University Press.

Lin, J.Y. 2011. 'New Structural Economics: A Framework for Rethinking Economic Development'. *World Bank Research Observer,* **26** (2), 193–221.

Lin, J.Y. 2012. *Demystifying the Chinese Economy.* Cambridge: Cambridge University Press.

Lin, J.Y. and H. Chang. 2009. 'DPR Debate: Should Industrial Policy in Developing Countries Conform to Comparative Advantage or Defy It?' *Development Policy Review* **27** (5), 483–502.

Lin, J.Y. and C. Monga. 2011. 'DPR Debate: Growth Identification and Facilitation: The Role of the State in the Dynamics of Structural Change'. *Development Policy Review* **29** (3), 259–310.

Lin, J.Y. and J. Nugent. 1995. 'Institutions and Economic Development'. In T.N. Srinivasan and J. Behrman (eds), *Handbook of Development Economics,* Vol. 3. Amsterdam: North Holland, pp. 2301–70.

Lin, J.Y. and D. Rosenblatt. 2012. 'Shifting Patterns of Economic Growth and Rethinking Development'. *Journal of Economic Policy Reform* **15** (3), 71–94.

Lin, J.Y. and D.T. Yang. 2000. 'Food Availability, Entitlements and the Chinese Famine of 1959–61'. *Economic Journal* **110** (460, January), 136–58.

Lin, J.Y., F. Cai and Z. Li. 1994. *China's Miracle: Development Strategy and Economic Reform.* Shanghai: Shanghai Sanlian Press. Chinese edition reprinted in 1996, Chinese University of Hong Kong Press. English edition reprinted in 2003.

Maddison, A. 2006. *The World Economy.* Paris: Organisation for Economic Co-operation and Development.

Maddison, A. 2010. Historical Statistics of the World Economy: 1-2008 AD. www.ggdc.net/maddison/Historical_Statistics/horizontal-file_02-2010.xls (accessed 19 April 2013).

Murphy, K., A. Shleifer and R.T Vishny. 1992. 'The Transition to a Market Economy: Pitfall of Partial Reform'. *Quarterly Journal of Economics* **107**, 889–906.

Naughton, B. 1995. *Growing Out of Plan: Chinese Economic Reform 1978–1993.* Cambridge: Cambridge University Press.

Pack, H. and K. Saggi. 2006. 'Is There a Case for Industrial Policy? A Critical Survey'. *World Bank Research Observer* **21** (2), 267–97.

Pomeranz, K. 2000. *The Great Divergence: China, Europe, and the Making of the Modern World Economy.* Princeton Economic History of the Western World Series, Vol. 4. Princeton, NJ: Princeton University Press.

Porter, M.E. 1990. *The Competitive Advantage of Nations.* New York: Free Press.

Prebisch, R. 1950. *The Economic Development of Latin America and its Principal Problems.* New York: United Nations.

Pritchett, L. 1997. 'Divergence, Big Time'. *Journal of Economic Perspectives* **11** (3), 3–17.

Ranis, G. and S. Mahmood. 1992. *The Political Economy of Development Policy.* Oxford: Basil Blackwell.

Rodrik, D. 2004. *Industrial Policy for the Twenty-first Century.* Cambridge, MA: Harvard University Press.

Romer, P.M. 1990. 'Endogenous Technological Change'. *Journal of Political Economy* **98**, s71–s102.

Rosenstein-Rodan, P. 1943. 'Problems of Industrialization of Eastern and Southeastern Europe'. *Economic Journal* **111** (210–11), 202–11.

Sachs, J.D. and A.M. Warner. 2001. 'Natural Resources and Economic Development: The Curse of Natural Resources'. *European Economic Review* **45**, 827–38.

Sachs, J.D., W.T. Woo and X. Yang. 2000. 'Economic Reforms and Constitutional Transition'. *Annals of Economics and Finance* **1**, 435–91.

Schumpeter, J.A. 1942. *Capitalism, Socialism and Democracy.* London: Routledge.

Shinohara, M. 1982. *Industrial Growth, Trade and Dynamic Growth in the Japanese Economy.* Tokyo: Tokyo University Press.

Singer, H.W. 1950. 'The Distribution of Gains between Investing and Borrowing Countries'. *American Economic Review (Papers and Proceedings)* **40**, 473–85.

Stern, J.J., J.H. Kim, D.W. Perkins and J H. Yoo. 1995. *Industrialization and the State: The Korean Heavy and Chemical Industry Drive.* Cambridge, MA: Harvard Institute for International Development and Korea Development Institute, distributed by Harvard University Press.

Subramanian, A and D. Roy. 2003. 'Who Can Explain the Mauritian Miracle? Meade, Romer, Sachs, or Rodrik?' In D. Rodrik (ed.), *In Search of Prosperity: Analytic Narratives on Economic Growth.* Princeton, NJ and Oxford: Princeton University Press, pp. 205–43.

Tsiang, S.C. 1984. 'Taiwan's Economic Miracle: Lessons in Economic Development'. In A.C. Harberger (ed.), *World Economic Growth: Case Studies of Developed and Developing Nations.* San Francisco, CA: ICS Press, pp. 301–25.

Wade, R. 1990. *Governing the Market.* Princeton, NJ: Princeton University Press.

Williamson, J. 1990. 'What Washington Means by Policy Reform'. In J. Williamson (ed.), *Latin American Adjustment: How Much has Happened?* Washington, DC: Institute for International Economics, pp. 7–20.

Williamson, J. 2004, 'A Short History of the Washington Consensus'. Paper commissioned by Fundación CIDOB for the conference, 'From the Washington Consensus Towards a New Global Governance', Barcelona, 24–25 September.

World Bank. 1993. *The East Asian Miracle: Economic Growth and Public Policy.* Oxford: Oxford University Press.

World Bank. 2002. *Transition, the First Ten Years: Analysis and Lessons for Eastern Europe and the Former Soviet Union.* Washington, DC: World Bank.

5. Why the 'Rest' doesn't need foreign finance

Luiz Carlos Bresser-Pereira

The relations between the West and the Rest, between the center and the periphery of capitalism, were always difficult. They originally assumed the form of colonial domination: mercantile domination of Latin America, mainly by Spain and Portugal, between the sixteenth and the eighteenth centuries; and industrial domination of Asia and Africa, mainly by Britain and France, in the nineteenth century and the first half of the twentieth century, as the industrial revolution in Europe made these countries strong enough to subjugate the old empires of these two continents. As colonized countries achieved independence – the Latin American ones in the early nineteenth century, the others after World War II – domination remained, but now relied on the West's soft power and on the dependency of the local elites.

After World War II, it was clear that the world had been divided between the West – the rich countries – and the Rest – the developing countries. With the theoretical support of a school of thought that emerged at this time – namely, development economics – the countries where the elites had been mostly nationalist in economic terms criticized the law of comparative advantage, adopted a developmental strategy, neutralized the Dutch disease when they contracted it,[1] and industrialized; and after the 1970s, the more successful ones – the newly industrialized countries (NICs), that is, the four Asian tigers (Hong Kong, Singapore, South Korea and Taiwan) and Brazil and Mexico – began to export manufactured goods to the West, actively competing with it. Soon other Asian countries, including China and India, successfully joined the competition, and the world economy

---

[1]   This was the case with Brazil, which industrialized between 1930 and 1980, and became an exporter of manufactured goods. The neutralization of the Dutch disease was achieved by adopting either a system of multiple exchange rates or a system of high tariffs on imported manufactured goods combined with high subsidies for exporters of such goods. This neutralization mechanism was dismantled when the country liberalized trade in 1990. Since then Brazil has been de-industrializing and growing much more slowly than in the period of industrialization.

changed. It ceased to be a world only of rich and pre-industrial countries, and became a world also of middle-income or emerging countries exerting pressure on the West. Today, the more successful ones – South Korea, Taiwan and Singapore – are already rich.

All successful cases of development among the Rest involved economic nationalism or a developmental strategy whereby the manufacturing sector was protected up to the moment it ceased to consist of infant industries.[2] No industrial revolution in these countries was achieved while their states were liberal; their states were always developmental, combining market coordination with moderate but firm government intervention. All of them privileged national business enterprises over foreign ones.

Yet the Rest's intellectuals and politicians failed to criticize foreign finance. They failed to recognize that in most cases a country would grow faster and with more stability if it avoided current account deficits that would have to be financed either by loans or by the direct investments of multinational enterprises. Many of the intellectuals joined forces with left-wing economists who since the 1990s had been criticizing 'financialization' – the speculative action of financiers searching to multiply the gains of rentier capitalists through financial innovations that involve leverage increase and fraud – but financialization is a general problem of capitalism as a whole. It was the main cause of the 2008 Global Financial Crisis. What the Rest's economists have failed to do is criticize the *received truth* that resorting to foreign indebtedness is a good way to achieve growth: the idea that current account deficits should be welcomed because these 'foreign savings' increase the investment rate of the country, provided that they are financed by direct investment or by loans formally attached to investments. Developing countries need finance, but domestic finance not only for short-term commercial activities but mainly for investment and exports, particularly exports of manufactured goods. Domestic private banks satisfactorily finance day-to-day commerce; public banks should be set up to finance investment and exports.

Since the nineteenth century developing countries have turned to foreign banks for finance in hard currency and have experienced currency crises, usually caused by increases in foreign debt associated with falling commodity prices. The World Bank was set up after World War II to rescue the European countries and to offer finance to developing economies. It was then that the strategy of 'growth cum foreign savings' was 'officially' adopted. At this time – the 1950s – classical developmentalism – the version of development economics that originated in Latin America and whose main advocates were Raúl Prebisch and Celso Furtado – was able

---

[2] See Bresser-Pereira and Ianoni (2015).

to criticize 'unequal exchange' but unable to criticize foreign finance. On the contrary, from its foundation text (Rosenstein-Rodan's 1943 paper on the 'big push'), development economics relied on foreign capital to promote economic growth. It is true that some economists, such as Ragnar Nurkse, maintained that 'capital is made at home,' but this didn't represent a critique of growth with current account deficits to finance loans or direct investment. At that time, developmental economists criticized investment by multinationals in the exploitation of mineral resources and bananas, which created modern enclaves in pre-industrial societies and involved large profit remittances to the West. But they made no critique of the multinational corporations that to circumvent the barriers imposed by developing countries began to invest directly in manufacturing industry from the 1950s on. On the contrary, a number of them understood that such investment refuted the contention of economic nationalism (or developmentalism) that the rich countries opposed the industrialization of the periphery, and moved from classical developmentalism to economic liberalism. Indeed, the West is not opposed to the industrialization of the Rest since such industrialization is carried out by multinational corporations.

Economic liberalism proposes an intuitively rational argument in favor of the policy of growth cum foreign indebtedness, namely, that 'capital-rich countries should transfer their capital to capital-poor countries.' This is an argument in favor of current account deficits and financing them either by long-term loans or by direct investment. But although this argument seems to be true, it is in fact false because, as we show below, it ignores two facts: (a) that a current account deficit is consistent with an overvalued currency that discourages domestic investment, and (b) that when a country duly neutralizes its Dutch disease, it will have a current account surplus consistent with the resulting competitive exchange rate. The argument for growth cum foreign indebtedness serves the interests of the West but not the interests of the Rest, except under certain special conditions. I maintain that developing countries will grow faster and catch up if they achieve current account balance or surplus. In this chapter my objective is to discuss this issue – an issue rarely debated by economists – and to offer an argument against current account deficits. I shall argue that developing countries (other than very poor ones) don't need foreign capital, and so should avoid current account deficits and any recourse to foreign finance. They may accept direct investment because it brings technology or because it opens new markets, but not because it brings capital.

I am not making an argument against domestic finance. Such finance is essential to economic development, whether in Schumpeterian terms, whereby the business entrepreneur has credit and innovates, or in Keynesian terms, whereby the investment, duly financed, determines savings. And I am not making an argument against multinationals so long as their legiti-macy is based on technology transfer and the generation of exports, not on the financing of current account deficits.

SOME EVIDENCE

This chapter is analytical rather than empirical. It assumes that there is already enough evidence to show that, in most cases, developing countries don't need foreign finance in order to grow. A very simple way of confirm-ing this fact is to show that the countries that run current account deficits and so resort to foreign finance usually grow less than if they achieve current account balance or surplus. In other words, the greater a develop-ing country's current account deficit, the more slowly it grows. A simple demonstration is presented in Figure 5.1, which shows the relation between current account deficits and per capita economic growth in a sample of middle-income countries with per capita purchasing parity (PP) incomes of more than US$10 000, other than oil exporters, between 1981 and 2007. The tendency line has a clear upward slope, confirming the negative rela-tion between current account deficits and growth. The majority of the middle-income countries run current account deficits, but the smaller they are, or the greater their current account surpluses, the faster they

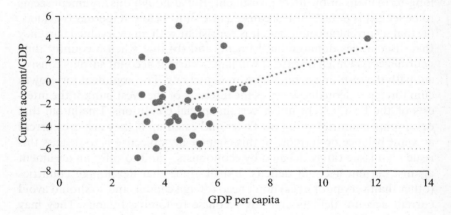

Note: PP income per capita above US$10 000, except oil exporters.

Source: World Bank.

Figure 5.1   Per capita income growth and current account in middle-income countries (1981–2014)

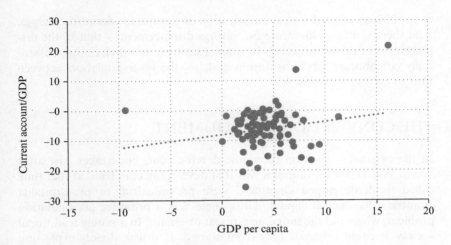

Note: PP income per capita below US$10 000, except oil and diamond exporters.

Source: World Bank.

Figure 5.2   Per capita income growth and current account in developing countries (1981–2014)

grow. This finding challenges the conventional wisdom, whose advocates will certainly argue that the data in Figure 5.1 are not enough to establish definitively an inverse relation between foreign savings and growth. I agree, but the data are a good indication.

In Figure 5.2 we have the other developing countries, those with per capita PP incomes of below US$10 000, other than oil exporters and diamond exporters, between 1981 and 2007. As expected, the relation is less clear because foreign capital may assist countries in the earliest stages of capitalist development, but even here the same tendency is evident.

There is further evidence of the inverse relationship between current account deficits and growth, beginning with the so-called 'Feldstein–Horioka puzzle' (1980) – the realization on the part of these two distinguished economists that domestic savings rates and domestic investment rates are highly correlated in the Organisation for Economic Co-operation and Development (OECD) countries, which refutes the belief that the savings of any country will flow to those countries with the most productive investment opportunities. In my first paper on the theme (Bresser-Pereira and Nakano, 2003) a clear inverse relationship is demonstrated between foreign savings and growth; in relation to Brazil, Bresser-Pereira et al. (2014a) verified a clear substitution of foreign for domestic savings. And there is a large literature on 'savings displacement' – that is, the displacement of domestic savings by foreign savings – in which findings essentially corroborate this substitution and, so, the inverse relation between foreign savings and growth.[3]

THE CONVENTIONAL ARGUMENT

In the original studies on economic development, undertaken just after World War II, the assumption was that developing countries, at that time called 'underdeveloped countries,' were pre-industrial or pre-capitalist countries that lacked capital. Thus, there was a primitive accumulation problem: where did the initial investment originate? In a purely traditional society, it could originate only from abroad. If it was already exploiting certain natural resources which complemented Europe's natural resources, the original accumulation could be domestic. That happened in most Latin American countries and, in a different way, in the Asian countries where previous civilizations, mostly destroyed in the colonial period, had somehow accumulated some capital. These countries enjoyed what came to be called 'Ricardian comparative advantage,' but, actually, what they produced could not be produced in the West for reasons of climate or of natural resource availability.

In this case, there were two possibilities: either the local elites had been able, over the centuries, to achieve primitive accumulation domestically by exporting agricultural goods, as in most of Latin America; or foreign firms took charge of this task, investing mostly in mining but also in agriculture, as in many African countries from the nineteenth century. Yet there was also a third possibility, associated with East Asian countries, which proved more fruitful: the country did not rely on natural resources to export commodities (so it did not face the Dutch disease problem), instead the pre-existing traditional system had developed a domestic market and an education system that served as instruments for a short-lived import substitution model of industrialization, soon followed by the export of manufactured goods.

Thus, only in the second of these three cases set out above did foreign finance play a significant role. Nevertheless, economic theory always assumed that foreign capital was essential to growth in all developing countries. The conventional argument in favor of growth cum foreign

[3] See Fry (1978), Schmidt-Hebbel et al. (1992), Edwards (1995), Reinhart and Talvi (1998), Uthoff and Titelman (1998).

savings and, so, in favor of foreign finance is simple and straightforward. And naturally it ignores historical and natural resource problems. Growth depends on investment, I, which is equal to total savings, S, which is equal to domestic savings, Sd, plus foreign savings, Sx. Domestic savings are by definition necessarily insufficient. Thus, when a country obtains foreign savings, its total savings and total investments will be proportionally higher, and growth will accelerate. The only problem with this argument is that it involves not economic but accounting reasoning, not *ex ante* but *ex post* reasoning. The accounting argument does not consider that, *ex ante*, investment can be higher or lower than savings; that foreign savings don't necessarily add to domestic savings but may substitute for them. I come back to this problem later.

Developing countries are taught that they should increase their savings and investment capacity, and the best way to do this is to run current account deficits, supposedly caused by increased investment, and finance them with foreign loans. Actually, the West explains, this is a second best, because there is no guarantee that the loans will finance additional investment rather than additional consumption. But there would be an obvious first best – foreign direct investment finance – because in this case it would not be possible to use the additional financial resources to finance consumption.

The country will have to pay interest on the additional foreign debt, or profit remittances on the additional foreign direct investment; but in the case of loans, the argument goes, the country should reason as individual business enterprises do: provided that the interest rate is lower than the rate of return on the additional investment, the country will grow faster and will not have any difficulty in paying its debts and in keeping its foreign account in balance. I remember hearing this argument again and again in the second half of the 1970s, when Brazil decided to grow with foreign savings. And I also remember how terrible its consequences were in the following decade, when the countries with high foreign debt, 'led' by Brazil, faced a huge financial crisis – the foreign debt crisis of the 1980s.

Actually, foreign finance, in the form of portfolio investment and especially foreign direct investment, is essentially in the interests of the West. It is key to the foreign policy of the United States and the other rich Western countries, which send much more investment abroad than they receive into their territories, and thus occupy without direct reciprocity the domestic markets of developing countries. When we examine the bilateral 'trade' agreements that the United States signs with other countries, or the multilateral agreements that the United States has signed on the one hand with Europe and on the other with Pacific countries, we see that they are not really trade agreements, in so far as tariffs are already quite low. The real objectives of these agreements are twofold. The first is to assure more guarantees for their direct investments, for instance, by ensuring that the problems that US multinational corporations face in other countries are resolved by 'independent arbitrage' rather than by those countries' legal systems. The second is to create additional protection for their intellectual property rights.

In both cases, the interests of the multinational corporations predominate. This is something that I can understand if I adopt the point of view of the rich countries. Today, they are increasingly less involved in production. They are essentially knowledge countries and rentier countries. They receive a substantial portion of their revenues in the form of remittances of profits and royalties from the multinational corporations, while, naturally, always arguing that this is a win–win game in which the interests of the developing countries are also duly considered.

THE ORIGINAL CRITICISM

Developmental politicians and intellectuals framed the original criticism of the policy of growth cum foreign indebtedness mainly in the 1950s and 1960s. They focused on the law of comparative foreign advantage and on the remittance of profit. The criticism of the Ricardians – the Prebisch–Singer law – was strong enough to legitimize the decision of many developing countries to build a tariff system protecting their infant industries. But the Rest failed to frame a persuasive argument against foreign loans. Developing countries didn't know how to reject logically the comparison between the indebtedness in foreign money of a country and the foreign indebtedness of a firm; they were unable to demonstrate that a loan to a business enterprise in the country's money is very different from a loan to this same enterprise in foreign currency. As to direct investment, it became a problem only in the 1950s, when the manufacturing corporations in the West responded to the developing countries' protection of their domestic markets by undertaking foreign direct investment. Again, the Rest didn't have a theory on which to base the framework of conditionalities to these investments. The developing countries' critique was either outdated or insufficient. It was outdated when they argued that the multinational corporations invested only in mining and in monopolist public services – something that was not true from the 1950s. It was insufficient when they founded their critique on the remittance of profits. But why be concerned about profits if the foreign corporation had made additional investment that increased the productive capacity of the country?

It was an objective fact that, originally, the more successful countries, namely, the East Asian countries including Japan, didn't open their markets to foreign investment. In the 1970s developmental economists and politicians used this fact to justify the adoption of developmental policies, while the United States, which was facing a domestic economic crisis and experiencing military defeat in Vietnam, was on the defensive. But soon the picture was reversed, as the foreign debt crisis of the 1980s weakened developing countries, strengthened rich ones, and enabled the latter to impose neoliberal reforms on highly indebted countries by means of the 1985 Baker Plan,[4] which requested the World Bank to carry out 'market-oriented reforms' and the International Monetary Fund (IMF) to implement 'structural adjustment.' Both policies were understood to be necessary: market reforms 'because the import substitution model had failed,' and structural adjustment because, indeed, many countries were bankrupted and facing high inflation. Actually, the import substitution model of industrialization had been exhausted long before, in the late 1950s, and the two more successful Latin American countries – Brazil and Mexico – were engaged in an efficacious strategy of exporting manufactured goods. For instance, Brazil's exports of manufactured goods, which represented only 6 percent of total exports in 1965, jumped to 62 percent in 1990. What had interrupted the growth of these countries in 1980 was the foreign debt crisis of the 1980s, the de facto moratoriums on debt servicing, and the high inflation associated with this balance of payment crisis.

In the 1980s the six original NICs fell apart; but while the four Asian tigers continued to grow fast, and today, 36 years later, are already rich countries, Brazil and Mexico fell behind. There are, essentially, two reasons for these different outcomes. First, the Asian countries didn't get involved in the growth cum foreign savings policy in the previous decade as the Latin American countries did, and so didn't face a real debt crisis in the 1980s;[5] and second, the East Asian countries continued to be developmental societies, while Latin America, under the pressure of the Washington Consensus, bowed to the West in the late 1980s. Developmentalism was forgotten, the industrialization project was abandoned, trade and financial liberalization was adopted, and countries got involved in large privatization programs that even included monopolistic public services. In addition,

---

[4]   This 1985 plan, formulated to solve the 1980s foreign debt crisis, was called the Baker Plan after James Baker, the then US Secretary of the Treasury, who gave to the World Bank the responsibility for the 'market-oriented reforms,' which would complement the 'structural adjustments' that were already being undertaken by the IMF.

[5]   Some Asian countries – specifically, South Korea, Thailand, Indonesia and Malaysia – would suffer a currency crisis in 1996, which, as had happened to Latin America, was also a consequence of the growth cum foreign savings policy.

growth rates fell as economies suffered a process of re-primarization, perversely transferring labor from manufacturing industry to low per capita income services, from sophisticated and well-paid activities to less sophisticated and poorly paid ones. Mexico, instead of experiencing re-primarization, experienced 'maquilization' – the transformation of most of its manufacturing industry (not only the maquilas in the frontier with the United States) into plants that assemble imported inputs using cheap labor – industries also producing low per capita added value.

At that time, developmental ideas were a shambles. Classical developmentalism or Latin American structuralism had little to offer. The 'associated dependency' theory, which became dominant in Latin America in the 1970s, made the first attack, as it dismissed the possibility of a national bourgeoisie emerging to lead the industrial revolution in developing countries, as had happened in the rich countries, and defended the association with (subordination to) the West. The crisis of Keynesian macroeconomics in the 1970s, and the simultaneous rise of monetarist and neoclassical economics, represented a second major blow. In the early 1980s Albert Hirschman (1981) wrote the epitaph of development economics in a paper whose title is self-explanatory: 'The rise and decline of development economics.' Thus, when the foreign debt crisis broke in the 1980s, the West ignored the fact that it was mainly a consequence of the growth cum foreign indebtedness policy adopted in the 1970s; and, profiting from the weakness of the developing countries, it was able to persuade their elites, other than the fast-growing Asian countries, that the cause of the crisis was the exhaustion of the import substitution model of industrialization, which would be inescapably a victim of fiscal populism. Actually, there was a problem of fiscal populism in the countries in crisis, but the direct cause of the crisis was not fiscal populism but exchange rate populism – the practice of the nation-state (not only the public sector but also the private sector) getting involved in current account deficits – which the West does not criticize but encourages.

From the mid 1980s developing countries, other than the fast-growing Asian countries, lost the capacity to resist neoliberalism and neoclassical theory, and so ceased to be able to argue against the growth cum foreign savings policy – a policy that the West assumed to be virtuous by definition. The same happened to other Washington Consensus reforms, such as financial liberalization and the privatization of public service monopolies, two reforms that were in the interests of the West, not the Rest.

It was in such a framework that Ha-Joon Chang (2002) and Erik Reinert (2007) published their books renewing criticism of the West. They argue and demonstrate that, since the 1980s, the Washington Consensus had been attempting to inhibit the adoption by developing countries of the very same policies and institutions that rich countries had embraced in the eighteenth and nineteenth centuries, when they were undergoing their national and industrial revolutions. These two remarkable books showed forcefully how the West was limiting the policy space of developing countries, but their criticism didn't include the growth cum foreign savings policy. At the same time, and mainly after the 2008 Global Financial Crisis, the economists associated with the only international institution that deals appropriately with the problems of developing countries centered their focus on the critique of financialization – or 'finance-driven globalization.'[6] The criticism is correct; it is a criticism of practices associated with leveraged speculation and fraudulent financial innovations that became dominant in financial markets and caused harm to rich as well as developing countries. But it should not be confused with the criticism of the growth cum foreign indebtedness policy that is key to new developmentalism.

NEW DEVELOPMENTALISM CRITICISM

In the 1990s many developing countries – now under neoliberal domination – were able to carry out fiscal adjustment and control inflation; but, predictably, they were unable to reduce economic inequalities and resume growth. This opened the way for the gradual formulation of a new theoretical framework, based on classical developmentalism and post-Keynesian macroeconomics, which came to be called new developmentalism – a work in progress that is oriented to middle-income countries. This theoretical framework already embraces a microeconomics, a macroeconomics and a political economy. The microeconomics is built on classical developmentalism's association of growth with structural change and productive sophistication; developmental macroeconomics is based on the tendency to cyclical and chronic overvaluation of the exchange rate and the problem of access to demand, and is focused on the exchange rate and on the current account deficit; and the political economy deals with the historical concept of the developmental state and the concept of developmental class coalitions associating business industrialists with the popular classes and the public bureaucracy.[7]

One of the key claims of the new theoretical approach is that developing countries don't need foreign capital in order to grow and catch up, except in certain special circumstances. The growth cum foreign savings policy is a hindrance rather than a help to developing countries, except in moments

6   Alfredo Calcagno (2015).
7   On this developmental macroeconomics, see Bresser-Pereira (2010) and Bresser-Pereira et al. (2014b).

when a country is already growing fast, the marginal propensity to consume falls, and the rate of substitution of foreign for domestic savings falls. Except in these circumstances, the orthodox claim – that current account deficits (foreign savings) will increase the investment and the growth rates provided that it is financed by direct investment or by loans directly associated with capital accumulation – is false. On the contrary, current account deficits are in most cases harmful to growth. They wouldn't be harmful if they were caused by, effectively, additional investment; but usually, even when they assume the form of foreign direct investment, they end up financing more consumption than investment.

On that matter, new developmentalism shows theoretically two things related to the exchange rate and the current account balance that reinforce each other: first, if a country has the Dutch disease, it should have a current account surplus in order to grow; second, even if this is not the case, the country should not adopt the growth cum foreign savings policy because such a policy involves a high rate of substitution of foreign for domestic savings.

I offer two arguments in this direction, both associated with the exchange rate. Both proceed from a core claim of developmental macroeconomics, namely, that growth depends on investment, which depends on the interest rate and on the expected rate of profit, which in turn depends on effective demand and access to demand, which a currency that is overvalued over the long term does not assure. The assumption is that long-term overvaluation is the rule rather than the exception in developing countries, in which a competent exchange rate policy does not neutralize the tendency to cyclical and chronic overvaluation of the exchange rate. The fact that the overvaluation persists over the long term – that it is not just a misalignment – is essential for the argument because, in this circumstance, the businessman who is deciding whether or not to invest will take into consideration this overvalued currency and will not invest. By contrast, when the exchange rate is experiencing a short-term misalignment, the businessman interested in the long term will consider the average exchange rate, which will not be overvalued, and may invest.

There are two causes for such a tendency, which correspond to the two arguments cited above. One cause is the policies that developing countries routinely adopt, and that overvalue the national currency; the other is the Dutch disease, which most developing countries face, but which today few, if any, neutralize.

I will begin with the Dutch disease. It is not a cause of current account deficits, because it is consistent with the current equilibrium – the value or level of the exchange rate which balances inter-temporally the country's current account. But a country that has a permanent Dutch disease must

have a current account surplus in order to have the exchange rate float-
ing around the competitive or industrial equilibrium; if the disease is less
severe and appears only during commodity booms, the country will have
to run a current account surplus at these moments.

The Dutch disease is a long-term appreciation of the exchange rate
caused by Ricardian rents that arise from the exploitation of natural
resources and/or by commodity booms which involve a long-term overvaluation of the exchange rate, because the exchange rate that makes such
commodities competitive and defines the current equilibrium exchange
rate is substantially more appreciated than the industrial equilibrium,
which makes competitive the non-commodity tradable goods and services
that utilize world state-of-the-art technology. The severity of the Dutch
disease, or natural resource curse,[8] is measured by the difference between
the two equilibriums. Neutralizing the Dutch disease means shifting the
value of the exchange rate around, which it floats from the current equilibrium to the industrial equilibrium – which will represent a current account
surplus and the corresponding competitive market exchange rate. Thus,
this amounts to a very strong argument against foreign savings or current
account deficits.

Let us turn now to the second argument, related directly to the growth
cum foreign savings policy. Developing countries usually don't run current
account balances corresponding to the current equilibrium, much less consistent with the industrial equilibrium – they run deficits. Deficits which,
as I have already demonstrated, are, essentially, desired deficits, in so far as
their causes are three usual policies adopted by developing countries: the
growth cum foreign indebtedness policy, a monetary policy defining a high
level of interest rate around which the central bank manages the market
interest rate, and the use of the exchange rate anchor to control inflation.

If we assume that the usual thing – and certainly what the West expects
from the Rest countries – is current account deficits, why don't such deficits contribute to economic development even when they are financed by
direct investment? Or, in other words, why don't foreign savings add to
domestic savings as nicely as most expect?

The theory is very simple. The current account deficit or surplus,
independently of how is it financed, corresponds to a more appreciated

---

[8]   There is a line of thought that distinguishes the Dutch disease, which would be a not
very well-defined economic problem, from the natural resource curse, which would be a political or moral problem associated with the rent-seeking involved in the exploitation of natural
resources. I don't deny that there are two problems, but I use the two expressions 'Dutch
disease' and 'natural resource curse' interchangeably to refer to the coincidence of the two
problems that is usually stronger, the poorer and less institutionalized a country is. In this way,
I avoid the problem of paying attention just to the political-moral problem while leaving aside
the economic problem which is fundamental.

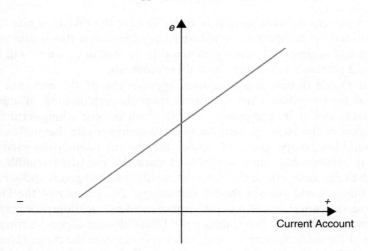

Figure 5.3   Relation between the current account and the exchange rate

currency, as we see in Figure 5.3. Given this relation, the theory has two explanations for why the rate of substitution of foreign for domestic savings increases with the current account deficit. Both proceed from that correspondence between current account balances and the exchange rate, and from the appreciation of the national currency due to the increase in the current account deficit. On the demand side, the model says that if we are already in the realm of deficit, the corresponding appreciated currency disconnects the competent firms of the country from existing domestic and foreign demand, and so discourages investment, and correspondingly reduces domestic savings; if we increase the current account deficit, the exchange rate will appreciate further, the disconnection will be stronger, and more and more firms will lose their market to other countries' firms. On the revenue side, the more appreciated the currency is, the greater will be the buying power of consumers or their disposable income. In consequence, they will spend more than a competitive exchange rate would allow, and the domestic savings of the country are reduced, with foreign savings substituting for domestic savings. In both cases, there is an implicit rate of substitution of foreign savings for domestic savings, which, as I argued in Bresser-Pereira and Gala (2008), depends mainly on the marginal propensity to consume.

Is this rate of substitution always high? Since this is a historical model, not a hypothetical-deductive syllogism, the answer is 'not always but most of the time.' The marginal propensity to consume is generally high in developing countries. But when a country is growing very fast, because investment opportunities are high and firms are investing strongly, investment perspectives attract consumers who reduce their marginal propensity to consume and invest, and, in consequence, the rate of substitution of foreign savings for domestic savings falls.

And what of the analogy between countries and firms – the claim that foreign finance will be benign provided that the return on the investment is higher than the interest rate paid on the loan? But a country is very different from a business enterprise. In the case of the country, there is the effect of the capital inflow on the exchange rate – a problem that does not exist for the business enterprise that incurs debts in foreign money. The problem lies not in the exchange rate risk, which the firm incurs, but in the fact that the capital inflows appreciate the exchange rate and discourage investment.

Another question: in the case of direct investment, how can it be diverted to consumption, since the capital inflow is deemed to finance real additional investment? First, not all the inflows that countries classify as foreign direct investment really finance additional investment. But even if they did, the additional investment may not materialize because capital inflows are fungible. It is impossible to know what, eventually, will be done with the extra capital inflows. They may directly finance investment, but as a trade-off, investments will be discouraged, or consumers' disposable revenues increased, or both; and the final outcome may well be a partial or even a total (100 percent) rate of substitution of foreign savings for domestic savings.

EAST ASIAN COMPARED WITH LATIN AMERICAN AND AFRICAN COUNTRIES

The conclusion that developing countries don't need foreign finance, that it is usually detrimental to their economic growth, may seem surprising to Latin Americans and Africans; but if we look to the fast-growing Asian countries, such as South Korea, Vietnam and China, we will see that they usually run current account surpluses, and are even free from the Dutch disease. The Latin American and African countries, which are cursed[9] with abundant and cheap natural resources, should run large current account surpluses because they have two arguments in this direction – the Dutch disease argument and the rate of substitution of foreign savings for domestic savings argument – while the fast-growing Asian countries have only the second. That is one (not the only) basic reason why they grow faster; that is

[9] Cursed either because the policymakers believe in reasonably efficient markets or because they don't neutralize the Dutch disease because they don't know how to.

why they seldom get caught up in balance of payment crises, which are frequent in Latin American and African countries. They seldom get involved in high current account deficits. In the 1990s, at a time when the American and neoliberal hegemony were unchallenged, four of them did get involved in current account deficits, and together faced a major currency crisis. But they learned the lesson, and since then they have run large current account surpluses and built up reserves.

The fact that a country does not need foreign finance does not mean that it should accept no investment from multinational companies. But such companies have lost the argument that their representatives cite to legitimize their occupation of the domestic markets of developing countries. They are welcome if they transfer technology, or if they export, or if their investments are compensated by foreign investments of the receiving country, as happens among rich countries. What is essential is that the receiving country has a current account balance or surplus: a current account balance if the country does not have the Dutch disease, a current account surplus if it does have the disease – and the more severe the disease, the larger the surplus should be. As a result, the country's exchange rate will not be over-appreciated but competitive; the domestic firms will not face a competitive disadvantage, but will compete on equal terms with firms of other countries.

Once this condition has been met, the country will be able to receive direct investment, legitimized not by 'the lack of capital' but rather by the commitment of multinational corporations to technology transfers or to exports – something that China, for one, requires from foreign investors. Clearly, the great bulk of direct investment in developing countries fails to meet these two conditions and, therefore, it is simply a means for rich countries to impose seigniorage on their domestic markets.

THE POLITICAL ECONOMY INVOLVED

Developing countries will grow faster if they run a current account balance or surplus because this is the way to neutralize the tendency to cyclical and chronic overvaluation of the exchange rate and maintain a competitive exchange rate. Thus, they don't need foreign finance. When they accept it, their economies are usually harmed, not improved. The question, therefore, is: why don't developing countries realize this and eliminate their current account deficits?

The answer is relatively simple. The deficits are in the interest of the West and in the short-term interest of politicians and consumers in developing countries. The interest of rich countries is obvious. They benefit from exporting to developing countries more than they import from them; more important, they gain from legitimizing their loans and the occupation of developing countries' domestic markets by their multinational corporations without real reciprocity.

As for the short-term interest of politicians and consumers in developing countries, this derives from the simple fact that an overvalued currency (a currency below the industrial equilibrium) means lower inflation (while the depreciation is taking place) and higher revenues for workers and the techno-bureaucratic middle class (wages and salaries) and for capitalist rentiers, in the form of the interest, dividends and real-estate rents that they receive. Thus, this is very attractive to populist politicians, who know that their societies have a strong preference for immediate consumption. But there is a second reason for the incapacity that the elites of developing countries often display in defending the national interest of their people: their weak idea of nation, and their ideological subordination to the economic theories and ideologies of the West, which they view as embodying the truth, and nothing but the truth.

In the political economy of current account deficits and foreign direct investment, the West uses all possible ideological weapons. Here, I shall comment on just one. The United Nations in Geneva has a division devoted to the study of foreign direct investment.[10] Every year this division distributes a press release listing the names of the ten countries that have received the most direct investment in the previous year. Rich countries – particularly the United States, Germany, Britain and France – usually come top in this small table; Brazil was usually around the eighth place of the list up to the 1990s; in the last 20 years, China has risen to the top of the list or near it. What ideological message does this innocent table convey, which only China in some way upsets? That foreign direct investment is a 'wonderful thing' – so wonderful that rich countries receive it with gusto. But this message is highly misleading. What is really important are the net figures: capital outflows versus capital inflows. These should give rise to two small tables: one with the ten most positive outflows, which will show the countries that made most direct investment without reciprocation, and the other with the most negative outflows, which will show the countries that received most direct investment without reciprocation. In the first table, we will see the major rich countries, and in the second the major developing countries. And the UN division would leave the interpretation

---

[10]   I refer to the FDI Statistics Division on Investment and Enterprise of the United Nations Conference on Trade and Development (UNCTAD). However, being part of UNCTAD, this division adopts an approach that has no relation to the developmental approach that the yearly *Trade and Development Report* has been adopting for years, with strong restrictions imposed by the West.

to each reader of its press release. But, on the contrary, it suggests that all countries should welcome foreign direct investments because the richer countries welcome them.

One interesting thing about this political economy of current account deficits is how the imperial interests of the West coincide with, in developing countries, the loss of the idea of nation of the dependent local elites and the high preference for immediate consumption of the people, to produce a perverse policy and a bad outcome.

CONCLUSION

The West's domination and the developmental response to such domination have undergone changes over the course of history. Imperialism appeared in the nineteenth century as a consequence of the increased power of the countries that first made the industrial revolution – the United Kingdom, Belgium and France – relative to the peoples of Africa and Asia, which, when the Americas were colonized, were powerful enough to resist European colonialism. This imperialism led the colonized peoples – the Chinese and Indians in particular – to massive economic decline. Meanwhile, Latin American countries freed themselves in the early nineteenth century from Spain and Portugal, and their decadent mercantilist metropolis developed, but slowly because their elites were culturally and economically dependent on the imperial center.

After World War II, all European colonies achieved independence and imperialism ceased to be explicit. The hegemony or the soft power that the West was already exerting in Latin America spread to the rest of the world. The imperialist rationale – occupation of developing countries' domestic markets – was now implemented by co-opting the peripheral elites, by persuading them of the benefits of trade liberalization and the growth cum foreign savings policy. Initially the West failed in this project, even in the Latin American countries, because national elites adopted developmental policies. After World War II, classical developmentalism was able to criticize the inequality involved in trade liberalization, but was not able to criticize growth with foreign finance. In the decade following the West's strong hegemony in the 1990s, new developmentalism was able to criticize the foreign savings policy, showing that developing countries don't need foreign finance and that it is usually harmful to their development since loans as well as foreign direct investment finance consumption rather than investment, while increasing the financial or the patrimonial foreign debt of the country.

ACKNOWLEDGMENT

I would like to express my thanks to Eliane Araújo for her comments and suggestions.

REFERENCES

Bresser-Pereira, Luiz Carlos (2010) *Globalization and Competition*. New York: Cambridge University Press.

Bresser-Pereira, Luiz Carlos and Paulo Gala (2008) 'Foreign savings, insufficiency of demand, and low growth', *Journal of Post Keynesian Economics* **30** (3), Spring, 315–34.

Bresser-Pereira, Luiz Carlos and Yoshiaki Nakano (2003) 'Economic growth cum foreign savings?' *Brazilian Journal of Political Economy* **22** (2), April, 3–27 (in the website edition, www.rep.org.br; in Portuguese, in the printed edition).

Bresser-Pereira, Luiz Carlos, Eliane Araujo and Paulo Gala (2014a) 'An empirical study of the substitution of foreign for domestic savings in Brazil', *Revista EconomiA* (ANPEC) **15** (1), 54–67.

Bresser-Pereira, Luiz Carlos, José Luis Oreiro and Nelson Marconi (2014b) *Developmental Macroeconomics*. London: Routledge.

Bresser-Pereira, Luiz Carlos and Marcus Ianoni (2015) 'Developmental class coalitions: historical experiences and prospects', EESP/Fundação Getúlio Vargas Working Paper 386, March.

Calcagno, Alfredo (2015) 'Rethinking development after the Global Financial Crisis', in UNCTAD (ed.), *Rethinking Development Strategy after the Financial Crisis: Volume I: Making the Case for Policy Space*. Geneva: UNCTAD, pp. 9–26.

Chang, Ha-Joon (2002) *Kicking Away the Ladder*. London: Anthem Press.

Edwards, Sebastian (1995) 'Why are saving rates so different across countries? An international comparative analysis', NBER Working Paper 5097, Cambridge, MA.

Feldstein, Martin and C. Horioka (1980) 'Domestic savings and international capital flows', *Economic Journal* **90** (358), 314–29.

Fry, Maxwell J. (1978) 'Money and capital or financial deepening in economic development?', *Journal of Money, Credit and Banking* **10** (4), November, 464–75.

Hirschman, Albert O. (1981) 'The rise and decline of development economics', in *Essays in Trespassing*. New York: Cambridge University Press, pp. 1–24.

Reinert, Erik S. (2007) *How Rich Countries got Rich . . . and Why Poor Countries Stay Poor*. New York: Carroll & Craf.

Reinhart, Carmen M. and Ernesto Talvi (1998) 'Capital flows and saving in Latin America and Asia: a reinterpretation', *Journal of Development Economics* **57**, 45–66.

Rosenstein-Rodan, Paul (1943) 'Problems of industrialization in Eastern Europe and South-eastern Europe', *Economic Journal* **53**, June, 202–11.

Schmidt-Hebbel, Klaus, Steven B. Webb and Giancarlo Corsetti (1992) 'Household saving in developing countries: first cross-country evidence', *The World Bank Economic Review* **6** (3), September, 529–47.

Uthoff, A. and D. Titelman (1998) 'The relationship between foreign and national savings under financial liberalization', in Ffrench-Davis and Helmut Reisen (eds), *Capital Flows and Investment Performance, Lessons from Latin America.* Paris: ECLAC and OECD, pp. 23–41.

6. Global 'disorder' and the rise of finance: implications for the development project

Jayati Ghosh

INTRODUCTION

Through history, there have been varying perceptions of the relevance and significance of global economic and political stability for the process of development. On the face of it, such stability would appear to be beneficial for the process of development, as stability dramatically increases the possibilities of expansion of trade and development of commerce both within and across nations. This appears to be confirmed by the long-term trends in both trade and economic development across the more advanced nations in particular (Maddison, 2001). The more optimistic vision of global economic integration is one that takes off from this, arguing that as countries are enabled to engage in more internal and external commerce, the enhancement of the material well-being of their population is supported, and this in turn leads to incentives for ensuring such peace and stability within and across borders.

This is of course a rather rosy view of human history, and certainly of the last five centuries. In fact, such stability – especially at an international level – did not come easily. In the phases when it did occur, it has most often been the outcome of violence, generating an imposed order that may have provided some stability, but at the cost of unequal outcomes for different sections of humanity. But this has often been seen as the necessary cost of achieving the larger good of human progress. Even some of those analysts who have recognized this truth have nonetheless argued that the imposition of such order, however bloody and otherwise unpleasant, has been critical in enabling the growth of commerce that has in turn been associated with rising incomes. For example, Findlay and O'Rourke (2007, p. xviii) argue that 'the greatest expansions of world trade have tended to come not from the bloodless *tâtonnement* of some fictional Walrasian auctioneer but from the barrel of a Maxim gun, the edge of a scimitar, or

91

the ferocity of nomadic horsemen'. Indeed, according to these authors, the relation between power and plenty was such that 'achieving either aim would promote further achievement of the other' (Findlay and O'Rourke, 2007, p. 191).

Yet there are contrary views, which point to different and potentially less positive implications of such stability, even for economic growth. These recognize that 'stability', however generated, may play and indeed has played a positive role in some phases of global capitalist growth – and most of all in particular regions and countries. But in other phases, and especially when some countries have already managed to industrialize and grow faster than others, such stability may actually serve to cement existing unequal divisions of labour in various ways. The most critical element of this process is that of increasing returns (both static and dynamic) that does much to ensure that those countries able to create more increasing returns activities faster are more likely to dominate over others, even in a context of supposedly 'free' trade on a 'level playing field'.

Thus, Erik Reinert (2007) notes that a significant lesson of the past five centuries of economic history is that of the different mechanisms set in motion by increasing returns and a large division of labour on the one hand and diminishing returns and monoculture on the other hand – and that these different mechanisms can be set off by the interaction of trade and power generating completely different results in different contexts. So 'stable' international economic contexts privilege those with larger increasing returns industries and create dynamic processes of greater differentiation over time – a phenomenon that was recognized by Lenin, for example, as 'uneven development' characteristic of capitalism. Similarly, Amiya Bagchi (2005), who also recognizes the emergence and growth of capitalism as a system driven by wars over resources and markets rather than one based on 'free market operations', notes that this has had immensely adverse consequences for the people of the 'periphery', not only in terms of subverting chances of economic diversification into higher value added activities, but also in terms of basic human development indicators such as nutrition and health. These consequences are in addition to those resulting from specific adverse circumstances such as colonial control – they tend to occur because of the implications of being confined to particular relative positions in the global division of labour, and all the effects this then has on incomes and development in general.

Patnaik (1997) makes the stronger point that it is such differences across regions – along with the possibility of pushing adjustments on to some regions and countries – that allows for the stability of the more advanced economies, and thereby creates the illusion of stability in global capitalism as a whole. The very existence of a periphery of less developed countries provides a buffer that allows the relatively crisis-free and non-inflationary growth in the capitalist core. To that extent, global 'stability' is both a cause and an effect of uneven development, and therefore capitalism as an international system needs such inequality in order to function smoothly. Certainly, the analysis by Robert Triffin (1964) of the operations of the 'Gold Standard' in the late 1870s to the outbreak of the First World War confirms that a system widely seen as the first 'Golden Age' of capitalism because it combined stability with growth worked essentially because it was able to push the costs of adjustment, in terms of not only exchange rate shocks but also trade and output losses, on to the countries in the periphery.

A corollary of this perspective is that – in contrast to stability (whether imposed by force or other means) that reinforces an existing international division of labour and thereby forces countries and peoples to persist at low levels of income and development – some degree of instability may actually benefit economies that hope and attempt to change their relative position in the international division of labour, moving up the ladder in terms of more diversified and higher value added activities. It is certainly true that in the past, periods of global economic instability – such as the 1930s or the 1970s and 1980s – have also been periods when certain countries in the periphery were able to embark upon or intensify their industrialization projects (Kindleberger and Aliber, 2005). The industrialization of India, Argentina and some other countries was given an impetus in the 1930s and thereafter during the Second World War when existing international supply chains were disrupted. Similarly, the East Asian and Southeast Asian countries that are today perceived as successful industrializers were able to increase their shares of global manufacturing exports and improve economic diversification during the period of global economic turmoil and stagnation in the 1970s and 1980s.

Essentially, when countries are open to external trade in a world in which increasing returns activities are significant, the chances are greater that such trade will cement existing divisions of labour between countries, because those countries with small or infant industries will be unable to compete with the competition from larger or more advanced industries elsewhere. When these trade patterns get disrupted, either through conscious commercial policies in some countries or because of other factors (such as wars, global recessions and so on), then there are greater chances of some countries breaking out of the existing division of labour to diversify into higher value added increasing returns activities. So 'instability' in global trade can indeed generate possibilities for industrialization under certain conditions – though it should be noted that the implications vary greatly depending upon the domestic economic conditions and policies adopted by such countries. It should also be noted that the mechanism of economic integration (or disintegration) being considered here is that of trade rather than financial flows, which can have very different outcomes.

What does this suggest for the more recent 'emergence' of some countries that have become significant in the global economy, and of the prognosis for the future? Unlike the East Asian economies of South Korea, Taiwan and Singapore that emerged in the late twentieth century, the recent rise of China and some other countries has essentially taken place during the recent period of globalization that many have seen as a stable period. However, it has not been a period of stability overall; rather, it has been one of phases of relatively high growth punctuated by crises that have affected advanced, developing and less developed regions.

Does this mean that the current period of stagnation and even greater propensity to crises that appears to be the fate of global capitalism in the immediate future is one that will once again create favourable conditions for the expansion of economies in the periphery? Unfortunately, that seems less likely than was the case earlier, largely because now these countries are integrated not only through trade but also through finance, and the nature of the domination of finance is such that even when trade patterns allow for greater economic diversification in the periphery, financialization is likely to inhibit it.

This argument is developed in more detail in subsequent sections. In the next section, I examine the extent to which there has really been a shift in global economic power in the past few decades, and whether the more optimistic projections of the 'rise of the Rest' are validated by recent experience. The third section contains a discussion of what 'rise' means in terms of development, and more specifically, structural change within economies. It is argued that financial liberalization and the associated financialization of the economy serve to retard or disrupt the process of development through various mechanisms. In the fourth section, the specific impact of the recent dominance of finance on growth and structural change in some Asian economies is considered, and it is argued that the rise of finance has actually impeded the development project in these countries. The fifth and sixth sections take up the very different cases of China and India, which despite their varying development trajectories are now showing somewhat similar tendencies with respect to the impact of financial deregulation. The final section provides a short conclusion.

HOW SIGNIFICANT IS THE 'RISE OF THE REST'?

Much has been made of how there has been a substantial shift in the balance of economic power between the advanced capitalist economies (or the 'North') and some economies of the global South. The associated geo-political shifts are also ascribed in great part to growing economic clout, as in the notions of the *Rise of the South* (UNDP, 2013). The narrative of a 'great convergence' became even stronger as newer groups of such economies were progressively celebrated by being awarded acronyms, from BRICS to MINTs, for example.[1] There were arguments that the evidence of convergence, particularly as driven by the two most populous nations on earth, implied a major structural shift in the dynamics of the global economy (Dervis, 2012).

It is true that recently some of the hype surrounding 'emerging markets' has died down, as international capital flows have swung away from them and many have shown decelerating growth or even declines in income as global exports fall. Nevertheless, the feeling persists that – in spite of a supposedly resurgent US economy – the advanced economies are generally in a process of relative decline, while the developing world in general and certain economies in particular have much better chances of future eco-nomic dynamism. And this process is generally seen to be the result of the forces of globalization, which have enabled developing countries, especially some in Asia, to take advantage of newer and larger export markets and improved access to internationally mobile capital to increase their rates of economic expansion.

But how significant has this process actually been? In fact, there has def-initely been some change over the past three and a half decades, but it has been more limited in time than is generally presumed. Figure 6.1 plots the share of the advanced economies in global gross domestic product (GDP) in current US dollar prices, calculated at market exchange rates. (Data for all the figures have been taken from the International Monetary Fund (IMF) World Economic Outlook October 2015 Database (accessed 23 September 2015), unless otherwise specified.) This shows that the share of advanced economies declined from around 83 per cent in the late 1980s to around 60 per cent currently, which is quite a substantial decline. However, the bulk of this change occurred in a relatively short period: the decade 2002 to 2012, when the share dropped from 80 per cent to 62 per cent. The

[1] BRICS refers to Brazil, Russia, India, China and South Africa, with Jim O'Neill of Goldman Sachs using the acronym for the first four, which became a formal grouping to which South Africa was subsequently added. MINTs refers to Mexico, Indonesia, Nigeria and Turkey, a term used first by Fidelity Investments, but this has no institutional basis.

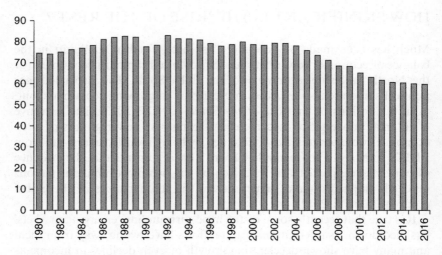

*Figure 6.1   Share of advanced economies in global GDP (%, current dollar
             prices at market exchange rate)*

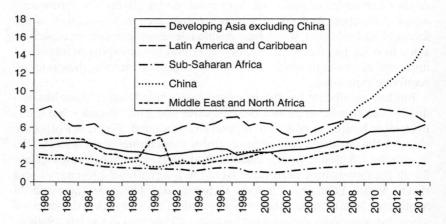

*Figure 6.2   Share of developing regions in global GDP (current dollar
             prices at market exchange rate)*

periods before and after have shown much less variation, and indeed, the
share seems to have stabilized at around 61 per cent thereafter.

Figure 6.2 looks at the obverse of this process – the change in the shares
in global GDP of the major developing regions, with China treated as
a separate category on its own. This shows a somewhat more surprising

pattern, because it indicates that the dominant part of this shift is due to the increase in China's share, which rose from around 3 per cent to more than 15 per cent. Once again, this happened essentially during the decade after 2005, when the share of China in global GDP at market exchange rates jumped by more than ten percentage points. Indeed, the change in China's share alone explains 87 per cent of the entire decline in the share of the advanced economies in the period 1980 to 2015. Considering only the last decade, that is, after 2005, the relative increase in China's GDP accounts for a slightly lower proportion of the change, at 67 per cent – which is still hugely significant.

The change in shares of other regions provides some interesting insights. The Latin American region experienced a medium-term decline in relative income share over the 1980s (the 'lost decade'), recovered somewhat in the 1990s before declining once again in the late 1990s and early 2000s. The global commodity boom of 2003 onwards was associated with a revival in the region's economic fortunes and the share of the region increased from 5 per cent in 2003 to more than 8 per cent in 2011, but thereafter it has stagnated and fallen with the unwinding of that boom.

The income shares of the MENA region (Middle East and North Africa) appear to have been very strongly driven by global oil prices, with sharp peaks in periods of high oil prices and stagnation or decline otherwise. Over the entire period there has been a stagnation in income share rather than any increase. An even more depressing story emerges for sub-Saharan Africa, which showed declining income shares for a prolonged period between 1980 and 2002, and subsequently a slight recovery (from 1.1 per cent in 2002 to around 2 per cent in 2012 and thereafter) that still left it well below the share of more than 3 per cent achieved in 1980.

As a result of these trends in various developing regions, the only developing region that shows a clear increase in global incomes share is developing Asia. But much of this is really driven by the rapid expansion of the Chinese economy. Since Figure 6.2 excludes China from developing Asia, it becomes evident that the increase in the income share of the other countries of the region taken together has been much less marked than that for China, and most of it occurred after 2002, as the income share rose from 3.5 per cent in 2002 to 6.4 per cent in 2015.

Figure 6.3 indicates the changes in shares of the largest Asian developing countries other than China. It is evident that in terms of increasing share of global GDP, India has been the most impressive performer over the past decade in particular, with its share increasing from 1.8 per cent in 2005 to 3 per cent in 2015. Note, however, that this is still tiny in comparison to China, and indeed, just the increase in China's share over that decade has been more than three times India's aggregate share. South Korea's share

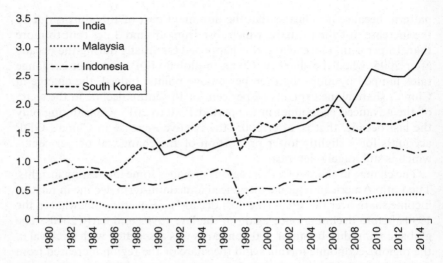

*Figure 6.3   Share of major non-China Asian economies in global GDP
(current dollar prices at market exchange rate)*

has also increased, mostly over the 1980s and early 1990s, while Indonesia's
share increase occurred mostly during the commodity boom of the 2000s.

In terms of per capita GDP, however, the Indian performance looks much
less impressive than those of its major Asian counterparts. Interestingly,
even the Chinese experience appears not as remarkable, although still
hugely better than that of India. Figure 6.4 tracks the movements of per
capita GDP, measured now in Purchasing Power Parity (PPP) exchange
rates rather than market rates. There are numerous problems with the use
of the PPP measure, but for current comparative purposes it does provide
some kind of indicator. This shows that by far the most impressive performance in terms of increasing per capita GDP has been in South Korea,
followed by Malaysia. India shows the least improvement among these five
economies, despite its apparently more rapid increase in terms of share of
world GDP in the last decade.

Overall, therefore, while the world economy has changed over the past
three decades, this change should not be exaggerated for most developing
regions (as also noted by Akyuz, 2012), or even for most countries in what
is apparently the most dynamic region of Asia.

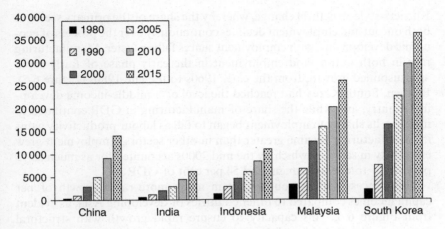

Figure 6.4   Per capita GDP at PPP exchange rates

GROWTH, STRUCTURAL CHANGE AND FINANCE

It is clearly important to establish how the term 'development' is being interpreted in this chapter. Obviously, there can be many varying definitions for a term trying to capture human and social progress. These have ranged from just looking at per capita income to more complex and multidimensional ideas of human development as the progressive realization of human rights, or of capabilities, of development as freedom and so on. But here I will focus on a more specific and limited indicator, on the basis of the argument that the diversification of productive structures in the economy towards higher value added activities is the essential basis for economic development (UNCTAD, 2016). Let us consider, for present purposes, development as productive transformation, in which industrialization in particular is therefore extremely important in the early stages. I shall argue that the process of financial liberalization and integration with global capital markets actually impedes the ability of an economy to undergo structural transformation and diversify towards more high value added activities in a sustained and stable way. In other words, the process of 'emerging' actually reduces the capacity to develop, as I shall illustrate with examples from some emerging markets in Asia over the past two decades.

Traditional development economists saw growth and structural change as closely intertwined, chiefly through the process of industrialization that was seen as delivering not only higher per capita incomes but also less inequality. Indeed, the case of South Korea can be described as the 'classic'

Kuznets-style structural change, whereby the share of the primary sector in both output and employment declines continuously over the process of economic development, with employment shares falling faster. Manufacturing rose in both output and employment in the early phase of fairly rapid and sustained growth, from the early 1960s to the late 1980s (Figure 6.5). By then, South Korea had reached the level of a middle-income developing country, and while the share of manufacturing in GDP continued to increase, its share of employment began to fall as labour productivity gains in manufacturing became greater than in other sectors. Employment grew essentially in services, which by the mid 2000s accounted for as much as 73 per cent of total employment and 54 per cent of GDP.

This process had its counterpart in much more rapid growth of per capita incomes compared to other countries of developing Asia, as evident from Figure 6.6. This capacity to ensure rapid growth with structural change in the Republic of Korea was not just reflective of a state-led export-oriented accumulation model, as widely accepted, but also crucially dependent on the state's ability to control and direct finance. Indeed, subsequent financial liberalization and greater integration with global capital markets has greatly reduced that potential.

There are several reasons for this adverse impact of financial liberalization. To begin with, it has resulted in an increase in financial fragility in developing countries, making them prone to periodic financial and currency crises. These relate both to internal banking and related crises, and currency crises stemming from more open capital accounts. The origin of several crises can be traced to the shift to a more liberal and open financial regime, since this unleashes a dynamic that pushes the financial system towards a poorly regulated, oligopolistic structure, with a corresponding increase in fragility. Greater freedom to invest, including in sensitive sectors such as real estate and stock markets, the ability to increase exposure to particular sectors and individual clients, and increased regulatory forbearance all lead to increased instances of financial failure. In addition, the emergence of universal banks or financial supermarkets increases the degree of entanglement of different agents within the financial system and increases the domino effects of individual financial failures.

Financial markets left to themselves are known to be prone to failure because of the public goods characteristics of information which agents must acquire and process. They are characterized by insufficient monitoring by market participants. Individual shareholders tend to refrain from investing money and time in acquiring information about managements, hoping that others would do so instead and knowing that all shareholders, including themselves, benefit from the information garnered. As a result, there may be inadequate monitoring leading to risky decisions

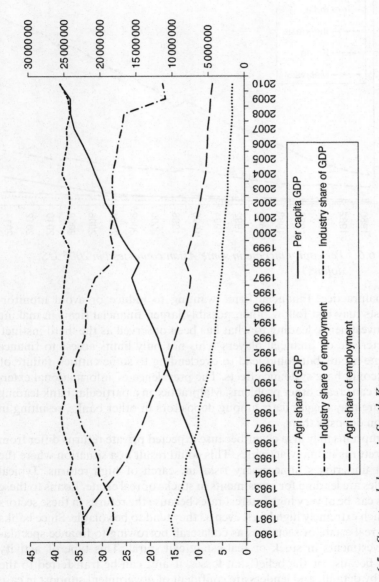

Figure 6.5 Structural change in South Korea

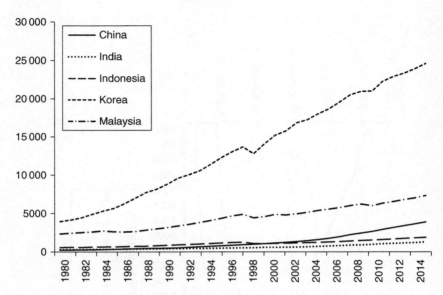

*Figure 6.6   Per capita income in some Asian countries (in 2005 US
             dollars)*

and malpractice. Financial firms wanting to reduce or avoid monitoring costs may just follow other, possibly larger, financial firms in making
their investments, leading to what has been observed as the 'herd instinct'
characteristic of financial players. This not only limits access to finance
for some agents but could lead to overlending to some entities, failure of
which could have systemic effects. The prevalence of informational exter-
nalities can create other problems. Malpractice in a particular bank leading
to failure may trigger fears among depositors in other banks, resulting in
a run on deposits there.

Disruptions may also occur because expected private returns differ from
social returns in many activities. This could result in a situation where the
market undertakes unnecessary risks in search of high returns. Typical
examples are lending for investments in stocks or real estate. Loans to these
sectors can be at very high interest rates because the returns in these sectors
can touch extremely high levels even as they tend to be volatile. Since banks
accept real estate or securities as collateral, borrowing to finance speculative investments in stock or real estate can spiral. This type of activity
thrives because of the belief that losses, if any, can be transferred to the
lender by default, and lenders are confident of government support in case
of a crisis. This moral hazard can feed a speculative spiral that in time may
lead to a collapse of the bubble and bank failures.

Meanwhile, all too often the expected microeconomic efficiency gains are not realized. In developing countries, the market for new stock issues is small or non-existent except in periods of a speculative boom. Deregulated bank lending tends to privilege risky high-return investment rather than investment in the commodity producing sectors like manufacturing and agriculture. This tends to generate housing and personal finance booms, which in many circumstances tends to increase the fragility of the system.

Another result of financial liberalization in imperfect markets is the strengthening of oligopolistic power through the association of financial intermediaries and non-financial corporations. Financial intermediaries that are part of these conglomerates allocate credit in favour of companies belonging to the group, which is by no means a more efficient means of allocation than could have occurred under directed credit policies of the government. Moreover, while financial liberalization does encourage new kinds of financial savings, total domestic savings typically do not increase in many cases, and expansion of available financial savings is often the result of inflow of foreign capital. Nor does liberalization necessarily result in intermediation of financial assets with long-term maturities, with deposits and loans of less than six months' duration dominating. And despite short booms in stock markets, there tends to be relatively little mobilization of new capital or capital for new ventures. In fact, small investors tend to withdraw from markets because of allegations of manipulation and fraud, and erstwhile areas of long-term investments supported by state intervention tend to disappear. Not surprisingly, investment performance does not usually reflect signs of either improved volume or more efficient allocation.

External financial liberalization, with associated capital inflows, only aggravates these consequences. Indeed, all the evidence on capital inflows and subsequent crises suggests that once an emerging market is 'chosen' by financial markets as an attractive destination, this sets in motion processes that are eventually likely to culminate in crisis. This works through the effects of a surge of capital inflows on exchange rates (unless the capital does not add to an increase in domestic investment but simply ends up adding to foreign exchange reserves).

An appreciating real exchange rate encourages investment in non-tradable sectors, the most obvious being real estate, and in domestic asset markets generally. At the same time, the upward movement of the currency discourages investment in tradables and therefore contributes to a process of relative decline in real economic sectors, and possibly even deindustrialization in developing countries. Given the differential in interest rates between domestic and international markets and the lack of any prudence on the part of international lenders and investors, local agents borrow heavily abroad to directly or indirectly invest in the property and

stock markets. Thus, it was no accident that all the emerging market economies experiencing substantial financial capital inflows also at a similar
time experienced property and real estate booms, as well as stock market
booms, even while the real economy may have been stagnating or even
declining. These booms in turn generated the incomes to keep domestic
demand and growth in certain sectors increasing at relatively high rates.
This soon results in macroeconomic imbalances, not in the form of rising
fiscal deficits of the government but a current account deficit reflecting the
consequences of debt-financed private profligacy.

However, once there is growing exposure in the form of a substantial
presence of internationally mobile finance capital, any factor that spells
an economic setback, however small or transient, can trigger an outflow
of capital as well. And the current account deficits that are necessarily
associated with capital account surpluses (unless there is large reserve
accumulation) eventually create a pattern whereby the trend becomes perceived as an unsustainable one, in which any factor, even the most minor or
apparently irrelevant one, can trigger a crisis of sudden outflows.

One very common argument relates to the importance of 'sound' macroeconomic policies, once financial flows have been liberalized. It has been
suggested that many emerging markets have faced problems because they
allowed their current account deficits to become too large, reflecting too
great an excess of private domestic investment over private savings. This
belated realization is a change from the earlier obsession with government
fiscal deficits as the only macroeconomic imbalance worth caring about,
but still misses the basic point. This point is that with completely unbridled
capital flows, it is no longer possible for a country to control the amount
of capital inflow or outflow, and both movements can create consequences
which are undesirable. If, for example, a country is suddenly chosen as a
preferred site for foreign portfolio investment, it can lead to huge inflows
which in turn cause the currency to appreciate, thus encouraging investment in non-tradables rather than tradables, and altering domestic relative prices and therefore incentives. Simultaneously, unless the inflows of
capital are simply (and wastefully) stored up in the form of accumulated
foreign exchange reserves, they must necessarily be associated with current
account deficits.

Large current deficits are therefore necessary by-products of the surge in
capital inflow, and that is the basic macroeconomic problem. This means
that any country which does not exercise some sort of control or modera-
tion over private capital inflows can be subject to very similar pressures.
These then create the conditions for their own eventual reversal, when the
current account deficits are suddenly perceived to be too large or unsustainable. In other words, once there are completely free capital flows and

completely open access to external borrowing by private domestic agents, there can be no 'prudent' macroeconomic policy; the overall domestic balances or imbalances will change according to the behaviour of capital flows, which will themselves respond to the economic dynamics they have set into motion.

This points to the futility of believing that capital account convertibility accompanied by domestic prudential regulation will ensure against boom-bust volatility in capital markets. Financial liberalization and the behaviour of fluid finance have therefore created a new problem analogous to the old 'Dutch disease', with capital inflows causing an appreciation of the real exchange rate that causes changes in the real economy and therefore generate a process that is inherently unsustainable over time.

There are also adverse implications for investment and therefore overall growth and diversification prospects of economies. Financial liberalization generates a bias towards deflationary macroeconomic policies and forces the state to adopt a deflationary stance to appease financial interests. The need to attract internationally mobile capital means that there are limits to the possibilities of enhancing taxation, especially on capital. Typically, prior or simultaneous trade liberalization reduces the indirect tax revenues of states undertaking financial liberalization, and so tax-GDP ratios often deteriorate in the wake of such liberalization. This imposes limits on government spending, since finance capital is generally opposed to large fiscal deficits. This not only affects the possibilities for countercyclical macroeconomic stances of the state but also reduces the developmental or growth-oriented activities of the government.

These tendencies affect real investment in two ways. First, if speculative bubbles lead to financial crises, they squeeze liquidity and increase costs for current transactions, and result in distress sales of assets and defla-tion that adversely impact on employment and living standards. Second, inasmuch as the maximum returns to productive investment in agriculture and manufacturing are limited, there is a limit to what borrowers would be willing to pay to finance such investment. Thus, despite the fact that social returns to agricultural and manufacturing investment are higher than for stocks and real estate, and despite the contribution such investment can make to growth and poverty alleviation, credit at the required rate may not be available.

This is why it is increasingly recognized that liberalization can disman-tle the very financial structures that are crucial for economic growth. When the financial sector is increasingly left unregulated or covered by a minimum of regulation, market signals determine the allocation of investible resources and therefore the demand for and the allocation of savings intermediated by financial enterprises. This can result in the problems conventionally associated with a situation where private rather than overall social returns determine the allocation of savings and investment. It aggravates the inherent tendency in markets to direct credit to non-priority and import-intensive but more profitable sectors, to concentrate investible funds in the hands of a few large players, and to direct savings to already well-developed centres of economic activity. The socially desirable role of financial intermediation therefore becomes muted. This affects employment-intensive sectors such as agriculture and small-scale enterprises, where the transaction costs of lending tend to be high, risks are many and collateral not easy to ensure. It also has a negative impact on any medium-term strategy of ensuring growth in particular sectors through directed credit, which has been the basis for the industrialization process through much of the twentieth century.

All this is the more significant because the process of financial liberalization across the globe has not generated greater net flows of capital into the developing world, as expected by its proponents. Rather, in recent years, the net outflows have been in the reverse direction. Even the emerging markets which have been substantial recipients of capital inflows have not experienced increases in aggregate investment rates as a consequence, but have built up their external reserves. This is only partly because of a precautionary measure to guard against possible financial crises; it also indicates a macroeconomic situation of *ex ante* excess of savings over investment resulting from the deflationary macroeconomic stance. The curious workings of international financial markets have actually contributed to international concentration, whereby developing countries hold their reserves in US Treasury bills and other safe securities, and thereby contribute to the fact that the US economy continues to absorb the bulk of the world's savings. At the same time, developing countries are losing in terms of seignorage costs of holding these reserves, as typically the reserves are invested in very low yielding 'safe' assets while capital inflows include debt-creating flows at much higher rates of interest. This inverse and undesirable form of financial intermediation is in fact a direct result of the financial liberalization measures which have simultaneously created deflationary impulses and increased financial fragility across the developing world.

SOME ASIAN EXAMPLES

Within developing Asia, the Asian crisis of 1997–98 marked a watershed as it heralded a period of significantly deeper financial integration of the countries of the region. This in itself is curious because it is now widely accepted that the most crucial proximate factor for the crisis was financial liberalization, specifically external or capital account liberalization. During the early 1990s, almost all East Asian countries liberalized their financial sectors and allowed local corporations, banks and non-bank financial institutions to freely access international capital markets with little commitment to earn the foreign exchange needed to service the costs of such access. This allowed inflows of capital that enabled short-term borrowing for long-term projects, which broke the link between domestic agents' ability to access foreign exchange and their need to earn it. This was associated with the use of new instruments, specifically derivatives contracts that were enabled by deregulation. The capital inflows into the region that increased as a result of the capital account liberalization and investor bullishness about export growth caused appreciation of the real exchange rate. This shifted incentives for investment within the economy from tradables to non-tradables (especially real estate and domestic asset markets), and it caused current account deficits to occur as exports effectively became more expensive and imports were cheaper. As a result, the capital inflows were associated with current account deficits and deceleration of exports that sowed the seed for the eventual reversal of investor confidence. All these economies consequently experienced property and real estate booms, as well as stock market booms, at some time in the years between 1993 and 1996, which in turn kept domestic demand and growth growing at relatively high rates. This soon resulted in signs of macroeconomic imbalance, not in the form of the government's rising fiscal deficits but as current account deficits reflecting the consequences of debt-financed private profligacy. This in turn threatened the export-driven model that underpinned the real economic growth of these economies.

It was inevitable that this would eventually result in a collapse of investor confidence. When that did occur, capital was pulled out and currencies depreciated; those with dollar commitments in the offing rushed into the market to purchase dollars early and cut their losses. The spiral continued, generating a liquidity crunch and a wave of bankruptcy. In retrospect, the more surprising result was that the crisis actually resulted in an intensification of the process of financial liberalization and increasing ownership and control of foreign financial institutions in domestic financial markets in these countries. This process has been marked in Korea, but it is also evident in several other 'emerging markets' in the region, which were and remain at much lower levels of per capita income.

In many of these countries, the post-crisis trajectory has been marked by something rather unusual: domestic investment rates fell even as domestic savings rates remained high. So they stopped being net recipients of foreign savings and instead showed the opposite tendency of net resource

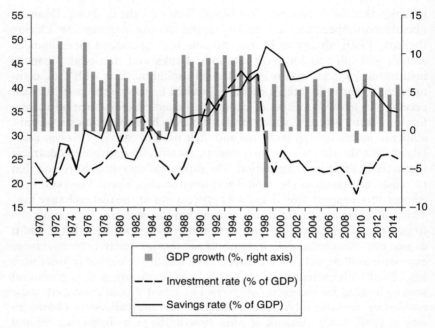

*Figure 6.7   Malaysia: savings, investment and GDP growth, percentage of
              GDP*

outflow, as domestic savings were higher than investment. This meant
that there was a process of squeezing out savings from the population as
a whole, but not investing it within the economy to ensure future growth.
Instead, these savings were effectively exported, either through capital
outflows or by adding to the external reserves of the central banks, which
were typically held in very safe assets abroad (such as US Treasury Bills).

Consider Malaysia and Indonesia, two economies in the region that
exhibit this tendency very clearly, and both of which were seen as emerging
markets with significant future potential as recently as 2014. Figures 6.7
to 6.9 show the experience of Malaysia and Figures 6.10 to 6.12 illustrate
the Indonesian pattern. These are very different economies, with somewhat different initial positions, varying political trajectories and even
dissimilar economic policies over the entire period. Yet they share some
basic similarities, from the emphasis on export orientation in the pre-Asian
crisis boom as well as subsequently, to the financial liberalization that was
already present to some extent in the 1990s but gathered pace thereafter
and particularly after 1998, when both countries also made significant
commitments to the World Trade Organization in terms of liberalizing

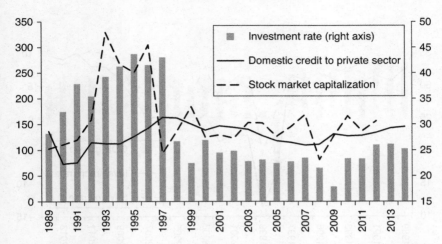

Figure 6.8   Malaysia: financial sector and investment, percentage of GDP

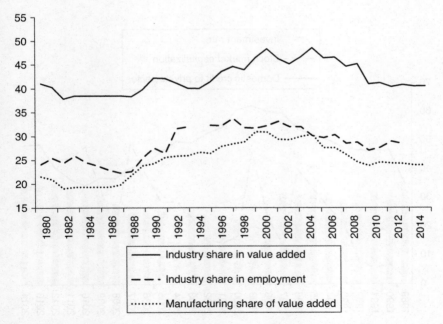

Figure 6.9   Malaysia: structural change, percentage of GDP

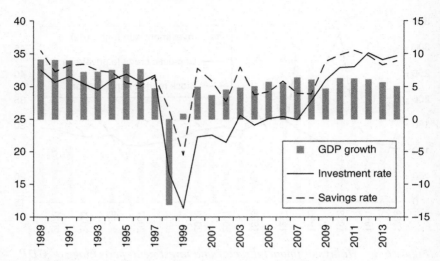

Figure 6.10   Indonesia: savings, investment and GDP growth

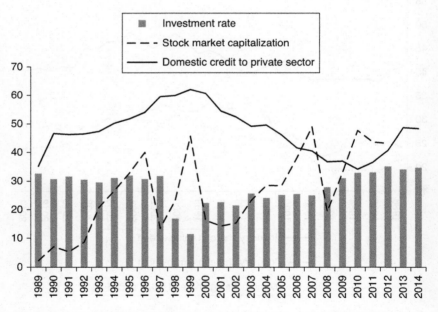

*Figure 6.11   Indonesia: financial sector and investment, percentage of
            GDP*

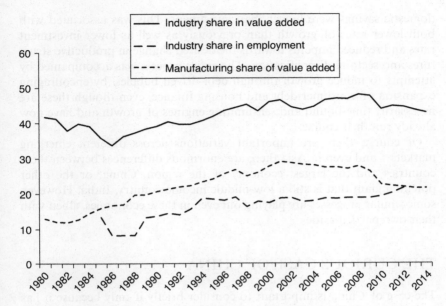

Figure 6.12   Indonesia: structural change, percentage of GDP

financial services. Both of these countries had rising investment rates that were generally higher than savings rates in the run-up to the Asian crisis.

Thereafter, investment rates fell sharply in each country, and remained low in Malaysia even as savings rates stayed high. In Indonesia, there was eventual recovery of the investment rate, but it only managed to reach and exceed the savings rate in 2012. Meanwhile, investment rates have shown little relationship with financial indicators like stock market capitalization and credit to the private sector. In other words, the recent financial boom that has been associated with these 'emerging markets' has not translated into real investment increases. Very significantly for present purposes, the processes of structural change in both economies seem to have been stalled or even reversed, with industry (and manufacturing) shares of value added and employment remaining stagnant in Indonesia and falling in Malaysia. Bear in mind that these changes are occurring at much lower levels of per capita income than occurred even in South Korea and certainly as compared to the experience of the currently advanced economies of the West.

So even as these economies became more 'open' in policy terms, especially with respect to rules regarding foreign investment, and were celebrated as 'emerging markets', they stopped being net recipients of foreign savings and instead showed the opposite tendency of net resource outflow, as domestic savings were higher than investment. This was associated with both lower rates of growth than previously as well as lower investment rates and reduced impetus towards the desired change in productive structures and sectoral diversification. The entire process was accompanied by attempts to induce growth through debt-driven bubbles, by encouraging expansion of consumer debt and housing finance, even though these are necessarily time-bound and self-limiting engines of growth and have now already run their course.

Of course, there are important variations across different emerging markets – and even in Asia there are enormous differences between these countries and the largest economy of the region, China, or the other potential giant that is still a low-middle income country, India. However, some similar processes are playing out even in these economies, albeit with their own particularities.

THE CURIOUS CASE OF CHINA

The case of China is important to consider briefly if only because it has such important implications for the Asian region as well as for the world economy. From the early 1990s, China adopted an export-led strategy that delivered continuously increasing shares of the world market, fed by relatively low wages and very high rates of investment that enabled massive increases in infrastructure. This was very successful over two decades, albeit accompanied by big increases in inequality and even bigger environmental problems. Once again, this was critically dependent upon the ability of the Chinese state to control and direct financial allocations, especially through the four large publicly owned banks that accounted for more than 85 per cent of all domestic transactions through most of this period.

But the strategy received a shock with the global crisis in 2008–09 when exports were hit, which showed very clearly that the Chinese economy was not really 'decoupled' from the West as claimed by some observers. The relatively small impact on the economy and the subsequent rapid recovery were the result of China (and much of 'emerging' Asia) shifting to a different engine of growth without abandoning the focus on exports. In a sense, just as the 1998 Asian financial crisis was the watershed moment for East Asian economies in terms of substantially altering the nature of their growth trajectories, the global financial crisis of 2008–09 was a turning point in China, particularly in terms of the state's relationship with financial markets and its consequent control over investment allocations. This is once again surprising, because the US sub-prime crisis had exposed the risks of financial deregulation so very clearly, and these lessons should have been heeded by countries that had succeeded precisely by not allowing such unfettered activity of their own financial markets.

The Chinese authorities could have generated more domestic demand by stimulating consumption through rising wage shares of national income, but this would have threatened the export-driven model. Instead, they put their faith in even more accumulation to keep growth rates buoyant, and in allowing much higher levels of debt (both controlled and through shadow banking activities) to finance this expansion, fed in turn by associated asset bubbles. The 'recovery package' in China essentially encouraged more investment, which was already nearly half of GDP. Provincial governments and public sector enterprises were encouraged to borrow heavily and invest in infrastructure, construction and more production capacity. To utilize the excess capacity, a real estate and construction boom was instigated, fed by lending from public sector banks as well as 'shadow banking' activities winked at by regulators. Total debt in China increased four times between 2007 and 2014, and the debt–GDP ratio nearly doubled to more than 280 per cent, with a significant part of this associated with shadow banking in various forms.

Curiously, the recovery of investment rates that this precipitated (with investment rising to even higher proportions of GDP from already unprecedented levels) did not lead to more rapid growth: quite the contrary, GDP growth decelerated in the period after 2009, as clearly shown in Figures 6.13 and 6.14. Growth rates of 7–8 per cent per annum would be considered creditable in most countries, but China's rapid accumulation strategy has been based on even higher growth expectations, which in turns means that this appears as underperformance relative to capacity creation and associated debt overhang.

It should be evident by now that such debt-driven bubbles end in tears. The property bubble began to subside in early 2014 and real estate prices across most cities in China have been stagnant or falling ever since, with the particular exceptions of Shanghai and Beijing. The policy response became one of assisting in (or at the very least allowing) the emergence of other asset bubbles to take up that slack – most particularly the stock market, and trading in the 'A' shares that can be held by Chinese residents.

As Chinese investors shifted to the stock market, it began to sizzle, actively encouraged by the Chinese government. Stock market indices more than doubled in a year, reaching a peak in early June 2015. For some stocks, the price-equity values crossed 200. This was clearly crazy, and had to be corrected. But the correction was untidy in the extreme, as quite typical in such markets when unregulated, and yet it probably still has some way to go. Stocks in late 2016 were trading approximately 40 per cent lower than the peak, but only because the Chinese government pulled out

Figure 6.13   China: savings, investment and GDP growth

all the stops in interventions to control further falls. This generates another source of instability and potential slowdown, as artificially inflated stock markets cannot stay that way beyond a point.

The mistake on the part of policy makers may well be that of persisting in the belief that the behaviour of the stock market is a relevant indicator of real economic performance. As evident from Figure 6.15, in China as in the other countries considered here, recent patterns of investment have been quite unrelated to stock market capitalization in the economy, even in the period when it has been more active and stocks of listed firms have begun to be more widely traded.

All this came in the midst of an overall slowdown in China's economy. Exports fell for some time in 2015–16, while imports fell much more substantially. Capital outflows were associated with a depreciation relative to the US dollar as well as a significant decline in the admittedly still very large holdings of foreign exchange reserves. Manufacturing output decelerated and construction activity almost halted, especially in the proliferating 'ghost towns' dotted around the country. Stimulus measures like interest rate cuts did not seem to be working. The recent devaluation of the Renminbi has not really helped to revive the economy. Demand from the advanced countries – still the driver of Chinese exports and indirectly of exports of other developing countries – will

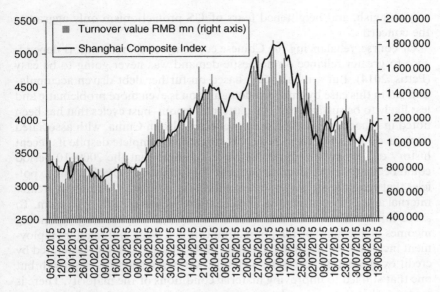

Source: CEIC (National Bureau of Statistics) China database.

Figure 6.14   Movements in the Shanghai Stock Exchange

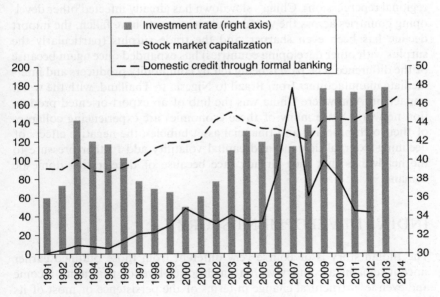

Figure 6.15   China: investment and financial indicators

stay sluggish, and heightened fears of US protectionism only aggravate the concern.

Of course, rebalancing the Chinese economy away from export dependence to greater reliance on domestic demand was never going to be easy (Pettis, 2014). But a rebalancing based on further debt-driven accumulation led in this case by financial deregulation is even more problematic and less likely to be sustainable. The pattern of boom–bust cycles that has been noted in other cases could then be reflected also in China, with associated impacts on a development project that is still incomplete despite its recent history of very rapid growth. There is a danger that the 2009–10 period could become the 'Asian crisis moment' for China in terms of a shift to policies that generate an unsustainable trajectory ultimately leading to greater internal and external financial liberalization but less growth dynamism. To avoid this, a course correction would be required emphasizing expanding incomes of the mass of the population through wage and regular employment increases, rather than increasing GDP through demand generated by credit expansion, if necessary with a slower aggregate rate of growth but one that still led to improving material conditions of the majority. There is evidence that this process has started to some extent, with rapid increases in wages. However, such a strategy is not compatible with the ongoing efforts at financial liberalization.

Meanwhile, the economic slowdown in China has major global and regional repercussions. China's slowdown has already infected other developing countries across the world: while its exports have fallen, the import decline has been even sharper, and the trade surplus (particularly the surplus with other developing countries) has expanded once again because of the difference. The pain is being felt by commodity producers and intermediate manufacturers from Brazil to Nigeria to Thailand, with the worst impacts in Asia where China was the hub of an export-oriented production network. Since many of these economies are experiencing collapses of their own property and financial asset bubbles, the negative effects of declining external demand and capital volatility add further pressure to the headwinds that they already face because of decelerating domestic demand.

INDIA'S DEVELOPMENT STORY

The Indian story is of course very different from those outlined earlier since it remains a country with a much lower level of per capita income and even less structural change in terms of the persistence of most of its labour in low productivity activities in agriculture and services. It was not

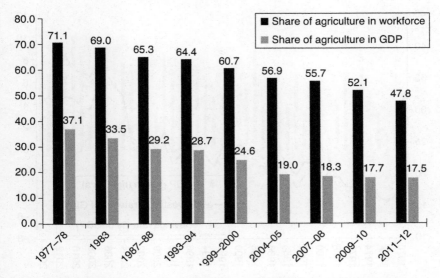

Source: National Sample Survey Office (NSSO), various rounds and Central Statistical Office (CSO), National Income Accounts, Ministry of Statistics, Government of India.

Figure 6.16   India: share of agriculture

a successful export-driven economy and generally had large and growing current account deficits throughout the period of its boom. Indeed, the relative absence of structural change, particularly in terms of employment shifts out of low value activities, is probably the most important stylized fact about the Indian economy over the past half century. Remarkably, it has persisted through different economic policy regimes and phases of low, moderate or rapid growth.

Yet in its essentials, the recent Indian boom was not fundamentally different from the debt-driven accumulation that has been noted elsewhere. Recent high economic growth in India was related to financial deregulation that attracted attention and mobile capital from abroad, and sparked a domestic retail credit boom and combined with fiscal concessions to spur consumption among the richer sections of the population (Ghosh and Chandrasekhar, 2009). In addition, relatively cheap access to natural resources provided a means of encouraging the 'animal spirits' of both local and foreign investors. There was a substantial rise in profit shares in the economy and the proliferation of financial activities. This combined with rising asset values (particularly in stocks and real estate) to enable a credit-financed consumption splurge among the rich and the middle classes. The earlier macroeconomic reliance on public spending as the

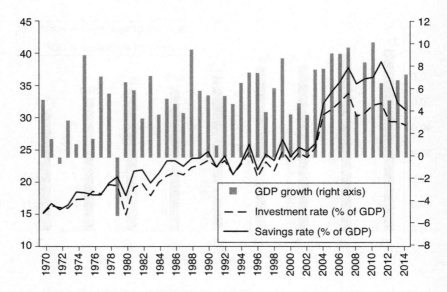

Figure 6.17   India: savings, investment and GDP growth

principal stimulus for growth in the Indian economy was thus substituted
with debt-financed housing investment and private consumption of the
elite and burgeoning middle classes. Similarly, in the current period of
deceleration, several of the features that were identified as problems
with respect to other countries – and particularly the growing emphasis
on financial liberalization and the use of credit-driven consumption and
investment as engines of expansion rather than demand generated by
rising income per se – have also been significant in India.

In the period of boom, investment rates rose rapidly and were higher
than savings rates, as is typical and indicated in Figure 6.17, and were
associated with growing current account deficits. However, while the boom
managed to continue despite the global financial crisis, with only a minor
blip in terms of GDP growth in 2008–09, effectively it came to an end
around 2011–12. Thereafter, GDP growth has decelerated and investment
and savings rates have both fallen.[2]

As Figure 6.18 suggests, in India as in other countries considered here,
the behaviour of the stock market had little to do with actual investment
rates, while domestic credit to the private sector was generally positively
associated with investment. This can work both ways: when the investment

---

[2] The old series of National Accounts Statistics is used here for all years, including
2013–14, to ensure comparability over time.

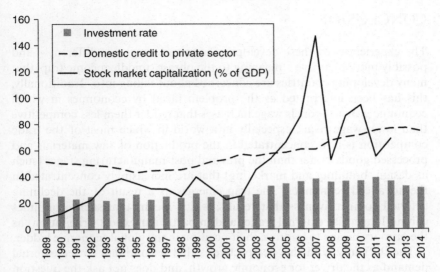

Figure 6.18   India: financial sector and development, percentage of GDP

outlook remains less optimistic for various reasons, creditworthy firms choose not to borrow while those that do are rationed out of the credit market either because of size (small and informal enterprises still receive a tiny share of total bank loans) or because they already have unpaid debt. The worry is with regard to the sustainability of the debt, and the possibility of the debt overhang affecting current and future investment. The problem is compounded in India by the fact that since development banks were effectively killed by the central government as part of its 'economic reform' process, the debt contracted by commercial banks (mostly public sector banks) is often directed to large, high-risk and long gestation period projects that are really not meant to be financed in this way. Loans to infrastructure (particularly the power sector) and sectors like aviation have been associated with the growing proportion of bad loans of commercial banks. Similarly, real estate and construction have also been significant areas of credit allocation, and the slump in these assets generates both financial and real economic fragility as well as potential stagnation. The lack of responsiveness of real investment to the change in political regime (the opposite of what was widely expected in early 2014) suggests that the forces that operated to constrain investment rates in the recent past, including the problem of debt overhang and the inability to raise domestic purchasing power through the expansion of wage incomes, remain significant even at present.

CONCLUSION

The experiences of these developing countries suggest a different – and possibly more plausible – meaning to the phrase 'middle income trap' that many developing countries are concerned about falling into. Traditionally, this has been interpreted as the problem faced by economies in which economic growth propels wage increases that render them less competitive than lower-wage rivals, especially in a world in which most of the trade competition is now concentrated in the production of raw materials and processed goods rather than the pre- and post-manufacturing stages (such as design, branding and marketing) that are increasingly concentrated in the advanced economies. The trap emerges as a result of the declining external competitiveness that results, which means that such economies can no longer use external trade (and in particular export orientation) as the primary means to improve their position in the global economic ladder.

The difficulty with this perspective is that it continues to see external demand as the driver for economic growth, and does not ask the question of why such countries cannot turn easily to a greater reliance on domestic demand as a sustainable and stable means of income expansion. What I have tried to suggest here is that this type of 'middle income trap' may be less of a problem than the other manifest trap that so many middle income countries seem to fall into: that of financial liberalization that affects both macroeconomic processes and the potential for future growth, even growth based on expanding domestic incomes in a stable way.

It is evident that financial liberalization can do more than simply create sharp and painful economic shocks for the residents of the country – they can also alter longer-term economic trajectories in unfortunate ways. An important fallout has been that the project of the developmental state, which was such an essential feature of economic progress in the region in the past, has effectively been abandoned. So the process of 'emerging' need not be celebrated – indeed, if it does in essence imply regression in terms of developmental objectives, it may be preferable not to emerge into global financial markets.

It may be asked whether this concern with financial liberalization glosses over other problems and constraints in the path towards economic diversification. Certainly, it is true that relatively few countries managed to use the period of greater control over finance that was widespread during the heyday of the import substituting strategy to their advantage in terms of transiting to rich/developed country status – South Korea being an important example of that success. The specific nature of the developmental state in South Korea as well as in Taiwan China was obviously important – but the external political economy figuration was equally important.

The geopolitics of the Cold War and South Korea's and Taiwan China's locations as frontline states vis-à-vis the Communist North, the People's Republic of China and the socialist bloc generally meant that the United States allowed and evenly actively encouraged state-led strategies that combined import protectionism with export-led industrialization, assisted by stable inflows of foreign capital and preferred access to major foreign markets. So, in addition to being developmental states, South Korea and Taiwan China benefited from a particular set of historical and geopolitical circumstances that are not easy to replicate.

Three conclusions emerge from this discussion. First, the process of economic diversification, and with it industrialization, is an essential part of development, and countries cannot hope to simply skip over it or benefit from periodic terms of trade advantages to somehow generate sustained and permanent increases in per capita income that lead to true convergence. Second, this process can be constrained or even reversed by financial liberalization policies that reduce the possibilities of using directed credit and stable financial allocations to promote industrialization. Third, external circumstances remain important, but even successful structural transformation requires institutional change that allows the domestic market to sustain industrialization. Insofar as 'emerging markets' hope to find a growth trajectory that ignores these processes, their development projects are likely to remain incomplete. In the context of an increasingly uncertain global order, the ability of developing countries to seize whatever opportunities for autonomous industrialization that may emerge from the current 'disorder' will depend on political economy processes that emphasise sustained emphasis on wage and employment-led growth.

REFERENCES

Akyuz, Yilmaz (2012) 'The staggering rise of the South', Background Paper No. 1 for ECIDC Report, UNCTAD, Geneva.

Bagchi, Amiya Kumar (2005) *Perilous Passage: Mankind and the Global Ascendancy of Capital*, London: Rowman and Littlefield.

Dervis, Kamal (2012) 'Convergence, interdependence and divergence', *Finance and Development*, September, IMF, Washington, DC.

Ghosh, Jayati and C.P. Chandrasekhar (2009) 'The costs of coupling: the global crisis and the Indian economy', *Cambridge Journal of Economics*, **33** (4), July, 725–39. doi: https://doi.org/10.1093/cje/bep034.

Findlay, Ronald and Kevin H. O'Rourke (2007) *Power and Plenty: Trade, War, and the World Economy in the Second Millennium*, Princeton, NJ: Princeton University Press.

Kindleberger, Charles P. and Robert Z. Aliber (2005) *Manias, Panics and Crashes: A History of Financial Crises*, Hoboken, NJ: John Wiley and Sons.

Maddison, Angus (2001) *The World Economy: A Millenial Perspective*, Paris: OECD Development Centre.

Patnaik, Prabhat (1997) *Accumulation and Stability under Capitalism*, Oxford: Clarendon Press.

Pettis, Michael (2014) *The Great Rebalancing: Trade, Conflict and the Perilous Road Ahead for the World Economy*, Princeton, NJ: Princeton University Press.

Reinert, Erik (2007) *How Rich Countries Got Rich, and Why Poor Countries Stay Poor*, London: Constable.

Triffin, Robert (1964) 'Myth and realities of the so-called "Gold Standard"', in *Our International Monetary System: Historical Reappraisal and Future Perspectives*, Princeton, NJ: Princeton University Press, pp. 2–20.

UNCTAD (2016) *Trade and Development Report (TDR) 2016: Structural Transformation for Inclusive and Sustained Growth*, New York and Geneva: United Nations.

UNDP (2013) *The Rise of the South: Human Progress in a Diverse World*, Human Development Report, New York: United Nations.

7.   Capitalism and India's democratic revolution

Prabhat Patnaik

The fact that several third world countries, especially in Asia, have experienced remarkably high rates of gross domestic product (GDP) growth has been a matter of much discussion. There has been talk of a development of 'multi-polarity' in the world, of a shift in the balance of economic power from the West to the East, and even of an overtaking of the traditional metropolitan economies by the newly emerging ones. India has been one of these high-growth economies, and has been branded as an 'emerging economic superpower' by many writers both within and outside the country.

But even if we leave aside the very recent slowdown in the Indian economy, which is a result inter alia of the world capitalist crisis and which has nevertheless left the country with a fairly respectable GDP growth rate to date, and focus our attention on the high growth phase that preceded this slowdown, the fact remains that this high growth has been accompanied by such an increase in economic inequality and such a process of 'social retrogression' that the country faces a real threat of social disintegration.

Those applauding India's high GDP growth and believing that they are witnessing the arrival of an economic superpower, fail, in my view, to see that this society, if it continues along its present course, is heading towards an 'implosion' which makes all this talk of 'an emerging economic superpower' somewhat ridiculous.

This proposition may or may not be true of other rapidly growing Asian economies, but, in my view, it is true of India. The 'democratic revolution' promised by the anti-colonial struggle, which provided the foundation for the emergence of a modern India, is not only being thwarted by the economic policies being pursued of late, the very same policies which generated the high GDP growth during a certain conjuncture in the world economy, but is actually being rolled back in crucial ways by these policies. And since any return, however partial, to an Indian society of yore characterized by its horrendously inegalitarian pre-modern social institutions is impossible to sustain today, given the fact that the intrusion of capitalism, albeit through the medium of colonial conquest, has caused a break-up of the self-contained isolation of the traditional society, any subversion of the 'democratic revolution' promises only social disintegration rather than some new 'equilibrium' of social oppression.

Since underlying the high growth of the economy has been a process of consolidation and entrenchment of capitalism, the argument of this chapter can be stated more accurately as follows. Capitalism has been often seen, on the basis of the Western experience, as a 'revolutionary' and 'modernizing' force which breaks up traditional societies that are marked by a certain 'communal life' but extreme internal oppression. Early in the twentieth century, however, Lenin had provided in his pamphlet, *Two Tactics of Social Democracy in the Democratic Revolution*, a modification of this argument based on the Russian experience, which was to inform the praxis of the revolutionary Left in the third world for well over a century afterwards. This Left argument, derived from Lenin, stated that the bourgeoisie in societies that came late to capitalism made an alliance with feudal elements, since any attack on feudal property at that late stage could well rebound into an attack on bourgeois property. It therefore did not play the same revolutionary role of breaking up the old society as its predecessors had done earlier, whence it followed that the working class had to play this role in lieu of the bourgeoisie in the new setting. This role consisted above all in liberating the peasantry from feudal oppression through land redistribution, which constituted the essence of the democratic revolution.

This argument, however, had been developed in a particular context where it was relevant; and that context was of a society on the threshold of a transition from feudalism where there were both bourgeoisie-led and working class-led democratic struggles, *with each class being relatively small*. The point at issue within that context was the relation between the two struggles, in particular, the attitude of the latter to the former. And here the argument stated that the democratic revolution got stalled if the bourgeoisie-led struggle acquired ascendancy, and because of which the working class-led democratic struggle had to retain its independence and carry forward the democratic agenda.

But in societies that have gone beyond that stage, where capitalism, even though it has destroyed neither land concentration nor the social institutions of the old society, has already entrenched itself, this very process of entrenching entails not just a *stalling* of the democratic revolution but an actual *rolling back* of it. And such a roll back is not just ethically objectionable; it actually leads to social disintegration in the absence of a push towards a transcendence of that capitalist arrangement. Capitalism in 'newly emerging societies', in other words, does not just arrest the democratic revolution; in a world conjuncture, which facilitates a rapid growth and consolidation of capitalism, it tends actually to roll back the democratic revolution. Hence, advancing the democratic revolution, and even retaining the democratic gains already made requires, in societies like India, a resistance against the capitalism that marks the current conjuncture, that is, 'neo-liberal capitalism'.

The fact that traditional Indian society was marked by a level of institutional inequality, enshrined in the caste system that included even 'untouchability' and 'unseeability' (which meant that 'upper' caste persons were supposed to get 'polluted' if they so much as set eyes upon a person belonging to the 'lower castes'), which was unparalleled anywhere else in the world, hardly needs reiteration. It is often said that colonial rule with its assertion of juridical equality dealt a blow to this system of institutionalized inequality. But this was scarcely the case. True, there was formal equality before the law for everybody under colonialism, but this hardly had any impact in weakening caste discrimination at the ground level, where, for instance, the 'lower castes' were never allowed to draw water from the same well as the 'upper castes', confined through coercion and the absence of alternative opportunities to the most menial and degrading occupations, and even prevented over large parts of the country from owning any land.

What is more, the 'lower castes' were among the worst victims of the economic exploitation of the country under colonial rule, through the twin processes of 'drain of surplus' (which meant a transfer without any quid pro quo of resources to the metropolis) and of 'deindustrialization' (which meant the destruction of local craft production by the import of machine-made manufactured goods from the metropolis).[1] The burden of this exploitation greatly increased the pressure of population on land through a process of pauperization of peasants and petty producers, and this growing pressure entailed a lowering of real wages of agricultural labourers (Chandra, 1968), among which of course the 'lower castes' had an overwhelming presence.

The real opposition to the social inequities of the old system came not from colonial rule itself but the resistance that built up against it. The late nineteenth and early twentieth centuries were characterized by two outstanding movements in India: one was the 'social reform movement' of the oppressed castes that took off in different parts of the country against the social order of institutionalized inequality; the other was the anti-colonial struggle. And these two were joined later, in the 1930s and 1940s by the Left movement, which in many ways descended from one or the other of these struggles but was inspired by the Bolshevik Revolution.

Since many of the leaders of the anti-colonial struggle, including

[1]   For a discussion of the 'drain', see Utsa Patnaik (2006) and on 'deindustrialization', see Amiya Bagchi (1976).

Mahatma Gandhi himself, professed a belief in the caste system even as they struggled against its inhumane practices such as untouchability, and since many of the leaders of the social reform movement like Ambedkar and 'Periyar' Ramaswamy Naicker kept away from the anti-colonial struggle because of their fear that the place occupied by the British would simply be taken by the local 'upper castes' after independence, there is often a tendency among modern authors to see these two struggles as being antithetical to one another.

This, however, is a facile reading of the situation. No matter what the attitudes of the leaders of each of the two struggles towards the other struggle and its leaders, the two struggles were complementary, and dialectically reinforced one another. They complemented one another in the consciousness of the people and brought about an unprecedented awakening in the country. The social reform movement would not have acquired the sweep it did if a general anti-imperialist struggle that opened up people's horizons towards a new world had not existed at the same time. And the anti-colonial struggle would not have acquired the sweep it did, if it did not, under the impact of the social reform movement and of the pressure from the Left, present to the people a picture of a 'free India' of *equal* citizens.

The expression of this promise of the anti-colonial struggle was the resolution of the Karachi session of the Indian National Congress in 1931, which for the first time put before the country a picture of what 'free India' would look like. And this included inter alia a system of parliamentary democracy based on universal adult franchise; equality before law irrespective of caste, religion, gender and ethnicity; a set of fundamental rights for all citizens; a separation of the State from all religions; free and compulsory primary education; and the provision of economic security to all. The Karachi Resolution, which constituted the first manifesto of India's democratic revolution, played a major role, in the context, of course, of the acute distress of the peasantry in the 1930s as a consequence of the Great Depression in increasing the sweep of the anti-colonial struggle; and its key elements were to be incorporated into the Constitution of independent India.

While colonial rule played a role in bringing the outside world and its ideas into the country (for which however it was not *necessary*, as the case of Japan shows), the attack against the old social structures became a part of the anti-colonial struggle and found expression in the political agenda of this struggle. India's democratic revolution was as much anti-feudal as it was anti-imperialist. Ambedkar, the outstanding leader of the social reform movement who played a key role as the architect of the new Constitution, had warned the Constituent Assembly while presenting the

Constitution that the political equality the Constitution embodied would be threatened if there was no progress towards socio-economic equality. His warning was most insightful.

Putting the matter differently, the 'modern India' that was to emerge was envisaged, and rightly so, as being *fundamentally different* from what the society had been earlier, and it is the promise of this *difference* that underlay the implicit 'social contract' upon which the new post-colonial order was founded.[2] The crux of this difference lay in striving towards *equality in all spheres* in place of the institutional inequality of the old order. *A striving towards equality in other words was central to the 'social contract' that underlay the emergence of modern India, not a striving for high GDP growth as such, or a striving for the status of an economic superpower.* This is why I believe that the exacerbation of social and economic inequality under the impact of neo-liberalism is a violation of this implicit 'social contract' that is not only 'unfair' in an ethical sense, but, even more importantly, also inimical to the fragile stability of this society, and hence a potent source of 'implosion'.

THE *DIRIGISTE* REGIME

What was the development strategy that was envisaged for the realization of this vision of 'modern India'? While the slogan was of a 'socialistic pattern of society', the idea was not to have social ownership of all the major means of production because capitalists too were supposed to contribute towards economic development. But clearly the State had to play a key role, not only through a public sector that was to act as a bulwark against the domination and technological monopoly of foreign capital and as the pioneer in developing long-gestation and high-risk projects that typically characterize basic and capital goods industries, but also through the discipline it exercised over the capitalists, to ensure that their profit-seeking behaviour did not violate the march towards the more egalitarian order that the 'socialistic pattern' was supposed to embody. A whole range of controls and licensing requirements were imposed upon them towards this end.

There was something in common here between this line of thinking and that of Keynesianism. Both believed in the autonomy of the State as an entity standing above classes which could act disinterestedly for the 'social good' and remain impervious to pressures emanating from capital. Both

---

[2]   My reference to a 'social contract' should not be taken to mean an invocation of the theoretical legacy of Hobbes, Locke or Rousseau.

strands of thinking visualized a democratic polity where the government, being elected by the people on the basis of universal suffrage, would be concerned with *their* interests rather than with the sectional interests of the capitalists. But the problem with such thinking was not so much that it misread the subjective vulnerabilities of the State personnel, which no doubt it did and which no doubt are important, but that it ignored the fact of capitalism being a 'spontaneous' system (to use a phrase of Oskar Lange, 1963).

It is driven by a set of immanent tendencies, the State's interference with which makes the system dysfunctional. Whenever such dysfunctionality arises, the State either has to interfere still further, and hence engage in a recursive process of ever increasing interference until the system itself gets effectively transcended, or it has to pull back from its original interference. This is the dilemma that the State engaged in demand management in accordance with the Keynesian prescription faced in the advanced countries, with the acceleration of inflation in the late 1960s. And this is also the dilemma that the *dirigiste* economic *regime* created by the post-colonial Indian State faced as the economy, facing a narrow domestic mass market in the absence of an egalitarian distribution of land and other assets, and hence dependent crucially upon an expansion of public spending to keep up its momentum, began to atrophy under a growing fiscal crisis of the State.

The mode of resolution of this dilemma was effectively taken out of the hands of the State because the process of centralization of capital at the level of the world economy had brought into being a new actor, 'globalized finance capital'. The post-colonial State, lacking the will to resist its pressure, and that of the domestic big capitalists who had by then lost their interest in pursuing a trajectory of capitalist development that was relatively autonomous of metropolitan capital, and had decided instead to become integrated to globalized finance capital, opted for dismantling the *dirigiste* structure and following the neo-liberal policies that were being pushed by them.

The result, until the impact of the world capitalist crisis which started in 2007–08 hit the economy somewhat belatedly, was an increase in the growth rate, especially between 2004–05 and 2011–12 and especially of the tertiary sector (the material commodity producing sectors have not witnessed much acceleration in growth compared to the pre-liberalization era), but also a massive increase in income and wealth inequality. No doubt inequality was increasing even during the period of the *dirigiste* strategy, but the pace of increase was much slower, and any such increase was held to be an undesirable phenomenon. Under neo-liberalism, however, growing inequality is officially accepted and justified as an inevitable accompaniment of higher growth, whose benefits, it is argued, would 'trickle down' over time, if not automatically then at least through enlarging the fiscal resources available to the State for redistribution towards the poor in various ways.

Such redistribution through fiscal means of course never materializes, since the need for providing 'incentives' to the capitalists to keep this growth process going, as well as spending on infrastructure for which an insatiable demand is created by the tendency towards perennial technological and structural change that characterizes a neo-liberal economy, absorbs whatever resources do, or could, come towards the State. This is true to such an extent that even the modest National Rural Employment Guarantee Scheme, set up against the wishes of the neo-liberal lobby by the Congress Party-led United Progressive Alliance government in 2006, when it was dependent upon Left support for its survival, is now being starved of funds, even though it is a rights-based programme on which the expenditure is supposed to be demand-driven.

But, even assuming that the neo-liberal State cannot effect any redistribution through fiscal means, the question still arises: why should there be an increase in economic, especially income, inequality in a neo-liberal regime even when there is high growth?

NEO-LIBERALISM AND ECONOMIC INEQUALITY

The answer to this question lies in the fact that the neo-liberal regime entails a restoration of the 'spontaneity' of capitalism compared with being regulated and controlled in some ways, which was the case under *dirigisme*. And this makes a difference in at least two spheres – first, with regard to peasant agriculture and petty production in general and second, the removal of restrictions on the pace of technological cum structural change.

The tendency of the capitalist sector to encroach upon the traditional petty production sector, and upon peasant agriculture in particular, which was kept in check under the *dirigiste* regime, now reasserts itself.

The anti-colonial struggle had taken off in a big way in India in the 1930s when the Great Depression inflicted acute distress upon the peasantry. It had done so on the promise that such distress would never again visit the peasantry, and in keeping with this promise the post-colonial State had protected and promoted peasant agriculture in various ways. It had undertaken large public irrigation programmes; it had promoted research in State-funded institutions for improved agricultural practices; the outcome of such research was made available to the agricultural sector through the creation of a massive network of State-sponsored extension services;

it had protected agriculture through quantitative restrictions and tariffs from competition abroad and had thus insulated it against world price fluctuations; it had procured crops domestically at remunerative prices announced each season on the basis of estimates of costs of production by a special Commission set up for the purpose; it had subsidized agricultural inputs, including credit from the banking system which was nationalized for this very purpose inter alia; it had obliged banks to provide a certain percentage of their credit at these lower rates to agriculture which had been designated a 'priority sector'; it had prevented the multinational agribusiness companies from having any direct dealings with the peasantry; and it had even prevented the domestic big capitalists from entering into any direct deals with the peasantry.

The benefits of all these measures of support of course did not accrue to all sections of the peasantry equally, but were cornered by the well-to-do peasants, who were developing into a class of proto-capitalists, and by that segment of the erstwhile landlords who had taken to direct cultivation, instead of through tenants, and represented the Indian version of 'junker capitalism'. Nonetheless, these measures brought a halt to the long drawn-out agrarian crisis of the colonial period that had become particularly acute during the last two decades of colonial rule.

This fact manifested itself in two ways. The first was a turnaround in the per capita production and availability of food grains. The figure for per capita availability, which had been 199 kilogrammes (kg) per annum for 'British India' for the quinquennium 1897–1902, had declined to 136.8 kg in 1945–46 (Blyn, 1966); and even if we take the quinquennium 1939–44 as a whole, the average annual figure comes to 148.5 kg. This started increasing until around the end of the 1980s, that is, until the introduction of neo-liberal policies in 1991, when it climbed up to 177 kg per annum for the triennium 1989–92 (U. Patnaik, 2007).

The second was that the process of 'primitive accumulation of capital', which refers to the capitalist sector enriching itself at the expense of the pre-capitalist sector and which had been rampant during the period of colonialism, was significantly restricted. Primitive accumulation has a 'flow' and a 'stock' form. The former consists of the appropriation *gratis* of a part of the *income* of the pre-capitalist producers by the capitalist sector; and colonialism was engaged in it from its very inception through the sheer appropriation of the proceeds of the taxes levied upon the people, especially the peasantry (referred to above as the 'drain of surplus'). Primitive accumulation in 'stock' form, which is what Marx discussed at length in *Capital*, is when the capitalist sector simply expropriates the *assets* of the pre-capitalist producers, or what comes to the same thing, purchases them at 'throwaway' prices.

While there was eviction of tenants in the 1950s and 1960s associated with the development of capitalism in Indian agriculture, which also can be said to constitute primitive accumulation in a certain sense, the capitalism that began to develop through such evictions *was from within the sector*. Primitive accumulation *at the expense of the sector itself* for the benefit of either the metropolis or the domestic big capitalists was restricted during the *dirigiste* era, which also meant an end to the earlier agrarian crisis. This is what paved the way for the increase in agricultural output in general, and the output and availability of food grains in particular.

What I have said about peasant agriculture is also true of petty production as a whole. Through a policy of 'reservation' of certain categories of products for handlooms, through significant subsidies for hand spinning and weaving, through measures of protection of petty producers in fishing, and through the establishment of several commodity boards which marketed cash crops like tea, coffee and rubber after purchasing them from petty producers at assured prices, the *dirigiste* regime sought to ensure the viability of petty production to an extent.

Neo-liberalism has ended all this. Quantitative restrictions on agricultural imports have been given up and tariff rates too are well below the 'bounds' allowed by the World Trade Organization (WTO), which means that peasants are no longer insulated from world price fluctuations; input subsidies have been cut and even the procurement operations have been abandoned in many crops (there is currently a big question mark over food grain procurement because of the WTO); institutional credit to agriculture has dried up, forcing the peasantry to turn to a new class of private moneylenders who charge usurious interest rates; multinational seed and fertilizer firms are having a field day selling their products to the peasantry; extension services by the government have been wound up; commodity boards have been shorn of their marketing function; the proactive role of the State in undertaking research has been whittled down; and public investment in irrigation and rural infrastructure has been curtailed.

Not surprisingly, the agrarian crisis is back with us, with more than 200 000 peasants committing suicide over the last decade and a half.

Primitive accumulation of capital is occurring not just in 'flow' terms in favour of big capitalists and the multinational corporations but also in 'stock' terms through the takeover of peasant lands at low prices for 'industrial' and 'infrastructure' projects (many of which are in fact real estate projects).

In exactly the same manner, a process of primitive accumulation of capital is occurring at the expense of other petty producers. A recent measure to allow multinationals like Wal-Mart into the retail business is going to affect hundreds of thousands of petty traders. *The effect of the resumption of primitive accumulation of capital, as in colonial times, though using different instruments, is to throw a large number of displaced petty producers onto the labour market in search of jobs.*

The second major difference that neo-liberalism has made, compared to the earlier regime, is to remove restrictions on the pace of technological cum structural change. Since the domestic elite wishes to imitate the life-styles prevailing in the West, this removal of restrictions has entailed a shift in the pattern of consumption and production towards newer goods prevalent in the West. And what is more, as product innovation occurs in the West, the tendency has been to imitate such innovation. Given that the production of such goods in the West economizes on labour use, and new products and processes there have a generally labour-saving character, the removal of restrictions on technological cum structural change has raised the rate of growth of labour productivity quite significantly, and meant that even when the GDP growth rate has been high, employment growth has been extremely slow.[3]

The net result of these two changes, therefore, has been a significant increase in the relative size of the labour reserves, *though these do not manifest themselves explicitly as labour reserves since employment rationing takes the form of greater 'casualization' and 'informalization'.* Instead of the 'active army' of labour and the 'reserve army' of labour being two distinct entities, what we increasingly observe is the disappearance of the distinction between them, through the disappearance of a more permanently employed 'active army' as such. And even in sectors where there is some security of employment, in the sense that some notice is required before a worker can be sacked, the effort now is to introduce 'labour market flexibility', which would mean unrestricted freedom of employers to 'fire' workers.

The effect of all these developments has been a weakening of trade unions and a stagnation of real wage rates including for 'organized' workers; for 'unorganized' workers matters have been worse. Given the high rate of growth of labour productivity, this has meant a rise in the share of the 'economic surplus' in output, which explains basically the increase in income inequality even in the midst of impressive rates of GDP growth.

But it is not just income inequality that has increased. There has been an increase in the incidence of absolute poverty, which is defined in India in terms of a nutritional 'norm', *even in the period of high GDP growth.*

---

[3]   Indeed, Chandrasekhar and Ghosh (2011) estimate from the National Sample Survey data that during the quinquennium 2004–05 to 2009–10, which coincided with India's high growth phase, the annual rate of growth of 'usual principal status' employment was a mere 0.8 per cent, far below the rate of population growth itself.

Poverty is officially defined in India as the inability to access 2200 calories per person per day in rural India and 2100 calories per person per day in urban India. Using data collected by the National Sample Survey, the proportion of the rural population that is 'poor' by this criterion went up from 69.5 per cent in 2004–05 to 76 per cent in 2009–10, precisely during the period of high growth, and from 64.5 per cent to 73 per cent in urban India (U. Patnaik, 2013). A subsequent survey commissioned by the government for 2011–12, on the grounds that 2009–10 was a drought year and therefore exceptional, revealed a similar *trend* though slightly better absolute figures for the terminal year (Ram Krishna, 2015).

This is hardly surprising, in view of the fact that the per capita net availability of food grains, which we noted earlier had increased to around 180 kg per year by the end of the 1980s, came down to around 162 kg by 2011–12 (a good crop year). In fact, the nutritional deprivation in India today is worse than in sub-Saharan Africa.

GROWING SOCIAL INEQUALITY

Let me turn now to the question of *social* inequality. Any increase in economic inequality, given that among the labouring poor there is a preponderance of the 'lower castes', of the tribal people, and of other marginalized segments of the population, implies *ipso facto* an increase in social inequality. There are, however, three additional factors that contribute towards such an increase in social inequality.

The first is the following. We have noted that the rate of growth in the number of jobs created by the growth process, even when it is rapid, falls perennially short of the rate of growth in the number of job-seekers, leading to an increase in the relative magnitude of unemployment (which however is camouflaged). But the jobs created are typically in sectors, such as IT-related services, that require some education. These jobs may not be very 'creative' but they are not completely unskilled. Historically, however, the 'lower castes' and marginalized groups have been excluded from education. Hence, those who are rationed out of employment typically belong to the 'lower castes' and marginalized groups, while those who do benefit from such employment as created by the high GDP growth in the era of neo-liberalism belong to the 'upper castes'. This, therefore, becomes an additional factor contributing to a widening of the social distance between the 'upper castes' on the one hand and the 'lower castes' and the marginalized groups (which includes Muslims) on the other.

Of course, if the education divide between the different social groups was getting narrower at the same time, then the importance of this fact should decrease over time. But the education distance gets increased over time, and this is my second point. This increase is because of the privatization of important services like education and healthcare which is a feature of neo-liberalism. This raises the cost of such services and puts decent education and quality healthcare out of the reach of the 'lower castes' and the marginalized groups.

We mentioned earlier that the magnitude of absolute poverty has increased during the period of high growth. This fact, however, is not apparent from official poverty estimates which adopt a particular method of estimating poverty. They take a 'poverty line' in the base year as that level of expenditure at which the specified calorie 'norms' were accessed; they then bring up this 'poverty line' to the current year by using a cost-of-living index; and estimate, finally, how many fall below this updated 'poverty line'. The reason why this procedure underestimates poverty is that the rise in cost of living owing to the privatization of essential services, and the concomitant running down of public services, is not taken into account in the index (P. Patnaik, 2013). Once this running down of public services is recognized, the increasing vertical distance between different social groups in the matter of education (and also access to healthcare) becomes obvious.

The third point relates to the fact that even such affirmative action as existed earlier ceases to be effective with the growing privatization of the economy. Affirmative action in India took the form of reservations for the 'scheduled castes' and 'scheduled tribes' in educational institutions and in jobs, *but only in the government sector.* As the government sector becomes relatively smaller compared to the private sector where no such reservation exists, even those opportunities available to this segment of the marginalized population (such opportunities did not even exist for the Muslims) begin to shrink, leading again to a widening of the distance between the different social groups.

THE EMERGENCE OF THE HINDU RIGHT

For all the reasons described above, in addition to the general fact of growing income inequality, there is a growing social inequality. But the contribution of neo-liberalism lies not just in this growing social inequality. There is also an additional factor of great importance.

Even for jobs demanding some degree of education and skills there is an excess supply of labour. This creates a general apprehension, in the minds of the socially privileged groups that access these jobs, that if the 'lower castes' and other marginalized sections did acquire education and skills, then the opportunities for them would shrink further. They therefore develop a vested interest in a social order that keeps the reach of education restricted, even as the limited opportunities that do come their way make them votaries of neo-liberalism. The neo-liberal regime, even while it increases economic and social inequality, creates a constituency for itself which additionally also has a vested interest in perpetuating the inequities of the social order. Neo-liberal capitalism in other words, far from dealing destructive blows on the old social order as commonly expected, actually plays the role of strengthening the inequities of the old social order, of worsening its fault lines.

And the ideological support for such a strengthening of prejudice against the oppressed of the old order is provided through a revival of the Hindu religious right. The appeal of *Hindutva* to the educated segment in recent years has surprised many, but it is rooted in the above-mentioned phenomena. Instead of the vision of an egalitarian order which the implicit social contract that formed the basis of India's modernity had promised and to which the *dirigiste* regime at least expressed its adherence, we now have an explicit reversion to the older prejudices against the 'lower castes' and against Muslims which underlies all the grandiose talk about India being an 'emerging superpower'.

Such a social retrogression, however, will call forth resistance, either of a creative kind for a new socio-economic order transcending neo-liberal capitalism or a destructive kind that embodies mere mindless militancy.

In either case there would be a tendency for a shift towards a more repressive bourgeois State. This tendency is likely to get strengthened by the persistent world capitalist crisis that is reducing employment opportunities in India even further. The fight for the defence and deepening of democracy in this context has to be accompanied by an alternative agenda that negates the rolling back of the democratic revolution in general under neo-liberal capitalism. Unless a transcendence of neo-liberal capitalism is put on the agenda in other words, and with it the guaranteeing of a set of economic rights that provide economic security to every citizen – that is, unless the vision of the 1931 Karachi Resolution is carried forward – India is in danger of drifting towards social disintegration, and political authoritarianism which, however, would not prevent such disintegration.

REFERENCES

Bagchi, A.K. (1976) 'Deindustrialization in India in the Nineteenth Century: Some Theoretical Implications', *Journal of Development Studies*, **12** (2), 135–64.
Blyn, George (1966) *Agricultural Trends in India 1891–1947: Output, Availability, and Productivity*, Philadelphia: University of Pennsylvania Press.

Chandra, Bipan (1968) 'Reinterpretation of Nineteenth Century Indian Economic History', *Indian Economic and Social History Review*, **5**, March, 35–7.

Chandrasekhar, C.P. and J. Ghosh (2011) 'Latest Employment Trends from the NSSO', *Business Line*, 12 July.

Lange, O. (1963) *Political Economy*, Vol. 1, Warsaw: Pergamon Press.

Patnaik, P. (2013) 'A Critique of the Welfare-theoretic Basis of the Measurement of Poverty', *Economic and Political Weekly*, **XLVIII** (14), 6 April, 16–19.

Patnaik, U. (2006) 'The Free Lunch: Transfers from Tropical Colonies and their Role in Capital Formation in Britain During the Industrial Revolution', in J.K. Sundaram (ed.), *Globalization Under Hegemony*, Delhi: Oxford University Press, pp. 30–70.

Patnaik, U. (2007) 'The Republic of Hunger', in *The Republic of Hunger and Other Essays*, Delhi: Three Essays Collective, pp. 115–50.

Patnaik, U. (2013) 'Poverty Trends in India 2004–05 to 2009–10', *Economic and Political Weekly*, **XLVIII** (40), 5 October, 43–58.

Ram Krishna (2015) The Relationship Between Calorie Intake, Real Income and Nutrition: Empirical Study Based on National and International Data Since 1990s, PhD thesis, Centre for Economic Studies and Planning, Jawaharlal Nehru University, New Delhi.

8. Latin America's development: a short historical account

José Antonio Ocampo*

The economic history of Latin America[1] ('the region,' as I shall refer to it throughout this chapter) is marked by three essential features. The first is that it was the part of the developing world[2] that (together with the Caribbean) was most deeply transformed by colonization, as well as the first to become politically independent in the early nineteenth century (with the exception of Cuba). The second, which it shares with other parts of the developing world, has been its position within the world's economic system as a commodity producer, a feature that, a few countries aside, it has been unable to overcome despite the industrialization drive that took place in particular from the 1930s to the 1970s. This has made the region vulnerable to trends and fluctuations in commodity prices. This vulnerability, that has been enhanced in different periods by highly unstable and pro-cyclical access to external financing, has given rise to severe crises when these two factors coincided. The third is that, together with parts of sub-Saharan Africa, it is the most unequal region of the world.

This chapter presents the broad strokes of the historical evolution of Latin America in the global context. It is divided into four sections. The first takes a brief look at the region's colonial heritage. The second analyses the forms of insertion into the global economy since independence. The third considers the region's growth record and the process of convergence and divergence vis-à-vis both the developed world and other developing countries. The last summarizes the historical record in terms of social and institutional development.

---

*   This chapter borrows from a joint economic history of Latin America written with Luis Bértola (Bértola and Ocampo, 2012).
[1]   I will follow here the convention of using the term 'Latin America,' but this chapter really refers to Ibero-America – that is, the Spanish and Portuguese-speaking part of the Americas – but excludes the French-speaking nation (Haiti) and territories, which have quite a distinct history.
[2]   Throughout this chapter, the concept of developing world/countries is meant to encompass the so-called 'emerging' economies.

The sections differentiate four different periods:[3] (1) the post-independence decades; (2) the commodity export-led growth period, which coincided with the 'first globalization';[4] (3) the period of state-led industrialization – a term that, as argued by Cárdenas et al. (2000) and Bértola and Ocampo (2012), is preferable to that of 'import substitution industrialization' because the latter captures only one element, and not necessarily the most important, of this period of development; this phase is bound by two major crises, one of a global character, the Great Depression of the 1930s, and another of a regional character, the debt crisis and associated 'lost decade' of the 1980s; and (4) the period of market reforms, which began in the 1980s (in some countries, notably Chile, in the 1970s) and has broadly coincided with the second globalization. Given regional diversity, these phases were not entirely synchronized nor did they have identical effects on different countries. So, I shall also point out some national differences.

THE COLONIAL HERITAGE

Commodity dependence was firmly established in Latin America during the colonial period, when it was characterized by the dominance of precious metals (silver and gold, in that order of importance) in Spanish America and sugar in Brazil. The Bourbon and Pombaline reforms of the Spanish and Portuguese empires were introduced in the late eighteenth century to revitalize their ties with the colonies in order to benefit from the expansion of the international economy. This led to the development of several new export activities. In turn, the successful slave revolution in Haiti in 1791 generated the collapse of the then major world exporter of sugar and coffee, which led to a sugar boom in Cuba and the spread of coffee to Brazil, Costa Rica and Venezuela, among other countries.

The colonial structures were also characterized by highly segmented societies, which left a legacy of high levels of economic and social inequality. This included three types of structures, which mixed in diverse forms throughout the region. In those countries with developed Indian

[3]   See Bértola and Ocampo (2012) and the complementary book by Bulmer-Thomas (2014).
[4]   Following the recent historiography, I will use the term 'first globalization' to refer to the period of global integration unleashed in the second half of the nineteenth century, and particularly in the last three decades, by the maritime and railroad transport revolutions, the spread of the telegraph and the very open trade policies of England and a few other countries (the Netherlands). This period came to an end with the Great Depression of the 1930s. In turn, I will use the term 'second globalization' to refer to the most recent process of global integration since the 1960s.

civilizations, their old political structures were destroyed and new ones were created to subordinate them to the colonial structures; several lesser developed indigenous societies disappeared altogether, whereas others were able to survive in the remote areas of both empires. Given the demographic catastrophe that took place in the first decades of colonial rule, largely because of the spread of European diseases but also due to the over-exploitation of indigenous labor, slaves were brought from Africa to fill the vacuum. Europeans constituted, in turn, the apex of the social structure, but also generated pockets of white smallholder economies in some countries. Whites mixed on a relatively large scale with both indigenous peoples and African descendants, generating large mestizo and mulatto populations.

The colonial period came to an end in most of Latin America as a result of the events unleashed by the Napoleonic wars and particularly by the French invasion of the Iberian Peninsula in 1808. The exception was Cuba, which would become independent as a result of its second independence war and the Spanish–American war of 1898. Puerto Rico also ceased to be a Spanish colony as a result of the Spanish–American war, but became de facto a territory of the USA, with some semi-colonial features that have persisted until the present.

Independence created the need to develop new political structures. This process developed in different ways in Spanish America and Brazil. In the former, the old colonies were transformed into a diverse set of countries which underwent a traumatic process of state building, which included independence and later a myriad of civil wars. The result of this, as well as the high levels of inequality that characterized all of them, generated in most countries a tradition of military (and later civilian) caudillos rather than democratic republican structures. Economic liberalism, which had started to spread in the late colonial period and was finally victorious in the nineteenth century, was not accompanied, therefore, with a tradition of political liberalism, except in a handful of countries. In contrast, the Portuguese king migrated to Brazil during the French invasion and his son remained in the former colony, creating a new empire. This guaranteed a greater institutional continuity, not exempted from regional rebellions; it would turn into a republic in 1889. As part of the Spanish empire, Cuba was also characterized by the continuation of its political institutions through most of the nineteenth century.

Political continuity also led to the preservation of slavery in Brazil and Cuba, whereas this system collapsed in independent Spanish America during the independence wars and under the pressure of the British to eliminate the slave traffic. This process was a gradual one that ended in several countries toward the middle of the nineteenth century, but was speedier in the countries that depended less on slave institutions, as well as in the Dominican Republic, where a Haitian invasion freed the slaves. The end of slavery came late in Cuba and Brazil, in 1886 and 1888, respectively.

Following a policy that had been put in place during the late colonial reforms, several Indian reservations were dismantled, but many survived through the nineteenth century and would be reinforced by the agrarian reforms of the twentieth century. The Indian tribute was also eliminated after independence, but survived longer in countries where it constituted a large proportion of government revenues. In any case, a large part of the indigenous as well as the growing mestizo rural population continued to be subordinated in the hacienda system well into the twentieth century, which included mechanisms that reduced labor mobility (notably debt peonage). The mechanisms of subordination of former slaves evolved in similar directions.

THE EXPORT ECONOMY AND THE INDUSTRIAL SECTOR

Export expansion was a fairly diverse experience in the first decades after independence. Cuba was the most successful early story, greatly benefiting from the destruction of the sugar industry of Haiti. The persistence of slavery in Cuba, as well as Brazil, contributed to export expansion during these years. Other examples of successful export development in the post-independence period included the Southern Cone countries (Argentina, Chile and Uruguay), Costa Rica and Peru, and Colombia from the mid nineteenth century.

The first major export commodity expansion of the region as a whole was part of the worldwide international trade expansion that characterized the 'first globalization' of the late nineteenth and early twentieth centuries. During this period, Latin America's share in world exports increased substantially (Figure 8.1), a success that was behind the region's rapid gross domestic product (GDP) growth during this period (see the next section). It was accompanied by a major diversification away from colonial or early independence export staples (precious metals, sugar, tobacco, hides and guano) toward new agricultural goods (cereals, wool and meat), minerals (nitrates, copper and tin) and, late in the boom, oil, with coffee continuing to be the only traditional staple to share in the boom. The Southern Cone countries and Cuba were the indisputable regional export leaders on the eve of the First World War, but were now accompanied by the renewed export success of Mexico, and the spread of coffee in Brazil, Colombia and several Central American countries.

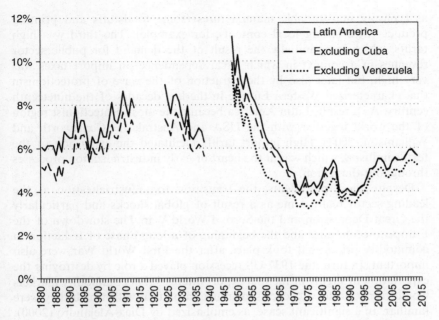

Sources: Bértola and Ocampo (2012) from 1820 to 1940. The United Nations Conference on Trade and Development (UNCTAD) from 1948.

Figure 8.1 Share of Latin America in world exports

The Southern Cone was strongly hit by the slowdown of Western Europe after the First World War, but other countries – notably Colombia, Peru, Venezuela, but also several Central American economies and, to a lesser extent, Brazil – sustained their growth or even speeded up given the opportunities provided by the continued expansion of the US economy. As a result, the region's share in world exports peaked in 1924–28 at levels slightly above those reached prior to the First World War. The Great Depression interrupted this expansion and led to the first significant reduction in Latin America's share in world trade.

Industrialization came as a by-product of three different processes unleashed by export expansion. The first was commodity processing, which was important for sugar and metals in particular. The second was the expansion of domestic markets, further facilitated by their integration thanks to the construction of railroads, and later car roads, and in some countries by steam navigation. Manufactures with high transport costs, such as beverages and construction materials, especially benefited, as well as typically non-tradable manufactures (some foodstuffs and printing products with strong local contents, for example). The third was high tariffs, which were initially the result of the demand for public sector revenues in a context in which fiscal dependence on import taxes was very high, but later also by the attraction of the wave of protectionism that characterized Western Europe in the last decades of the nineteenth century. As a result, Latin America became the most protectionist region of the world together with the USA and Australasia (Coastworth and Williamson, 2004). High import tariffs facilitated the expansion of the textile industry, which was at the heart of early industrialization processes throughout the region.

Despite these precedents, the transition to industrialization as the leading sector really came as a result of global shocks and particularly the Great Depression and the Second World War. The slowdown of the European economies and the beginning of a long phase of reduction in commodity prices that took place after the First World War were also important. In turn, the 1937 US recession played a role by destroying the expectation of highly influential export interests that commodity markets would recover after a cyclical downturn, a pattern with which they were familiar. In a significant sense, as emphasized by Diaz-Alejandro (2000), the shift toward industrialization during the 1930s was essentially the result of the incentives generated by relative price changes induced by external shocks. Following the past regional pattern, but now also a broad-based world trend, heightened protectionism played a role, now including the spread of a new instrument of protection, quantitative import controls. The lack of essential goods during the Second World War also generated the idea that it was essential to promote 'strategic industries,' including investment by a growing group of public sector development banks.

In a significant sense, therefore, industrialization came more as a result of external shocks rather than the rise of a new theory or strategy of development. As expressed with particular clarity by Love (1994, p. 395), 'Industrialisation in Latin America was fact before it was policy, and policy before it was theory.' Such theory came in the late 1940s and early 1950s under the leadership of the United Nations Economic Commission for Latin America (ECLA, later ECLAC when the Caribbean joined the organization), with Raúl Prebisch at the helm. The essential message, conveyed with strong force in the 1949 *Economic Survey of Latin America* (published also as Prebisch, 1973) – a document later referred to by Albert Hirschman as the 'Latin American manifesto' – was that manufacturing development was a better mechanism of transmission of technical progress and absorption of labor in a context in which commodity markets faced downward long-term terms of trade.[5] The most important of these concepts, which coincided with those of other contemporary classical development economists writing at the time, was the association of industrialization with technical progress. ECLAC crafted, therefore, the theoretical justification for the new strategy, with a strong sense of regional identity. It was also the major promoter of regional integration agreements in the 1960s: the Latin American Free Trade Area, the Central American Common Market and the Andean Group. These agreements did help expand intraregional manufacturing trade, but their development would be limited by national industrial interests as well as by recurrent crises.

Commodity interests were never totally replaced, however. Indeed, commodities and natural resource-based manufactures still represented more than three-quarters of Latin American exports around 1980 (see Figure 8.3). They also provided, therefore, the foreign exchange needed to finance the imports of capital and intermediate goods required by the rising manufacturing sector. This is the basic reason for Hirschman's (1971) argument that one of the distinctive features of the Latin American industrialization process vis-à-vis the 'late industrializing' Western European countries analysed by Gerschenkron (1962) was the weakness of industrial interests relative to those of commodity exporters. Furthermore, the industrialization of small economies did not go very far, and their export diversification since the 1950s relied essentially on new commodities; in a sense, in this case industrialization was overlaid upon what continued to be essentially commodity export-led models. New commodities were also important for larger countries, with oil in Mexico in the 1970s an important example.

State-led industrialization was largely an inward-oriented process. It evolved since the mid 1960s from import substitution to a 'mixed model' that combined the older strategy with export diversification and regional integration. Export diversification allowed several countries of the region to join the growing world markets for developing country manufactures, whereas regional integration was from the beginning highly intensive in manufactures. In any case, state-led industrialization was characterized by a significant anti-export bias. The major reflection of this fact was a massive fall in Latin America's share in world trade, to slightly more than 4 percent in the early 1970s, about half the level reached in the 1920s or prior to the First World War (a higher share was achieved for a few years after the Second World War years, but it reflected the major disturbances

[5]   Dosman (2008) provides an excellent biography of Prebisch set against the backdrop of the intellectual controversies of this time.

that world trade continued to face in the early post-war years). The loss in the region's share in world trade was even more massive if we exclude Venezuelan exports, largely of oil. This process stopped and started to reverse in the 1970s, reflecting the transition to the 'mixed model' (see Figure 8.1).

Falling market shares in world commodity trade was the major explanation for the decline experienced up to the 1960s (Bértola and Ocampo, 2012, Table 4.10; Ffrench-Davis et al., 1998). This was in part the effects of agricultural protectionism in developed countries, which hit Argentina, Cuba and Uruguay particularly hard, but also of policy discrimination against major agricultural staples such as coffee and sugar (Anderson and Valdés, 2008) including through industrial protection but also export taxes on commodity sectors, discriminatory exchange rates and currency overvaluation, with the particular mix depending on the specific country. Import-competing agricultural goods benefited, however, from protection (Anderson and Valdés, 2008, Figure 1.3) and agriculture more broadly from special financing mechanisms, domestic technological adaptation and transfer, and other forms of state intervention. The decrease in export share was even more striking in the case of oil, as world exports shifted from Venezuela and Mexico to the Middle East. Oil and minerals were also nationalized in several economies. The nationalization of oil in Mexico in 1938 was the landmark in that regard, and it was followed by those of tin in Bolivia, copper in Chile and oil in Venezuela in later decades. State-owned enterprises were active in oil and mining in many other countries. International regulation of commodity markets was also common from the late 1950s, with coffee as the best example (with precedents going back to the early part of the twentieth century). In turn, Venezuela became the leader behind the creation of the Organization of Petroleum Exporting Countries (OPEC) in 1960.

Given the persistent dependence on commodity exports, trends and fluctuations in commodity prices generated major regional effects. The downward trend of real non-oil commodity prices (relative to manufactures) from the 1920s until the end of the twentieth century was one such trend, which oil shared for a shorter period, but even more importantly were the effects of long-term price cycles (Figure 8.2; see Erten and Ocampo, 2013). The effects of the downward swing in the 1920s and 1930s has already been noticed, but equally important were the downward swing from the mid 1950s that followed the post-Second World War boom, and the new collapse that took place in the last two decades of the twentieth century (from 1986 in the case of oil). Commodity cycles had particularly troublesome effects when they were accompanied by boom–bust cycles in external finance, typical of the cycles of the 1920s/1930s and the

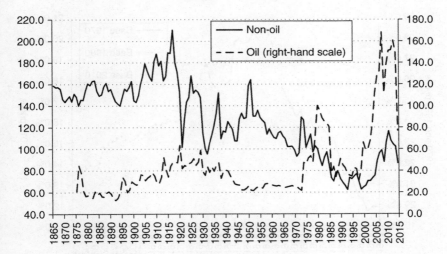

Note: Nominal prices have been deflated by the manufacturing unit value in international trade.

Source: Erten and Ocampo (2013) and updates by the author.

Figure 8.2   Real commodity prices (1980 = 100)

1970s/1980s. The 'sudden stop' in external financing during periods of downward commodity prices led to major financial crises, mainly a mix of default and strong exchange rate depreciation in the 1930s, and of debt crisis, major exchange rate adjustment and several domestic banking crises in the 1980s (Bértola and Ocampo, 2012, Figure 1.2)

The last two decades of the twentieth century were characterized, therefore, by the joint effects of a collapse of commodity prices and the Latin American debt crisis. This led to a major shift in regional development paradigms away from state intervention and toward market reforms. At the regional level, there had been an earlier shift in that direction in the Southern Cone countries, and notably Chile, in the second half of the 1970s, but the broader regional shift took place from the mid 1980s. The major effect of reforms was on the manufacturing sector. The rapid industrialization drive that had started in the 1930s and continued until the 1970s (peaking toward the middle of that decade) was followed by a fairly broad-based and strong de-industrialization from the 1980s to the present (Figure 8.3).

Countries have followed two basic specialization patterns after market reforms, which broadly followed a 'North–South' divide (Bértola and

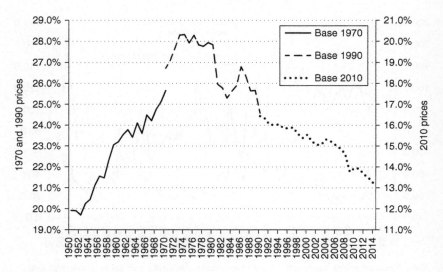

Source: Author estimates based on ECLAC data.

Figure 8.3   *Latin America: share of manufacturing in GDP,*
                1950–2014

Ocampo, 2012, Chapter 5; ECLAC, 2001). The 'Northern' pattern is characterized by a larger share of manufacturing exports, most of them with large import contents (in its most extreme form, maquila) and oriented to the US market. The launch of the North American Free Trade Agreement (NAFTA) in 1994 was crucial in this regard, as well as the later US agreement with Central American countries and the Dominican Republic. Mexico was an exception to the de-industrialization trend in the early phase of NAFTA (though not later on), and several Central American countries have also shown a stable or small rise in the share of manufacturing in GDP.[6] The 'Southern' pattern has changed less compared to the past, as market reforms reinforced the comparative advantage in natural resource sectors. It is characterized by a mix of extra-regional natural resource-based exports and a diversified menu of manufactures in intraregional trade. Brazil positioned itself between the two groups, since it already had a much more diversified export structure prior to liberalization, including some technology-intensive manufactures (Bértola and Ocampo, 2012, Table 5.5). There is also a third specialization pattern

---

[6] Costa Rica, El Salvador, Honduras and Nicaragua, though not Guatemala and Panama.

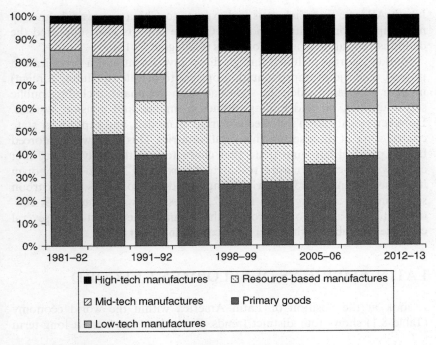

Source: ECLAC, using the classification designed by Sanjaya Lall.

Figure 8.4   Natural resource and technological contents of Latin American exports

of a few smaller economies, in which service exports dominate: transport and financial services in Panama, and tourism in Cuba and the Dominican Republic.

The Mexican manufacturing export boom that took place after the launch of NAFTA, together with falling commodity prices, implied that the diversification of Latin American exports away from commodities that had started in the mid 1960s continued during the last two decades of the twentieth century (Figure 8.4). The revitalization of the regional integration processes around 1990 and the creation of MERCOSUR in 1991 supported this diversification, given the high manufacturing intensity of intraregional trade. This process was followed by a significant re-primarization of the export structure as a result of the commodity price boom that started in 2003–04 and lasted for about a decade. The re-primarization was enhanced by growing trade with China, which became a major trading partner of Latin America in the 2000s, particularly after the 2007–09

North Atlantic financial crisis,[7] as exports to China are overwhelmingly made up of commodities. Booming Chinese imports also supported the de-industrialization of most countries (Gallagher, 2016).

Market reforms included foreign direct investment and a privatization process. Their joint implementation opened to private (including foreign) investor sectors in which the state had been dominant, including public sector utilities, oil and mining, domestic finance and pension systems. However, privatization followed a myriad of models, and kept under state control some of these sectors in several countries. This trend was reinforced by the political left-wing trend that characterized the early twenty-first century. In the case of natural resources, for example, Mexico did not open its oil sector until 2015, Bolivia strengthened control of its hydrocarbon sector in 2006 and Argentina in 2012,[8] and state-owned enterprises continued to play an important role in the oil and mineral sectors in several countries (notably, in the latter case, copper in Chile).

LATIN AMERICA'S DEVELOPMENT RECORD

A look at the position of Latin America within the world economy (Table 8.1) shows four distinct trends. First, there has been a long-term

Table 8.1   Relative position of Latin America in the world economy

	1820	1870	1913	1929	1950	1973	1980	1990	2008	2014
Per capita GDP versus										
Developed countries (%)	55.5	35.8	36.7	39.6	36.2	31.9	34.2	26.0	27.0	29.0
Other developing regions (%)	118.4	128.3	179.1	224.7	223.5	215.6	229.5	186.9	145.3	128.2
World average (%)	101.8	87.8	100.1	116.0	115.8	109.0	120.6	98.4	93.5	96.5
Share in world GDP (%)	1.9	2.6	4.2	5.2	7.2	8.2	9.5	8.0	7.8	8.0

Sources: Bértola and Ocampo (2012). Original data, except for Latin America, from Angus Maddison. 2014 estimates according to United Nations growth for the 2008–14 period.

---

[7]   This is the term I use here instead of 'global financial crisis' because although it had global effects, the crisis concentrated in the USA and Western Europe.

[8]   In the cases of both Bolivia and Argentina there had been a privatization earlier on that was reversed in the years indicated. Although in both cases the reversals were called 'nationalizations,' they really involved majority control by the state rather than full-scale nationalizations.

divergence vis-à-vis the developed countries (about 27 percentage points), concentrated in the post-independence period (20 percentage points) and during the lost decade of the 1980s (8 points). In contrast, only during a period of commodity export-led growth of the nineteenth and early twentieth centuries did the region converge with developed countries. This has also been true later on during shorter periods, including the recent commodity boom, but these positive phases have only temporarily and partially compensated the adverse long-term trend.

Second, although the region lost ground relative to the developed world, it gained vis-à-vis the rest of the developing world. This strong relative position within the developing world was reinforced during the phase of commodity export-led growth, when the region reached a per capita income that was more than twice the average of other developing countries, a position that it maintained during the era of state-led industrialization. The market reform period is, therefore, the only one during which the region lost ground relative to other developing countries, and, in particular, to Asia.

Third, as a result of these combined trends, Latin America's per capita GDP relative to the world average underwent a fully inverted U-curve from the late nineteenth century: it increased during the commodity export-led growth phase and held its position during state-led industrialization, but fell in the market reform era, largely due to the retrogression during the lost decade. On average, the region's per capita GDP has fluctuated between 90 and 120 percent of the world average, and in this sense it has constituted the 'middle class of the world.'

Fourth, despite this relatively stable long-term trend, rapid population growth through the nineteenth and twentieth centuries implied that the region's share in world GDP increased persistently up to 1980, from 1.9 percent in 1820 to 9.5 percent in 1980; it then fell to 8.0 percent during the lost decade, and has remained around that level since then. Rapid population growth has been essentially associated with high fertility, but it has been reinforced by international migration in specific countries during some periods (Argentina and Uruguay, in particular, but also Brazil, Chile, Cuba and Venezuela).

Looking at growth rates tells a complementary story. In particular, it indicates that the fastest growth was achieved during state-led industrialization (Figure 8.5 shows economic growth in moving averages for the decades ending in the year indicated in the graph).

The annual growth rates of over 5 percent during the whole post-Second World War industrialization period, and 6 percent toward its end had been achieved only briefly before – during the decade before the First World War and in the 1920s – but not afterwards. Rapid economic expansion

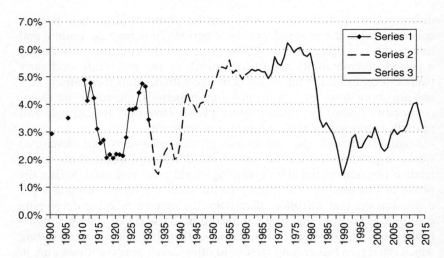

Notes: Series 1 includes Argentina, Brazil, Chile, Colombia, Cuba, Ecuador, Mexico, Peru, Uruguay, and Venezuela (the first two data points exclude Cuba and Ecuador); Series 2 includes all countries, except Bolivia, Panama, Paraguay, and the Dominican Republic; Series 3 includes all countries.

Sources: Series 1 and 2 from Bértola and Ocampo (2012); Series 3 estimated from ECLAC data.

Figure 8.5   Latin America: moving average of decade-long growth rates

during state-led industrialization indicates that per capita GDP growth during that period was brought down by explosive population growth. This fact can be interpreted in a positive way, as the capacity that Latin America had during this period to absorb one of the fastest-growing populations in world history, and the very rapid urbanization that accompanied it. In contrast, the slow growth that has characterized the market reform period – around 3 percent per year, except during the commodity boom of the early twenty-first century – has not benefited from the 'demographic dividend' (the fall in demographic dependency ratios) that has characterized recent decades.

These patterns show that the apparently narrow per capita GDP gap that separated Latin America from the developed world in the early nineteenth century fails to capture the limited capacity the region had to join the first industrial revolution, as it lacked the technological and institutional capacities required. However, the region did better than the average of the developing world during the post-independence years, positioned as a leading role within that group during the first globalization and maintaining that position during the period of state-led industrialization. Therefore, the most recent development period, which broadly coincides with the second globalization, is the only one in which the region has experienced a clear relative decline. The strong loss experienced during the debt crisis of the 1980s is the major explanation of that lag, but the decline vis-à-vis Asia has other determinants, notably the strong de-industrialization and technological lags that the region has faced.

A look at development patterns during different historical periods can further help to understand the features of the regions' development successes and failures. Aside from the success in responding to the developed countries' demands by developing new commodity sectors during the first globalization, the region also started its modern industrialization process during that period. This indicates that the development of a dynamic commodity export sector was not viewed as being opposed to modern industrialization under high tariff protection. Although the basic rationale for high tariffs was to generate public sector revenues, many countries did not resist the temptation to use them for protectionist purposes – and the rising entrepreneurial elite as an opportunity to diversify their investments. The structural changes that took place during this period left the region far behind the industrial countries in terms of the educational system (see below) and level of industrialization. As a result, Latin America also failed to join what has been called the second industrial revolution.

The fact that the period of state-led industrialization was one of rapid economic growth indicates that the 'Black Legend'[9] about industrialization and state intervention spread in the orthodox analyses of Latin American development during this period is fundamentally wrong. Part of that 'Black Legend' is related to the view that state-led industrialization was a period in which the region lacked macroeconomic discipline. This is also largely wrong. Until the early 1970s, high inflation and lack of fiscal discipline were absent except in the Southern Cone and Brazil, and even in those countries these problems were present only in specific periods. The lack of macroeconomic discipline was only a feature of a larger number of countries during the second half of that decade, when large flows of external financing associated with recycling 'petrodollars' poured into the region. Moreover, runaway inflation was only a feature of the 1980s, and in this sense more an effect than a cause of the debt crisis (Bértola and Ocampo, 2012, Chapters 4 and 5). The state-led industrialization model obviously had flaws, the main ones being the incapacity to significantly

---

[9] This term has been used mainly to refer to the demographic effects of the European conquest of the Americas.

Table 8.2   GDP growth: dynamics and volatility

	Average growth (%)	Standard deviation (%)	Coefficient of variation (%)
1950–80	5.5	1.7	31.3
1990–2015	3.1	2.2	73.5

Source: Author's estimates based on ECLAC data.

change the export structure – though this started to happen from the mid 1960s during what I called the 'mixed model' of development that characterized the last phases of this period – and, particularly, the incapacity to build a solid scientific-technological base.

Although the region's export performance has been good during the market reform period, as well as its capacity to attract foreign capital, the major reason for weak performance is the de-industrialization that has taken place since the 1980s (see Figure 8.3). This is confirmed by the empirical observation that there is a strong association of development success and industrialization, as reflected in the fact that persistent industrialization is the feature of the most successful developing country regions, notably East Asia (see, for example, Rodrik, 2014). Furthermore, Latin America's de-industrialization has been premature, in the sense that it has taken place at an early stage of development (Palma, 2011). It has also been associated with the slowing of the rising productivity trend that most of Latin American economies experienced until the mid 1970s (see, for example, IDB, 2010). Indeed, the mix of de-industrialization and inadequate attention to science and technology has generated a large technological lag vis-à-vis both East Asia and the developed economies whose production structures rely on natural resources (ECLAC, 2012).

Although runaway inflation was controlled in the late 1980s or early 1990s (the 1994 Brazilian Real plan being the last of the major anti-inflationary programs), and fiscal discipline has been generally maintained since the early 1990s (a few countries aside), a major feature of the period of market reforms has been sharply volatile economic growth. This feature is seen clearly when comparing growth rates in 1990–2015 versus 1950–80, which indicates that the recent market reform period has not only been a stage of slower but also of more volatile economic growth (Table 8.2). The greater volatility reflects not only persistent external shocks associated with commodity prices and external financing but also the dominance of pro-cyclical macroeconomic policies – expansionary fiscal, monetary

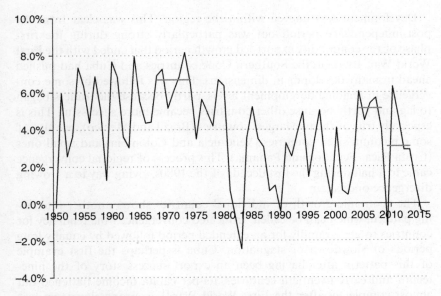

Note: The grey horizontal lines are average growth rates for the periods indicated in the graph.

Source: ECLAC (2016) according to IMF projections.

Figure 8.6   Annual GDP growth, 1950–2016

and exchange rate policies during booms, contractionary policies during crises – again a few exceptions aside.[10]

The adverse trends typical since the 1980s were temporarily interrupted by strong regional performance during the 'super-cycle' of commodity prices that took off in 2003–04. However, performance was only exceptional in 2003–08, and there was already a strong slowdown in 2008–13, which turned into a recession in 2015–16 that has largely affected South America (Figure 8.6). Part of the additional export revenues during the initial phase of the commodity boom were used to reduce external debt ratios. The lower debt ratios achieved by the time of the North Atlantic financial crisis gave room for some counter-cyclical policies and rapid, renewed access to external financing. But due again to pro-cyclical macroeconomic policies that characterized the region after that crisis, room for counter-cyclical policies was much more limited when the collapse of commodity prices hit in 2014.

---

[10]   These exceptions include the counter-cyclical fiscal rules adopted by Chile from 2000 and Colombia in 2011, and the counter-cyclical monetary policies of some central banks during the North Atlantic financial crisis and the succeeding recovery.

Development was uneven within the region. This was clear from the post-independence period but was particularly strong during the first phase of the commodity export-led growth period that ended with the First World War. By then, the Southern Cone countries and Cuba had pushed ahead in many development dimensions. This was followed by some convergence in regional development levels, partly because the leaders began to lag and partly because other countries became more successful. This is especially true of the two largest countries (Brazil and Mexico), but also of some medium-sized countries (Venezuela and Colombia) and small ones (Costa Rica, Ecuador and Panama). This process of regional convergence came to a halt during the lost decade of the 1980s, giving way to a growing divergence once again.

The economic growth of individual countries shows another interesting pattern, which can be called 'truncated convergence': the tendency for countries to grow rapidly for an extended period followed by equally long periods of slowdown or stagnation. Cuba is perhaps the first example of this pattern: after having been an export success story of the nineteenth and early twentieth centuries, its per capita income flattened out almost completely after the First World War.[11] A strong slowdown was also observed in the Southern Cone countries at that time, and notably in Argentina, which was one of the world's development success stories during the first globalization. This pattern was followed by Venezuela, the region's star from the 1920s to the 1960s, thanks to its oil boom, but followed by long-term stagnation in per capita income from the mid 1970s. Brazil and Mexico, the success stories of state-led industrialization, have also experienced very slow growth after the lost decade. Colombia is the major exception to this rule and, therefore, the best example of more stable growth rates.

SOCIAL AND INSTITUTIONAL DEVELOPMENT

Social progress lagged behind economic development. This is reflected in the two major social indicators that are included in the human development index (Figure 8.7). The lag in educational attainment in the late nineteenth century vis-à-vis developed countries was particularly remarkable, even in the region's leading countries (the Southern Cone and Cuba in terms of economic development, joined by Costa Rica in terms of social development). Years of schooling reached just over three for the working

---

[11]   So, this pattern preceded the 1958 revolution, and was reinforced by it in economic, though certainly not social, terms.

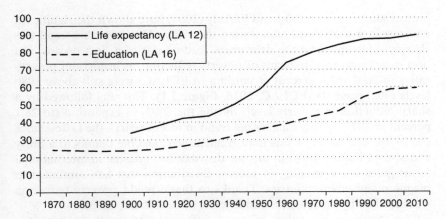

Source: Bértola and Ocampo (2012).

Figure 8.7 Latin America: human development indices versus developed countries

population in the Southern Cone countries and overall regional illiteracy affected more than half the region's adult population in 1930 (Bértola and Ocampo, 2012, Table 3.14). Lags in life expectancy were somewhat lower in Argentina and Uruguay (over 50 years in 1930) but still deplorable in the region as a whole (36 years), also indicating major lags in the development of health systems. Both indicators started to converge to those of more developed countries in the early twentieth century, but at a slow rate. Convergence speeded up during state-led industrialization, and was already fairly advanced in terms of life expectancy by 1980, but with lags in some countries (such as in Central America, except for Costa Rica and Panama, and Bolivia in South America). In turn, and in contrast to its generally poor economic performance, Cuba advanced substantially in social terms after the 1958 revolution and reached some of the highest levels of social development in the region. Lags in average educational attainment were still substantial at the end of state-led industrialization but continued to improve during market reforms, thanks to the increase in social spending induced by the broad-based return to democracy in the region. The average educational gap vis-à-vis developed countries continued to be large, and was compounded with significant quality problems.

Fewer studies are available to capture trends in poverty reduction and income distribution. Prados de la Escosura's (2007) estimates show that the most significant advance in terms of poverty reduction during the twentieth century took place from 1950 to 1970s – that is, during state-led industrialization. Londoño and Székely (2000) have shown the significant advance in poverty reduction during the 1970s. This favorable trend was sharply interrupted by the debt crisis, leading not to a 'lost decade' but 'lost quarter-century' in terms of poverty reduction, as headcount poverty ratios in 2002 (43.9 percent, according to ECLAC) were still above 1980 levels (40.5 percent) (ECLAC, 2016, Figure I.1). This was followed by a sharp reduction in poverty levels during the 2003–13 expansion (to 28.1 percent in 2013, with a small rising trend in recent years), the fastest since the 1970s. The speed of this improvement was possible thanks to a fairly widespread improvement in income distribution, unusual in international terms given the worsening of income distribution that has continued to plague many other countries. Thanks to these trends, poverty reduction was matched by the rise of a middle class (World Bank, 2013).

The trends in inequality followed different patterns throughout the region but there were also common factors that affected groups of countries in a similar direction. The colonial legacy of highly segmented economic and social structures continued to weigh upon the region's societies, but it was affected by many other factors over the past two centuries, both in positive and negative directions. In historical sequence, an initial step forward in terms of social equality was the abolition of slavery in the nineteenth century, which came late, as we saw, in Brazil and Cuba. This did not represent, however, major new economic opportunities for the freed blacks, who generally continued to belong to the lower strata of society. Massive immigration of European labor in the late nineteenth and early twentieth centuries had positive distributive effects on Argentina, Uruguay and, to a lesser extent, Chile, as they created the need to offer good wages to attract migrants, who brought with them skills, knowledge and institutions (trade unions, in particular) that helped to spread the benefits of development. However, this was matched with rising inequality trends generated by the first globalization, which pushed up the rewards on land and mining property.

The large labor surpluses that characterized most countries outside the Southern Cone exercised a downward pressure on unskilled wages and, therefore, a negative effect on income distribution throughout the twentieth century in most countries. In contrast, the rapid urbanization process that took place during state-led industrialization opened up new opportunities for people who had been subject to the strict social segmentation characteristic of the region's rural areas, even if those opportunities were initially in informal jobs in urban areas. The erosion of the various forms of rural servitude was slow to take place and only marginally affected by the generally weak agrarian reform processes that were put in place at different times; it did have greater effects in countries where those reforms were stronger (in Mexico, Bolivia and Cuba, and to a lesser extent Chile and Peru). But, again, like the abolition of slavery, agrarian reform did not generally open large economic opportunities for the rural poor.

Advances in education, which took a long time in coming, generated an adverse initial effect on income distribution, given the very uneven initial access to school and, even more, to university for different social groups. However, it had positive effects on income distribution in the long term. In particular, it is arguably the main driving force behind the improvement in income distribution experienced in the early twenty-first century. These benefits could have come earlier had it not been for the adverse distributive effects of the military dictatorships (particularly those of the Southern Cone in the 1970s), the debt crisis of the 1980s and the economic liberalization measures that spread throughout the region in the late twentieth century, which also had adverse distributive effects initially according to the literature.

These varying forces mixed in dissimilar ways in different countries. It is possible, however, to discern two major cycles.[12] The first was characterized by a deterioration in income distribution that lasted until the beginning of the twentieth century in the Southern Cone countries but much longer in economies that had extensive labor surpluses. This was followed by an improvement in distribution, which started in the 1920s/1930s in the Southern Cone countries thanks to the institutional forces mentioned above, but only in the 1960s/1970s in some other countries for which early national studies are available (Colombia, Costa Rica, Mexico and Venezuela), though not Brazil, where this late improvement in income distribution during state-led industrialization failed to take place at all.

The second cycle opened with a deterioration in distribution that once again began in the Southern Cone during the military dictatorships of the 1970s but then spread across the region in the late twentieth century, reflecting the adverse distributive effects of the debt crisis and market reforms. Most countries then witnessed an improvement in distribution in the first decade of the twenty-first century associated, according to a growing literature, with a reduction in wage skill premiums generated by increases in educational levels, and to a lesser extent by increased social transfers.

Different political histories also led to a diverse trajectory of state building and, more broadly, the organization of society to supply social and public goods. There are also, however, common elements. A first one is that, as already noticed and with the partial exception of a handful

---

[12] See in this regard the relevant sections of Chapters 3 to 5 of Bértola and Ocampo (2012).

of countries, economic liberalism was not synchronized with political liberalism in the nineteenth and most of the twentieth centuries. Strong caudillos and recurrent military dictatorships have been more common than democracy in the region's history. The major democratic wave is indeed of a very recent origin: it started in 1979 with the downfall of the military dictatorship in Ecuador and ended with the defeat of Pinochet in the 1988 referendum that led to the democratic transition in Chile. With some partial retrogressions, this democratic wave has lasted until the present – with the exception of Cuba. Another common denominator has been a tendency of most elites to embrace 'rentism,' understood as reliance of the rents derived from natural resources and special benefits granted by a privileged relationship with political power.

As for the relationship between the state and the market, modern institutions started to take shape during commodity export development, as reflected in the development of modern legal systems but also an increasing but still modest role of the state in the development of infrastructure (railroads and ports) and social services, but the greatest progress was again made during state-led industrialization. However, and in contrast with widespread views, during this period the level of state control of the economy was much lower in Latin America than in the now independent countries of Asia and Africa, and certainly than the communist countries of Eastern Europe and Asia. The region rather moved toward a mixed economic model closer to that of Western Europe, though with a much more limited welfare state; the exceptions were Cuba and a few other nations during their short-lived experiments with socialism. Development planning also evolved in a similar direction, taking the shape of 'indicative planning,' to use a French concept.

Economic liberalization led to a major redefinition of the roles of the state and the market, though with much more diversity than generally recognized. This is why the term 'market reforms' is more adequate than 'neo-liberalism' to refer to the late twentieth century. The most significant difference with orthodox economic views was the increase in social sector spending that took place from 1990 in all countries and that led to a significant expansion in access to social services and the development of the new social transfer mechanism (conditional cash transfers being the best known Latin American innovation). Several public sector banks and firms also survived in most countries – notably in the latter case in oil and mineral resources. Some government agencies became stronger – notably finance ministries and central banks – but others weakened or disappeared altogether, particularly planning agencies and those responsible for productive development policies. Also, the upturn in social expenditure was not coupled with a similar trend in investment in infrastructure, leading to a sizeable backlog in this area (CAF, 2014).

Disappointment with some of the results of market reforms led to a renewed view of the positive role of the state at the turn of the century. This was not only true of the various left-wing political movements that arose in several countries (a trend now in reverse) but also of center and even right-wing political parties. Latin America became, therefore, one of the leaders of renewed state building at the global level. Nonetheless, this process has differed across countries and shows some clear flaws. Aside from infrastructure, perhaps the most important is the lack of renewed attention to productive development policies and the inadequate attention to the need to generate a strong science and technology system.

REFERENCES

Anderson, Kim and Alberto Valdés (2008), 'Introduction and Summary', in Kim Anderson and Alberto Valdés (eds), *Distortions to Agricultural Incentives in Latin America*, Washington, DC: World Bank, pp. 1–58.

Bértola, Luis and José Antonio Ocampo (2012), *The Economic Development of Latin America since Independence*, Oxford: Oxford University Press.

Bulmer-Thomas, Victor (2014), *The Economic History of Latin America since Independence* (3rd edn), Cambridge: Cambridge University Press.

CAF (Development Bank of Latin America) (2014), *Infraestructura en el desarrollo de América Latina*, Caracas: CAF.

Cárdenas, Enrique, José Antonio Ocampo and Rosemary Thorp (eds) (2000), *Industrialization and the State in Latin America: The Postwar Years, Volume 3, An Economic History of Twentieth-century Latin America*, Houndmills: Palgrave, in association with St Antony's College, Oxford.

Coastworth, John H. and Jeffrey Williamson (2004), 'Always Protectionist? Latin American Tariffs from Independence to Great Depression', *Journal of Latin American Studies*, **36**(2), 205–32.

Diaz-Alejandro, Carlos F. (2000), 'Latin America in the 1930s', in Rosemary Thorp (ed.), *Latin America in the 1930s: The Role of the Periphery in the World Crisis*, Houndmills: Palgrave, in association with St Antony's College, Oxford, pp. 15–42.

Dosman, Edgar J. (2008), *The Life and Times of Raúl Prebisch, 1901–1986*, Montreal: McGill-Queen's University Press.

ECLAC (Economic Commission for Latin America and the Caribbean) (2001), *A Decade of Light and Shadow: Latin America and the Caribbean in the 1990s*, Santiago: ECLAC.

ECLAC (Economic Commission for Latin America and the Caribbean) (2012), *Cambio estructural para la equidad: Una visión integrada del desarrollo*, Santiago: ECLAC.

ECLAC (2016) (Economic Commission for Latin America and the Caribbean), *Panorama social de América Latina 2015*, Santiago: ECLAC.

Erten, Bilge and José Antonio Ocampo (2013), 'Super Cycles of Commodity Prices since the Mid-nineteenth Century', *World Development*, **44**, 14–30.

Ffrench-Davis, Ricardo, Oscar Muñoz and Gabriel Palma (1998), 'The Latin American Economies, 1959–1990', in Leslie Bethell (ed.), *The Cambridge*

History of Latin America, Volume 6, Latin America since 1930: Economy, Society and Politics, Cambridge: Cambridge University Press, pp. 159–250.

Gallagher, Kevin P. (2016), *The China Triangle: Latin America's China Boom and the Fate of the Washington Consensus*, New York: Oxford University Press.

Gerschenkron, Alexander (1962), *Economic Backwardness in Historical Perspective*, Cambridge, MA: Harvard University Press.

Hirschman, Albert O. (1971), 'The Political Economy of Import-substituting Industrialization in Latin America', in *A Bias for Hope: Essays on Development and Latin America*, New Haven, CT: Yale University Press, Chapter 3.

IDB (Inter-American Development Bank) (2010), *The Age of Productivity: Transforming Economies from the Bottom Up*, Washington, DC: IDB.

Londoño, Juan Luis and Miguel Székely (2000), 'Persistent Poverty and Excess Inequality: Latin America, 1970–1995', *Journal of Applied Economics*, **3**(1), 93–134.

Love, Joseph L. (1994), 'Economic Ideas and Ideologies in Latin America since 1930', in Leslie Bethell (ed.), *The Cambridge History of Latin America, Volume 6, Latin America since 1930: Economy, Society and Politics*, Cambridge: Cambridge University Press, pp. 391–450.

Palma, José Gabriel (2011), 'Why has Productivity Growth Stagnated in Latin America since the Neo-liberal Reforms?', in José Antonio Ocampo and Jaime Ros (eds), *The Oxford Handbook of Latin American Economics*, Oxford: Oxford University Press, Chapter 23.

Prados de la Escosura, Leandro (2007), 'Inequality and Poverty in Latin America: A Long-run Exploration', in Timothy J. Hatton, Kevin H. O'Rourke and Alan M. Taylor (eds), *The New Comparative Economic History: Essays in Honor of Jeffrey G. Williamson*, Cambridge, MA: MIT Press, Chapter 12.

Prebisch, Raúl (1973), *Interpretación del proceso de desarrollo latinoamericano en 1949* (2nd edn), Serie conmemorativa del XXV aniversario de la CEPAL, Santiago: ECLAC.

Rodrik, Dani (2014), 'The Past, Present and Future of Economic Growth', in Franklin Allen, Jehr R. Behrman, Nancy Birdsall et al. (eds), *Toward a Better Global Economy*, Oxford: Oxford University Press, Chapter 2.

World Bank (2013), *Economic Mobility and the Rise of the Latin American Middle Class*, Washington, DC: World Bank.

9. Russia and the European Union: the clash of world orders

Richard Sakwa

The breakdown in relations between Russia and the European Union (EU) is one of the most significant events of the last quarter-century. The end of the Cold War confrontation and the fall of the Berlin Wall promised the creation of a 'Europe whole and free', as enunciated in the *Charter of Paris for a New Europe* adopted by a plenary meeting of all the heads of state or government of the Conference on Security and Cooperation in Europe (CSCE) on 19–21 November 1990. The document announced that 'The era of confrontation and division in Europe has ended. We declare that henceforth our relations will be founded on respect and cooperation ... Europe whole and free is calling for a new beginning.'[1] Instead, on the 25th anniversary of the dismantling of the 'iron curtain' across Germany and Europe, a new confrontation once again divides the continent. The quarter-century between 1989 and 2014 was one of 'cold peace', in which none of the fundamentals of European security and political community was resolved (Sakwa, 2017). Since 2014 we have entered a new period of contestation that some call a 'new Cold War' (Legvold, 2016; for a contrary view, see Monaghan, 2015).

How can we explain this betrayal of expectations? Three fundamental processes shape the relationship, undermining trust and confidence in the other party and reducing the scope for pragmatic interest-based cooperation. These issues are: (1) the tension between spatial and normative configurations of European politics, which can also be seen as the contrast between spatial and temporal projects; (2) the failure to devise an adequate mode of reconciliation between 'smaller/wider' and 'greater' European agendas, in other words, between monist and pluralist conceptions of European order; and (3) the struggle between universalist representations of global engagement against particularist articulations of national identity in the international sphere, which can also be interpreted as the tension

---

[1] *Charter of Paris for a New Europe*, Paris, 19–21 November 1990, available at www.osce.org/node/39516.

between critical geopolitics and uncritical normativism. Let us examine each of these in turn.

BETWEEN NORMS AND SPACE

The tension between representations of the EU as a post-modern entity committed to a normative agenda of universal values and its spatial configuration as an expanding body locked in negotiating boundaries and interactions with an endless series of geographical neighbours has long been noted (Rumelli, 2004). This provokes a conflict at the very heart of Europe's self-identity. The normative representation of the EU as a values-based rule-governed entity seeks to combine both time and space to transcend the very notion of limits. The fact that discussion of the *finalité* of Europe, encompassing the meaning and purpose of the European project as well as its physical limits, has been so desultory suggests a refusal to constrain the expansive character of the endeavour. This is a universal programme that is both progressive in temporal terms and of universal application across space. This is why the EU has come to represent the utopia of our times to those nations struggling at its borders. The idea of 'Europe' has become the representation of a desirable future instantiated in a physical space. The contrast between this idealist representation of the EU and the endless fragmentation, contestation and regulation of its daily workings could hardly be starker. The tension between the quotidian reality and the soaring ambitions is both a source of frustration and inspiration for its friends and foes alike (Copsey, 2015).

The EU is today typically portrayed as a post-modern entity committed to a post-Westphalian agenda of universal values, accompanied by a commitment to a set of normative principles (Cooper, 2003). These norms are the basis for the EU's conditionality in dealing with external actors and its neighbours, now typically described as 'external governance' (Lavenex, 2012). Internally, the EU has assumed the characteristics of a neo-medieval polity, with overlapping jurisdictions and no settled sovereign centre (Zielonka, 2007). More profoundly, it is an arena in which differences are exposed to each other, transcending any rigid distinction between universalism and particularism (Lindberg et al., 2014). However, externally in recent years it has assumed an increasingly hard spatial configuration. Its external borders are mostly governed by Schengen regulations, allowing a single visa to operate across the participant countries while dissolving internal boundaries. The pressure of refugee and migratory flows, however, prompted a wave of suspensions and wall building. It is still too early to talk of a 'fortress Europe', especially in light of Germany's decision in 2015 to accept about a million refugees from Syria and other conflict zones. The global financial crisis from 2008 exposed the flaws in the eurozone model of monetary union, above all the perverse economic effects in peripheral economies (Streeck, 2015). The crises threw into sharp relief the tension between socio-economic and normative post-modernism and the securitization of relations with the neighbourhood and the world. Time and space came into collision.

Decades of enlargement pushed the EU into uncharted territory, in both symbolic and political terms (Zielonka, 2008). The expansionary dynamic through accession has now slowed, but there is no *finalité* in either spatial or normative terms. The EU remains an ambitious transformative agent in what are increasingly contested neighbourhoods. It is this which has brought the EU into confrontation with Russia. This is a conflict that neither wanted, and which both sought to avoid. The EU sought to devise a neighbourhood policy to ensure that the outer limits of EU territory did not harden into new lines of division, though the lack of differentiation was later criticized. Romano Prodi (2002), the President of the European Commission, introduced the European Neighbourhood Policy (ENP) in Brussels on 5–6 December 2002 with the words 'I want to see a "ring of friends" surrounding the Union and its closest European neighbours, from Morocco to Russia and the Black Sea.' This was one of the more imaginative and inclusive attempts to mediate between the ins and outs, as part of the EU's permanent deliberation over boundaries and interactions with neighbours (Rumelli, 2004; Whitman and Wolff, 2010). With the mass accession of a number of post-communist countries, most of which had been part of the Soviet bloc or even the Soviet Union itself, in 2004 and 2007, the character of 'negotiation' changed, and it became less of an interactive process (to the degree that it ever was), and became far more didactic (Prozorov, 2014). The specific manifestation of this new didacticism was the launching of the Eastern Partnership (EaP) in May 2009, an idea sponsored by some of Russia's most resolute critics in Poland and Sweden (Copsey and Pomorska, 2014). Although tempered by the bureaucratic and mediating practices of Brussels, EaP encapsulated an intensified combination of normative and didactic challenges that assumed a harshly physical form. A new line of division was drawn between Russia and the EU, with an overt struggle for influence over the lands in between.

This exacerbated the tension between the universalistic aspirations of the EU as a post-modern norm-based project and the physical manifestation of the EU as a territorially based entity permanently negotiating its physical engagement with neighbours (Browning, 2005). Engagement deploys a range of traditional diplomatic and other instruments, accompanied by a dynamic of conditionality that tempers realist interactions. The key point, however, is that the EU's idealist normative claims undermined the classic patterns of realist diplomacy. As the EU grew and embraced the post-communist region, its dualism became increasingly sharply delineated and exposed the tensions between norm and space. Both lost their original transformational impetus. The norms were tempered and modified as conditionality itself in certain circumstances became 'conditional', dependent on specific local conditions (Kochenov, 2008). This is the charge, for example, about the accession of Estonia and Latvia with a large number of predominantly Russian 'non-citizens' who, until special regulations were drawn up at the EU's insistence, effectively became stateless.[2] And when it came to space, instead of transcending the 'borderness' of borders, as it had so long tried to do and had achieved with such spectacular success among the original members of the European Economic Community (EEC) and relatively effectively through the Northern Dimension programme, borders were back with a vengeance, but now posited as the 'frontier' between the empire of good governance and all that was normatively progressive, and the dark and savage lands of corruption and neo-Sovietism on the other side.

Not surprisingly, relations with Russia soured and an increasingly overt struggle for influence intensified in the so-called 'shared neighbourhood', the traditional borderlands between the two major zones of Europe in the *intermarium* between the Baltic and Black seas (DeBardeleben, 2008). For the EU, this meant that pragmatism threatened to undermine its normative idealism as hard choices had to be made when dealing with a new type of recalcitrant regime. Hitherto it had been mostly plain sailing for the EU, extending its influence to regions that welcomed the EU as the path to political and economic modernization. The complexities of the Balkans were a foretaste of the problems to come, but for the first time in the *intermarium* the EU came up against a rival hegemonic enterprise. Countries such as Belarus and Ukraine were faced with stark choices, and sought to exploit the geopolitical competition for their own advantage. A new mode of engagement was called for, one more sensitive to the ideational and developmental ambiguities. After all, the Soviet Union had also been a progressive combination of time and space, and had delivered a type of modernization. The EU as a model of normative superiority and transcendence of space could not but be ambivalently received in a region that had already experienced the ambiguities and contradictions

---

[2]   In Latvia some 260 000 people are still stateless, down from the 730 000 who were not granted automatic citizenship at independence in 1990 because they could not trace their family's presence to the territory before the Soviet occupation in 1940. Louise Osborne and Ruby Russell, 'We Were Born and Grew Up in Italy, Yet We Are No People with No Nation', *Guardian*, 28 December 2015, p. 23.

of such a project. The contestation in the *intermarium* was thus far from being simply geopolitical, and even its designation as civilizational is inadequate (Huntington, 1993, 1996). The struggle was over developmental models, representations of the past and, above all, about didacticism and autonomy. In other words, the tension between 'values' and 'interests' took on a starkly dichotomous form, even though the two are typically balanced in any normal diplomatic relationship.

The result was disastrous. Russia's traditional mode of engagement with the EU as a mix of conflict and cooperation gradually gave way to a more antagonistic relationship (Haukkala, 2015). For the EU, this provoked conflict at the very heart of Europe's self-identity, while for Russia the struggle for autonomy assumed almost existential proportions. Nowhere was this clash between norms and spatiality seen more vividly than in the case of Ukraine (Samokhvalov, 2015). No other external actor has more poisoned relations between Russia and the EU. Indeed, the Ukraine crisis fundamentally damaged the development of both the EU and Russia, to the point that we can talk of Ukraine as the nemesis of Europe. By representing 'Europe' as Ukraine's future, the collapse of time and space was complete. The abstract ideal of 'Europe' had long been posited as the future of the EU's neighbours, with the spatial reality becoming a temporal ideal (Judt, 2010). Already in Mikheil Saakashvili's Georgia this ideal had become radicalized and lost its transformational quality. Instead of seeking to combine the post-modern with the normative transcendence of the logic of spatial conflict, 'Europe' became the ideology of a militant liberation creed, and thus became the opposite of itself. The Maidan revolution in Ukraine took this a step further, with Europe becoming the focus of a new national identity in opposition to what was constructed as the neo-Soviet backwardness, corruption and national constriction of the past. Traditional contestation over religion and class had by no means lost their traction, but now the over-riding conflict was formulated as some sort of post-colonial struggle for national emancipation (Sakwa, 2015a).

The concept of 'Europe' became the proxy for the absence of traditional ideologies of emancipation. In the process, its meaning became radically subverted. Instead of transcending the constraints of time and space, the nationalist project concretized EU normativity in a spatial form in opposition to what was defined as the imperial hegemon while idealizing it as the path out of the harsh conditions actually existing. From a post-modern project, the EU became appropriated into a harshly modernist struggle for national self-affirmation. Equally, as we shall see below, in global terms the EU conclusively became part of the new Atlanticist geopolitical construct. The Ukraine crisis acted as the catalyst to accelerate processes that had long been in the making. It was a symptom of the larger failure to establish both the institutions and processes that could have fostered trust and genuine interdependence between Russia and the EU (Sakwa, 2016a). Instead, on a whole series of issues, ranging from the energy relationship to neighbourhood policies, a pattern of antagonistic dependency emerged. These were relationships that both Russia and the EU needed but which did not lead to the creation of some sort of partnership community (Keohane and Nye, 1989).

As probably the most pro-European leader Russia has ever had, in the early days of his presidency Vladimir Putin sought to deepen Russia's relationship with the EU. This resulted in the adoption in November 2003 of the Common European Economic Space (CEES) concept, based on the St Petersburg declaration in May of that year, which later resulted in various roadmaps to develop the four spaces: economic; external security; justice and home affairs; and research and culture. However, there was always a sense that Russia was too big and too rough to be able to join the EU. Instead, relations between Russia and the EU steadily deteriorated, in large part because neither side had a clear vision of where the relationship was heading. The absence of a strategic goal meant that the association was easily derailed, especially when a number of former Soviet satellite states joined with a heavy burden of historical grievances and recriminations. The Copenhagen criteria of June 1993 laid down accession conditions including democracy, the rule of law, a functioning market economy and the protection of minorities, but missing was socialization in the mores of the EU as a peace project. With the accession of the 'new Europe', the EU was in danger of being transformed from a body that transcended the logic of conflict to one that perpetuated conflict in new forms.

In this line, the EaP was devised not as a mode of reconciliation between the EU and its neighbours but was posed from the start as a type of geopolitical project. This does not mean that its every move was geopolitical, since this was tempered by the normative agenda, but in the end neither strategy – the norm-based one and the attempt to stabilize relations with neighbours – was pursued with either consistency or coherence. The EU's idealist aspect meant that it failed to acknowledge the power consequences of its own actions; while the geopolitical aspect was managed not in the traditional manner of diplomatic negotiations with all interested parties but through a set of effectively unilateral actions. This increasingly irreconcilable dualism only reinforced the drift in the EU from a post-modern normative power to a securitized political actor. Although sovereignty remained decentred, the EU began to act as a Westphalian power.

By contrast, Russia resorted to the most basic of power responses, seeking in 2013 to influence Ukraine's decision about signing the Association Agreement (and the associated Deep and Comprehensive Free Trade

Area (DCFTA)) with the EU by exerting various forms of crude pressure (Dragneva and Wolczuk, 2015). Much of this reflected not Russia's strength but the remarkable paucity of instruments in its toolbox to deal with neighbours. In other words, whereas the EU has a dual identity – both normative and power-centred – and thus can with protean flexibility alternate between different modes of engagement with external actors, Russia is a resolutely traditional power. Indeed, the ideational basis of the power system created by Putin is defiantly particularistic. It may not in theory reject the universal principles governing international relations today, and is certainly committed to the adjudicating role of the United Nations Security Council (UNSC), but this is combined with a profound commitment to the traditional model of the Westphalian state. While Putin did not formally endorse Vladislav Surkov's notion of 'sovereign democracy', his practices certainly drew on the idea. There was thus an incommensurability built into Russia's relations with the EU, and this inevitably shaped the way that they related to neighbours and third parties.

PAN-CONTINENTALISM AND THE CLASH OF INTEGRATIONS

Two models of continental politics have come into collision – wider Europe and greater Europe. The core EU can be defined as the 'smaller Europe', but its 'wider European' agenda reflected a restless expansionary dynamic whose implications were barely understood. Wider Europe, the original name of the ENP, is based on the tried and tested model of the EU, whose arc of good governance, economic liberalism and societal welfare was projected ever further to the East This was an attractive prospect to those living in the shadow of authoritarianism, corruption and poverty, but it also came at the cost of forcing a choice between two integration projects. The wider Europe project is based on a series of concentric rings emanating from Brussels, weakening at the edges but nevertheless focused on a single centre. Spatiality is instantiated in the very name, and is one reason for the title being changed to ENP.

The neighbourhood policy seeks to have the best of both worlds. By transforming the neighbourhood into a zone of friendly and democratic states, the EU resolves the problem of security at its borders while consolidating its influence and power over the region. This is a monist vision, with a single centre (however fragmented and mediated by the power of the member states) that excludes any normative equivalence between the various powers on the continent. In the absence of a philosophy of *finalité*, all the other states on the European continent potentially come under the aegis of the EU. Indeed, given its normative impetus, any state that resists incorporation into the wider Europe is assumed to be defective in some way, and thus the EU's didacticism is accompanied by an implicit threat. Behaviour that is considered incompatible with the values of the EU is liable to become the target of normative normalization discourses.

The idea of greater Europe advances a very different, although not necessarily incompatible, vision of Europe. Greater Europe draws on pan-European ideas of some sort of political community from Lisbon to Vladivostok. Although inspired by geopolitical interpretations of territorial space, the greater European idea seeks to find ways to overcome the logic of conflict that inevitably arises from geopolitics. This is a more pluralistic representation of European space, and draws on a long European tradition ranging from various plans for the integration of the continent by Richard Coudenhove-Kalergi to Gaullist ideas of a broader common European space from the Atlantic to the Pacific. In the post-communist era it is Gorbachev's dream of a 'Common European Home' transcending the bloc politics of the Cold War era to create a single but plural space across Europe that predominated. With more than one centre and without a single ideological flavour, this is the regional equivalent of the concept of multipolarity. The greater European project explicitly seeks to overcome the division of the continent. This is a Europe that respects the various cultural and civilizational traditions yet is united on the principles of free trade, visa-free travel and the creation of a single cultural and educational community. A multipolar but united continent in world affairs is proposed to act as a moderating force vis-à-vis the alleged militarism of the hegemonic power (Gromyko, 2014). This plural conceptualization of Europe obviates struggle over the 'shared neighbourhood' between the great powers while consolidating the sovereignty of the countries in between (Krastev and Leonard, 2010). The downside, from the normative perspective of the EU, is that it provides space for authoritarian regimes. To this the partisans of greater Europe would counter that the removal of the intense logic of contestation would provide a more benign environment for democratic development.

With a healthy dose of pragmatism and good leadership, these two visions of Europe – wider and greater – were compatible. However, the inability to find a 'mode of reconciliation' between the two is yet another failure of the cold peace period. Reconciliation in this context would have built on the already existing 'variable geometry' of European integration to create a genuinely multipolar and pluralist model of continental unity. Instead, the wider European project was increasingly subsumed into the Atlantic security community, forcing the countries in between the EU and Russia to choose between the two (Korosteleva, 2015). Instead of the continent working together to create institutions and processes that could transcend the legacy of mistrust and division, North Atlantic Treaty Organization (NATO) enlargement and associated processes only confirmed the divisions. Many of the new Eastern Europe members of the EU and NATO came to these bodies with long histories of grievance against the various imperial and Soviet precursors to Russia, and these sins of the fathers were now placed at Russia's door.

There was much more that Russia could have done to allay these fears, above all by devising its own practices of reconciliation with its embittered former partners. Russia's insistence on its great power status and autonomy in world affairs generated new layers of mistrust, yet throughout the cold peace years there was no hint that Russia was interested in recreating some sort of imperial community. The country certainly sought to enhance its influence, above all in the core Soviet area, yet even here much of the activity was defensive and pre-emptive rather than aggressive and expansive. Exacerbated by disparate interpretations of history and by struggles over energy policies and security issues, a cycle of distrust set in. The mistrust that came to characterize relations between Russia and the European Commission spread to Brussels institutions, although most member states furthest from the old communist bloc (notably Italy) retained a traditional openness towards Russia.

The pan-European institutions of reconciliation in the cold peace years proved inadequate to the challenges of the post-communist era. The Organization for Security and Co-operation in Europe (OSCE) became a more ramified security body, above all dealing with election monitoring and the like through its Warsaw-based Office of Democratic Institutions and Human Rights (ODIHR), but in all substantive matters it was overshadowed by NATO. The OSCE's election monitoring focus on Eastern Europe rather than the whole OSCE space, including the United States, increasingly irked Russia. As for the Council of Europe and its Parliamentary Assembly (PACE), Russia repeatedly became the object of sanctions and suspensions, especially over the conduct of the two Chechen wars and the Yukos expropriation. Russia ratified the European Convention on Human Rights (ECHR) in 1998, and since then has been the subject of a number of adverse decisions in the European Court of Human Rights (ECtHR). The largest of these was the 2014 ruling by the ECtHR to pay the shareholders of the now defunct Yukos oil company 1.866 billion euros in compensation. The company was broken up following a series of adverse tax decisions and court rulings after the arrest of its head, Mikhail Khodorkovsky, in October 2003. Moscow has so far refused to pay the sum. On the other side, the development of the Collective Security Treaty Organization (CSTO) from the 1990s and what was to become the Eurasian Economic Union (EEU) gave institutional expression to Europe's multipolar pluralism, but at the same time only made more obvious the absence of pan-continental reconciliation.

The immediate catalyst for the Ukraine crisis in 2013 was the clash of integrations (Tolstrup, 2014). The signature theme of Putin's third term as president was Eurasian economic integration. His major programmatic article on the subject outlined a plan to create a Eurasian Union. He lauded the success of the Customs Union with Belarus and Kazakhstan, which was completed on 1 July 2011, and the imminent creation on 1 January 2012 of the Single Economic Area with three countries – Belarus, Kazakhstan and Russia – including standardized legislation and the free movement of capital, services and labour. Putin outlined plans for the enlargement of this project and its evolution into the EEU and eventually a Eurasian Union (EaU) (Putin, 2011). The EEU was formally established on 1 January 2015 and now includes Armenia, Belarus, Kazakhstan, Kyrgyzstan and Russia. At the same time, Eurasian integration is contested on a number of grounds. None of its three founding members are comfortable with the loss of sovereignty that regional integration involves. Even Putin's enthusiasm waned when confronted by the reality of the loss of sovereignty and the difficulties of ensuring foreign policy coordination with EEU partners and their lukewarm support for Russia's positions during the Ukraine crisis. The EEU proved to be a poor instrument to advance the greater European agenda, and instead was in danger of consolidating the long-term rift with the West (Dragneva and Wolczuk, 2013; Dutkiewicz and Sakwa, 2015; Kanet and Sussex, 2015; Lane and Samokhvalov, 2015). The EEU became the kernel of greater Eurasian ambitions, formalized by the agreement between Putin and the Chinese president, XI Jinping at the Ufa summit in May 2015 for Eurasian integration with China's Silk Road Economic Belt (SREB). This was yet another manifestation of the division of the continent between the Atlantic and greater Asian poles. Dmitry Suslov argues that 'For the first time in their relations, Russia and the EU must now formulate a model of interaction that focuses not on the strategic goal of building a common space. A new model presumes that Moscow and Brussels de facto belong to different political and economic communities' (Suslov, 2016).

In the 1990s the implicit condition of Russia's engagement with the EU was that it would not try to create a substantive alternative pole of integration around itself in Eurasia. In the twenty-first century the attempt to create just such a Eurasian pole was both cause and consequence of the growing gulf with the EU. Nevertheless, Putin insisted that the EEU was not an alternative but a complement to European integration. This reinforced the argument that Russia makes to this day that the greater

European cooperative and plural path of development is not dead. The idea is that the EEU will become one of the pillars of greater Europe, along with the EU, and thus provide a multilateral framework for engagement with the Atlantic community (and indeed, with greater Asia). In 2015 bilateral discussions between the EU and the EEU were encouraged by Angela Merkel as well as by the new team at the head of the EU from November 2014, notably Jean-Claude Juncker as the President of the European Commission and Federica Mogherini at the head of the European External Action Service (EEAS) and Vice President of the European Community (Sakwa, 2016b). This was virulently opposed by Lithuania and some other hardline countries, who considered engagement with Russia in the context of the Ukraine crisis a form of appeasement (Sytas, 2015).

The advocacy of greater Europe reflected Russia's attempt to shift the terms of discourse to an alternative vision of the character of European unity. This would not deny the achievements and reality of the EU, but it envisages a multipolar destiny for the continent in which a larger continental process would allow separate integration projects to thrive without coming into conflict with each other (Sakwa, 2015b). The greater European idea encompasses Turkey, but it puts Russia, not surprisingly, at the heart of an alternative, although complementary, project. It does not deny the EU, but it seeks to look at Europe from less of an institutional perspective, with more emphasis on practical economic and energy integration accompanied by a focus on broader civilizational trajectories. Although based on transactional practices, it has a transformational imperative. There is also a barely disguised geopolitical objective. Europe represented above all by the EU is frequently lambasted in Moscow for its inadequacies on the international stage: its inability to devise an independent policy of its own; its excessive fealty to the United States that reduces it to a 'little brother'; and its lack of consistency in propounding its own proclaimed norms. This engendered a distinctive strain of Russian 'Euroscepticism' in which classic British themes are reprised: the EU's alleged excessive bureaucracy, pettifogging interventionism and neo-socialism. In Putin's third term this was accompanied by a cultural critique, asserting that Europe was repudiating its own Christian heritage and had succumbed to a liberalism that eroded the very basis of civilizational coherence and community (Putin, 2013).

Despite the emphasis on Eurasian integration and the intensification of relations with China and 'greater Asia' following the imposition of Western sanctions in 2014, Putin and the Russian leadership refused to accept that Russia would become an outcast from Europe. The turn to Asia is accompanied by attempts to rebuild the relationship with significant European powers, notably Germany, France and Italy. Russia remained studiously neutral in the Brexit vote of 23 June 2016, although there was a barely disguised satisfaction that one of the staunchest US allies and the most consistent supporter of sanctions planned to leave the EU. Russia's relations with the Atlantic community, and its specific manifestations in the form of NATO and the EU, will be strained for years to come.

The symptom of this is the Ukraine crisis, the result of what Gorbachev and Putin never ceased to argue was an artificial attempt to impose a paradigm of Cold War victory over what they considered to be the common achievement of a peaceful end to the Cold War. Putin is heir to the greater Europe tradition, and even to this day repeatedly refers to the idea. Putin spoke of creating a free trade zone from the Atlantic to the Pacific at the Russo–EU summit in Brussels on 28 January 2014 (Putin, 2014). This was to be the last of the biannual summits, and put an end to the whole epoch of EU–Russian relations premised on a commonality of purpose and vision. In his speech to the UN General Assembly on 28 September 2015, discussing the resolution of the Ukraine crisis in the framework of the Minsk peace process, Putin argued that 'Such steps would guarantee that Ukraine will develop as a civilized state, and a vital link in creating a common space of security and economic cooperation, both in Europe and Eurasia' (Putin, 2015). It was not that Russia rejected the substantive values of the EU, but refused to accept the specific normative configuration described as 'Europeanization' (Kratochvíl, 2008). The EU's didacticism appeared to become a type of post-modern imperialism, where power was exerted while denying the essence of a power relationship (Kurki, 2011).

RETHINKING SPATIALITY: CRITICAL GEOPOLITICS AND UNCRITICAL NORMATIVISM

The Russian condemnation of Western double standards assumes a specific meaning. At issue is not just the apparent gulf between rhetoric and action, between declared principles and practices, but the EU with which Russia is trying to deal is structurally operating on at least two levels at the same time, each with its own logic and purposes. The tension between spatial and temporal dimensions is conventionally described as the contradiction between values and interests, or even more crudely between a pragmatic realist foreign policy and one based on a distinctive set of normative criteria. For the EU this dualism entails all sorts of coordination problems, but for Russia, operating as a traditional Westphalian power, the problems in the end became insuperable. It is not only that Russia prefers to engage with member states on a bilateral basis, but in the end this is the only way that Russia can have any relations at all. There was a fundamental incommensurability between Moscow and Brussels – one was a traditional great power, the other an amorphous and endlessly complex shape-shifting entity that assumed an increasingly hostile stance as the Union enlarged to the East.

The EU's normativism is driven by the view that the internal constitution of states determines their international behaviour. This postulate was long ago challenged by Waltz, who argued that the suggestion that only democracies are the foundation for a peaceful international system is little more than a self-serving argument of militant elites in the governments of the dominant powers. His model of structural realism has little role for values, and instead the exigencies of hard power and resources structure the conduct of international affairs (Waltz, 2000). Such views are balm to the ears of the Russian leadership, and build on E.H. Carr's (2001) critique of the idealism of the interwar years, which in the end helps precipitate the renewal of conflict.

After the disappointments of the early 2000s, with the effective stalling of the common spaces enterprise and despite the short-lived 'Partnership for Modernisation' programme launched by President Dmitry Medvedev with the EU, Russian foreign policy entered the phase of neo-revisionism. Russia's behaviour became more assertive, in part derived from economic recovery bolstered by windfall energy rents, political stabilization and a growing alienation not so much with the structures of hegemonic power but its practices. From a status quo state Russia became a distinctive type of neo-revisionist power, claiming to be a norm-enforcer and not just a norm-taker. Russia did not seek in any substantive sense to become a norm-maker – it was not interested in creating an alternative set of values, but sought adherence to the existing world order centred on the UN. The essence of neo-revisionism is not the attempt to create new rules or to advance an alternative model of international order but to ensure the universal and consistent application of existing norms. It is not the principles of international law and governance that Russia condemns but the practices that accompany their implementation. This reflected Russia's broader perception that it was locked into a strategic stalemate, and that the country was forced into a politics of resistance. As far as Moscow is concerned, it is the West that has become revisionist, not Russia. In its relations with the EU, Russia's neo-revisionist stance means that it was unable to become simply the passive recipient of EU norms, and instead tried to become a co-creator of Europe's destiny (Haukkala, 2008a, 2008b, 2009, 2010). The struggle is not only over contested norms but also over who has the prerogative to claim their norms as universal in Europe (Haukkala, 2015).

Contrary to the despatializing discourses of contemporary globalization ideology, integration efforts are all about respatialization and, in Eurasia, giving this substantive political form. For Carl Schmitt, 'the new spatial order based on states' took the form of several landmark events of spatial ordering of global linear thinking (Schmitt, 2006, Part II). However, the Monroe Doctrine of 2 December 1823 instituted a different form of political subjectivity, reflected in American ideas of *Grossraum* (greater space) which proclaimed predominance over the Western hemisphere and began the journey from isolationism to universalism and, ultimately, Wilsonian idealism and the League of Nations, accompanied by today's 'humanitarian interventionism' (Schmitt, 2006, Part IV, Chapter 5). This entailed an attempt by liberalism

> to turn the pluriverse of international politics into a universe, in which the effects of difference are controlled from a 'meta-sovereign' site through current US-driven attempts to reformulate international law by conferring a special status on liberal democracies, as well as by reintroducing a 'discriminatory concept of war' in the form of a right to different forms of intervention to preventive ones. (Odysseos and Petitio, 2007, p. 13)

Such a universe has no space for other *Grossraume*, of the sort posited by the Eurasianists and even the traditional Euro-Gaullists, and instead a homogeneous liberal order is proclaimed. It is hardly surprising that the EU project has prospered in the folds of the greater Atlanticism, since its post-modern relative desovereignization is homologous to the liberal universalism enshrined in the Atlantic Charter of August 1941. The Schuman proposals, as Jean Monet insisted, entailed the abnegation of sovereignty in a specific field, but with the expansive potential to undermine sovereignty in its entirety operating in the logic of neo-functional spillover from one sphere to another. The fundamental idea, as Burgess puts it, is that 'European peace would thus be assured not by diplomacy between nation-states, but by dismantling the political economic sovereignty of nation-states, albeit gradually and only in selected areas' (Burgess, 2007, p. 199, fn. 3). Russia's fundamental refusal to accept such a functionalist new order renders it an outsider, and possibly even an outcast, with commensurate effects on its domestic political evolution. Russia's reaction to despatializing discourses and the eruption of violence in Ukraine demonstrates that, in both ideological and spatial terms, the expansive dynamic of the EU is approaching its limits. However, although the idea of greater Europe gave both Russia and Turkey a way of escaping from the burden of history and marginality, and to create a positive post-enlargement agenda of European inclusion, the crisis of wider Europe was also that of greater Europe. The ideological framework of greater Europe has both a progressive logic of building an inclusive peace order, but it also has certain archaic elements. These neo-traditional features are both spatial and philosophical, stressing traditional Westphalian ideas of state sovereignty, the Concert of Powers in the management of international affairs, and Yalta ideas of geopolitical and ideological pluralism. The classic Gaullist idea of a Europe of nation states, nevertheless, still has a certain normative power, especially since so much of the continent, in the EU and beyond, is now drawn to resovereignization agendas.

Europe today is often used as a synonym for the EU, as an entity that is evolving and enlarging. However, it is precisely because Europe thus understood has begun to reach what is some sort of *finalité* that the greater Eurasian project has emerged as the continuation of the European idea in a new form and in a new arena. Although negotiations over Turkey's accession to the EU have been continuing since 2004, the prospect of Turkey actually joining is receding. Equally, although negotiations have started with some Balkan states, following Croatia's accession in July 2013, no more are likely to join in the near future. As for the EaP countries, the undignified and ultimately disastrous struggle over Ukraine from autumn 2013 revealed the radical degeneration of the EU as an instrument for the transcendence of the logic of conflict in Europe into an instrument for its perpetuation in new forms. This is where the EU's coadjuvancy with Atlanticism proved disastrous. The absence of some sort of defined *finalité* allowed accession to become an ideology of almost endless enlargement, until this was exposed as a hubristic illusion as the Union encountered a both deepening and widening crisis. The European project had clearly been hijacked by those who used it as an instrument of geopolitical ambition.

The advocacy of greater Europe ideas reflected Russia's attempt to shift the terms of discourse to an alternative vision of European unity. This does not deny the achievements and reality of the EU, but it envisages a more multipolar destiny for the continent in which a larger continental process would allow separate integration projects to thrive without coming into conflict. The greater European idea encompasses Turkey, but it puts Russia, as mentioned, at the heart of an alternative, although complementary, project. It contains a geopolitical objective not in the form of contestation but with the representation of Europe as a pluriverse in which no regional 'Monroe Doctrine', however finely it may be dressed in the language of wider Europe, is given legitimacy.

Today we are faced with the emergence of alternative integration projects, restoring a forced geopolitical pluralism to the heart of the continent. This is accompanied by an Asianist inflection to integrative projects reflecting the growing tilt in economic and political power to the East. Eurasian integration indicates the increasingly contested nature of the EU's hegemony on the continent and the development of alternative architectures. The double failure – to ensure that EU enlargement would be non-antagonistic to Russia and the failure to instantiate a broader vision of pan-European integration – is an unpropitious environment for Eurasian integration at a time when Russia itself has become a more assertive player. Mutual energy and other dependencies in Europe have been unable to overcome the competitive logic of the Cold War. This assumed a viscerally spatial aspect in imposing a choice upon Ukraine to turn decisively either West or East, when the country by definition was rooted in both wider and greater Europe. The inherently conflictual nature of the asymmetrical post-Cold War integrative model, in which the EU enlarged and projected a normative shadow deep into its borderlands, was ultimately challenged by attempts to find a new model, focused above all on Eurasia as an autonomous subject of international politics.

The pattern of mutually beneficial world order predicated on liberal internationalism from Russia's perspective had given way to the cold peace. Russia's response was to intensify plans for Eurasian integration. In the context of an era of renewed great power rivalry, the militarization of international politics, the structural erosion of the post-communist peace, and the assertion of elements of a post-ideological cold war (the cold peace), the pursuit of Eurasian integration in the context of greater Eurasian and greater Asian ambitions appears to make sense.

CONCLUDING REFLECTIONS

Russia's renewed bicontinental focus is driven by the perception that the West as a concept, a geopolitical actor and as a cultural project is showing signs of unravelling, accompanied by the rise of new geopolitical representations of 'the East'. Predictions about the imminent demise of the West are premature, yet its relative standing in the world is clearly being challenged. As a concept, the notion of the West has always contained numerous ambiguities, but it has effectively represented a certain ideal of progress and modernity. This ideal has become tarnished in Russian eyes. The EU's normative impetus is now overshadowed by perceptions of geopolitical threat, as institutionalized in NATO enlargement. Nevertheless, despite the hostile rhetoric, the Kremlin understands that the West retains an extraordinary cultural and economic dynamism. Yet the East is also reinventing itself, and is beginning to offer an alternative that is particularly attractive to the traditionalists within Russia. Russia's relations with the EU will not be able to return to anything like the status quo ante. Given its increasingly ramified orientation to multilateral bodies such as BRICS (Brazil, Russia, India, China, South Africa), the Shanghai Cooperation Organization (SCO) and various Silk Road endeavours, as well as increasingly close relations with China, a fundamental strategic rethink by all parties is required.

Putin's disillusionment with the West and Europe has entailed not simply a shift to a greater Asian orientation, but also a much more substantive attempt to give shape and substance to a re-energized vision of Russia as part of a greater Europe as well as a core element of greater Asia. By asserting a bicontinental identity, Russia seeks to avoid being ground between the EU and the rising powers of Asia. Hence, the EEU initiative was a way of mediating relations with the EU and China. While there has been an estrangement from the West in strategic and cultural terms, Russia has certainly not turned its back on Europe. Equally, the greater intensity of engagement with Asia, and in particular China, does not entail a shift from 'strategic partnership' to a far more exclusive 'strategic alliance', despite the calls for just such an alliance following the chilling of relations with the West. Russia's 'pivot' to Asia in this context is more than a contingent response to disappointments in the West, but reflects attempts to give substance to Russia's inherent bicontinentalism.

How to break out of the deadlock in Russo-EU relations? The only path out of the stalemate is to start thinking about new forms of spatiality. This does not necessarily entail the creation of new institutions, but of thinking about processes that may one day require formal institutionalization. Here the idea of an 'international regime' may be of help. The notion of an 'international regime', defined by Keohane as 'institutionalized patterns of cooperation', provides a conceptual key to the relationship (Keohane, 1982, p. 325). Keohane argues that interdependence creates the demand for an international regime, otherwise interdependence is liable only to exacerbate conflict and increase the risk of 'market failure'. As opposed to realist models of international relations, forms of international cooperation are sometimes generated that transcend the narrow and immediate interests of those concerned. This is more than the theory of 'hegemonic stability', which in contemporary Europe does not apply since two potential hegemonic powers are locked in a covert, and at times overt, struggle for mastery in their respective parts of the continent in general and in the overlapping 'near abroad' in particular. The 'liberal peace' to a large extent was always little more than a temporal form of hegemonic dominance, and even the democratic peace theory has been challenged. Russia's neo-revisionism challenges the classical postulates of liberal internationalism while rhetorically arguing that its plans for Eurasian integration do not repudiate these principles. It also offers the EU a chance to temper its own hegemonic potential, and thus allow it to remain true to its original ambitions. Schemes to give pan-European aspirations concrete form offer a way of making all of Europe once again a greater Europe.

REFERENCES

Websites were last accessed 14 February 2017.

Browning, Christopher S. (2005). 'Westphalian, Imperial, Neomedieval: The Geopolitics of Europe and the Role of the North', in Christopher S. Browning (ed.), *Remaking Europe in the Margins: Northern Europe after the Enlargements*, Aldershot: Ashgate, pp. 85–101.

Burgess, J. Peter (2007). 'The Evolution of European Union Law and Carl Schmitt's Theory of the *Nomos* of Europe', in Louiza Odysseos and Fabio Petitio (eds), *The International Political Thought of Carl Schmitt: Terror, Liberal War and the Crisis of Global Order*, London: Routledge, pp. 185–201.

Carr, E.H. (2001). *The Twenty Years' Crisis, 1919–1939: An Introduction to the Study of International Relations*, reissued with a new introduction and additional material by Michael Cox, London: Palgrave Macmillan.

Cooper, Robert (2003). *The Breaking of Nations: Order and Chaos in the Twenty-first Century*, New York: Atlantic Monthly Press.

Copsey, Nathaniel (2015). *Rethinking the European Union*, London: Palgrave Macmillan.

Copsey, Nathaniel and Karolina Pomorska (2014). 'The Influence of Newer Member States in the European Union: The Case of Poland and the Eastern Partnership', *Europe-Asia Studies*, **66** (3), 421–43.

DeBardeleben, Joan (2008). *The Boundaries of EU Enlargement: Finding a Place for Neighbours*, Basingstoke: Palgrave Macmillan.

Dragneva, Rilka and Kataryna Wolczuk (eds) (2013). *Eurasian Economic Integration: Law, Policy and Politics*, Cheltenham, UK and Northampton, MA, USA: Edward Elgar Publishing.

Dragneva, Rilka and Kataryna Wolczuk (2015). *Ukraine Between the EU and Russia: The Integration Challenge*, London: Palgrave Macmillan.

Dutkiewicz, Piotr and Richard Sakwa (eds) (2015). *Eurasian Integration: The View from Within*, London and New York: Routledge.

Gromyko, Aleksei (ed.) (2014). *Bol'shaya Evropa*, Moscow: Institute of Europe.

Haukkala, Hiski (2008a). 'A Norm-maker or a Norm-taker? The Changing Normative Parameters of Russia's Place in Europe', in Ted Hopf (ed.), *Russia's European Choice*, Basingstoke: Palgrave Macmillan, pp. 35–56.

Haukkala, Hiski (2008b). 'The European Union as a Regional Normative Hegemon: The Case of European Neighbourhood Policy', *Europe-Asia Studies*, **60** (9), November, 1601–22.

Haukkala, Hiski (2009). 'Lost in Translation? Why the EU has Failed to Influence Russia's Development', *Europe-Asia Studies*, **61** (10), December, 1757–75.

Haukkala, Hiski (2010). *The EU–Russia Strategic Partnership: The Limits of Post-sovereignty in International Relations*, London and New York: Routledge.

Haukkala, Hiski (2015). 'From Cooperative to Contested Europe? The Conflict in Ukraine as a Culmination of a Long-term Crisis in EU–Russia Relations', *Journal of Contemporary European Studies*, published online 3 February.

Huntington, Samuel P. (1993). 'The Clash of Civilizations?', *Foreign Affairs*, **72** (3), Summer, 23–49.

Huntington, Samuel P. (1996). *The Clash of Civilizations and the Remaking of World Order*, New York: Simon & Schuster.

Judt, Tony (2010). *Postwar: A History of Europe since 1945*, London: Vintage.

Kanet, Roger E. and Matthew Sussex (eds) (2015). *Power, Politics and Confrontation in Eurasia: Foreign Policy in a Contested Region*, London: Palgrave Macmillan.

Keohane, Robert O. (1982). 'The Demand for International Regimes', *International Organization*, **36** (2), Spring, 325–55.

Keohane, Robert O. and Joseph Nye Jr (1989). *Power and Interdependence*, 2nd edn, New York: HarperCollins.

Kochenov, Dimitry (2008). *EU Enlargement and the Failure of Conditionality: Pre-accession Conditionality in the Fields of Democracy and the Rule of Law*, Alphen and den Rijn: Kluwer Law International.

Korosteleva, Elena (2015). 'The European Union and Russia: Prospects for Cohabitation in the Contested Region', in David Lane and Vsevolod Samokhvalov (eds), *The Eurasian Project and Europe*, London: Palgrave Macmillan, pp. 187–202.

Krastev, Ivan and Mark Leonard, with Dimitar Bechev, Jana Kobzova and Andrew Wilson (2010). *The Spectre of a Multipolar Europe*, October, London: European Council on Foreign Relations.

Kratochvíl, Petr (2008). 'The Discursive Resistance to EU-enticement: The Russian Elite and (the Lack of) Europeanisation', *Europe-Asia Studies*, **60** (3), May, 397–422.

Kurki, Milja (2011). 'Governmentality and EU Democracy Promotion: The European Instrument for Democracy and Human Rights and the Construction of Democratic Civil Societies', *International Political Sociology*, **5**, 349–66.

Lane, David and Vsevolod Samokhvalov (eds) (2015). *The Eurasian Project and Europe: Regional Discontinuities and Geopolitics*, London: Palgrave Macmillan.

Lavenex, Sandra (2012). *EU External Governance*, London: Routledge.

Legvold, Robert (2016). *Return to Cold War*, Cambridge: Polity.

Lindberg, Susanna, Mika Ojakangas and Sergei Prozorov (eds) (2014). *Europe Beyond Universalism and Particularism*, London: Palgrave Macmillan.

Monaghan, Andrew (2015). 'A "New Cold War"? Abusing History, Misunderstanding Russia', May, Chatham House Research Paper, London.

Odysseos, Louiza and Fabio Petitio (2007). 'Introduction: The International Political Thought of Carl Schmitt', in Louiza Odysseos and Fabio Petitio (eds), *The International Political Thought of Carl Schmitt: Terror, Liberal War and the Crisis of Global Order*, London: Routledge, pp. 1–17.

Prodi, Romano (2002). 'A Wider Europe: A Proximity Policy as the Key to Stability', 5–6 December, Brussels, available at http://europa.eu/rapid/press-release_SPEECH-02-619_en.htm.

Prozorov, Sergei (2014). *Understanding Conflict between Russia and the EU: The Limits of Integration*, Basingstoke: Palgrave Macmillan.

Putin, Vladimir (2011). 'Novyi integratsionnyi proekt dlya Evrazii: budushchee, kotoroe rozhdaetsya segodnya', *Izvestiya*, 3 October, p. 1, available at http://izvestia.ru/news/502761.

Putin, Vladimir (2013). 'Zasedanie mezhdunarodnogo diskussionogo kluba "Valdai"', 19 September, available at http://kremlin.ru/news/19243.

Putin, Vladimir (2014). 'Russia-EU Summit', 28 January, available at http://eng.kremlin.ru/transcripts/6575.

Putin, Vladimir (2015). '70th Session of the UN General Assembly', 28 September, available at http://kremlin.ru/events/president/news/50385.

Rumelli, Bahar (2004). 'Constructing Identity and Relating to Difference: Understanding the EU's Mode of Differentiation', *Review of International Studies*, **30** (1), 24–47.

Sakwa, Richard (2015a). *Ukraine and the Postcolonial Condition*, 18 September, available at www.opendemocracy.net/od-russia/richard-sakwa/ukraine-and-post colonial-condition.

Sakwa, Richard (2015b). 'Dualism at Home and Abroad: Russian Foreign Policy Neo-revisionism and Bicontinentalism', in David Cadier and Margot Light (eds), *Russia's Foreign Policy*, London: Palgrave Macmillan, pp. 65–79.

Sakwa, Richard (2016a). *Frontline Ukraine: Crisis in the Borderlands*, paperback edn with new Afterword, London and New York: I.B. Tauris.

Sakwa, Richard (2016b). 'How the Eurasian Elites Envisage the Role of the EEU in Global Perspective', in David Lane and Vsevolod Samokhvalov (eds), *Eurasia in a Global Context*, Special issue of *European Politics and Society*, **17** (S1), 4–22.

Sakwa, Richard (2017 forthcoming). *Russia Against the Rest: Pluralism and the Post-Cold War International System*, Cambridge: Cambridge University Press.

Samokhvalov, Vsevolod (2015). 'Ukraine between Russia and the European Union: Triangle Revisited', *Europe-Asia Studies*, **67** (9), November, 1371–93.

Schmitt, Carl (2006). *The Nomos of the Earth in the International Law of the Jus Publicum Europaeum*, trans. and annotated by G.L. Ulmen, New York: Telos Press.

Streeck, Wolfgang (2015). 'Why the Euro Divides Europe', *New Left Review*, **95**, September–October, 5–26.

Suslov, Dmitry (2016). 'Without a "Common Space": A New Agenda for Russia-EU Relations', Valdai Papers No. 49, June, Moscow, p. 3, available at http://valdai-club.com/files/11016/.

Sytas, Andrius (2015). 'EU's Juncker Dangles Trade Ties with Russia-led Bloc to Putin', Reuters, 19 November, available at http://uk.reuters.com/article/2015/11/19/uk-eu-russia-trade-kremlin-exclusive-idUKKCN0T82O920151119.

Tolstrup, Jakob (2014). *Russia vs. the EU: The Competition for Influence in Post-Soviet States*, Boulder, CO: Lynne Rienner.

Waltz, Kenneth N. (2000). 'Structural Realism after the Cold War', *International Security*, **25** (1), Summer, 5–41.

Whitman, Richard and Stefan Wolff (eds) (2010). *The European Neighbourhood Policy in Perspective: Context, Implementation and Impact*, Basingstoke: Palgrave Macmillan.

Zielonka, Jan (2007). *Europe as Empire: The Nature of the Enlarged European Union*, Oxford: Oxford University Press.

Zielonka, Jan (2008). 'Europe as a Global Actor: Empire by Example?', *International Affairs*, **84** (3), May, 471–84.

10. Contemporary imperialism*

Samir Amin

LESSONS FROM THE TWENTIETH CENTURY

Lenin, Bukharin, Stalin and Trotsky in Russia, as well as Mao, Zhou Enlai and Den Xiaoping in China, shaped the history of the two great revolutions of the twentieth century.[1] As leaders of revolutionary communist parties and then later as leaders of revolutionary states, they were confronted with the problems faced by a triumphant revolution in countries of peripheral capitalism and forced to 'revise' (I deliberately use this term, considered sacrilegious by many) the theses inherited from the historical Marxism of the Second-International. Lenin and Bukharin went much further than Hobson and Hilferding in their analyses of monopoly capitalism and imperialism and drew this major political conclusion: the imperialist war of 1914–18 (they were among the few, if not the only ones, to anticipate it) made necessary and possible a revolution led by the proletariat.

With the benefit of hindsight, I will indicate here the limitations of their analyses. Lenin and Bukharin considered imperialism to be a new stage ('the highest') of capitalism associated with the development of monopolies. I question this thesis and contend that historical capitalism has always been imperialist, in the sense that it has led to a polarization between centers and peripheries since its origin (the sixteenth century), which has only increased over the course of its later globalized development. The nineteenth-century pre-monopolist system was not less imperialist. Great Britain maintained its hegemony precisely because of its colonial domination of India. Lenin and Bukharin thought that the revolution, begun in Russia ('the weak link'), would continue in the centers (Germany in particular). Their hope was based on an underestimate of the effects of imperialist polarization, which destroyed revolutionary prospects in the centers.

Nevertheless, Lenin, and even more Bukharin, quickly learned the

---

* This chapter first appeared in *Monthly Review* in July 2015 and is republished here with the kind permission of the author and editor of the *Monthly Review*.
[1] I am limiting myself to examining the experiences of Russia and China, with no deliberate intention of ignoring the other twentieth-century socialist revolutions (North Korea, Vietnam, Cuba).

necessary historical lesson. The revolution, made in the name of socialism (and communism), was, in fact, something else: mainly a peasant revolution. So what to do? How can the peasantry be linked with the construction of socialism? By making concessions to the market and by respecting newly acquired peasant property; hence by progressing slowly toward socialism? The New Economic Plan (NEP) implemented this strategy.

Yes, but . . . Lenin, Bukharin and Stalin also understood that the imperialist powers would never accept the revolution or even the NEP. After the hot wars of intervention, the cold war was to become permanent, from 1920 to 1990.[2] Soviet Russia, even though it was far from being able to construct socialism, was able to free itself from the straightjacket that imperialism always strives to impose on all peripheries of the world system that it dominates. In effect, Soviet Russia delinked. So what to do now? Attempt to push for peaceful coexistence, by making concessions if necessary and refraining from intervening too actively on the international stage? But at the same time, it was necessary to be armed to face new and unavoidable attacks. And that implied rapid industrialization, which, in turn, came into conflict with the interests of the peasantry and thus threatened to break the worker-peasant alliance, the foundation of the revolutionary state.

It is possible, then, to understand the equivocations of Lenin, Bukharin and Stalin. In theoretical terms, there were U-turns from one extreme to the other. Sometimes a determinist attitude inspired by the phased approach inherited from earlier Marxism (first the bourgeois democratic revolution, then the socialist one) predominated, sometimes a voluntarist approach (political action would make it possible to leap over stages).

Finally, from 1930 to 1933, Stalin chose rapid industrialization and armament (and this choice was not without some connection to the rise of fascism). Collectivization was the price of that choice. Here again we must beware of judging too quickly: all socialists of that period (and even more the capitalists) shared Kautsky's analyses on this point and were persuaded that the future belonged to large-scale agriculture.[3] The break in the worker-peasant alliance that this choice implied lay behind the abandonment of revolutionary democracy and the autocratic turn.

In my opinion, Trotsky would certainly not have done better. His attitude toward the rebellion of the Kronstadt sailors and his later equivocations

---

[2] Before the Second World War, Stalin had desperately, and unsuccessfully, sought an alliance with the Western democracies against Nazism. After the war, Washington chose to pursue the Cold War, while Stalin sought to extend friendship with the Western powers, again without success (see Roberts, 2007 [2014]). See the important preface by Annie Lacroix Riz to the French edition, *Les guerres de Staline: De la guerre mondiale à la guerre froide* (2014).

[3] I am alluding here to Kautsky's (1899 [1988]) theses in *The Agrarian Question*, 2 volumes.

demonstrate that he was no different than the other Bolshevik leaders in government. But, after 1927, living in exile and no longer having responsibility for managing the Soviet state, he could delight in endlessly repeating the sacred principles of socialism. He became like many academic Marxists who have the luxury of asserting their attachment to principles without having to be concerned about effectiveness in transforming reality.[4]

The Chinese communists appeared later on the revolutionary stage. Mao was able to learn from Bolshevik equivocations. China was confronted with the same problems as Soviet Russia: revolution in a backward country, the necessity of including the peasantry in revolutionary transformation, and the hostility of the imperialist powers. But Mao was able to see more clearly than Lenin, Bukharin and Stalin. Yes, the Chinese revolution was anti-imperialist and peasant (anti-feudal). But it was not bourgeois democratic; it was popular democratic. The difference is important: the latter type of revolution requires maintaining the worker-peasant alliance over a long period. China was thus able to avoid the fatal error of forced collectivization and invent another way: make all agricultural land state property, give the peasantry equal access to use of this land, and renovate family agriculture.[5]

The two revolutions had difficulty in achieving stability because they were forced to reconcile support for a socialist outlook and concessions to capitalism. Which of these two tendencies would prevail? These revolutions only achieved stability after their 'Thermidor,' to use Trotsky's term. But when was the Thermidor in Russia? Was it in 1930, as Trotsky said? Or was it in the 1920s, with the NEP? Or was it the ice age of the Brezhnev period? And in China, did Mao choose Thermidor beginning in 1950? Or do we have to wait until Deng Xiaoping to speak of the Thermidor of 1980?

It is not by chance that reference is made to lessons of the French Revolution. The three great revolutions of modern times (the French, Russian and Chinese) are great precisely because they looked forward beyond the immediate requirements of the moment. With the rise of the Mountain, led by Robespierre, in the National Convention, the French Revolution was consolidated as both popular and bourgeois and, just like the Russian and Chinese Revolutions – which strove to go all the way to communism even if it not on the agenda due to the necessity of averting

---

[4] There are pleasant exceptions among Marxist intellectuals who, without having had responsibilities in the leadership of revolutionary parties or, still less, of revolutionary states, have nonetheless remained attentive to the challenges confronted by state socialisms (I am thinking here of Baran, Sweezy, Hobsbawm and others).

[5] See Amin (2013b) for analyses concerning Maoism's treatment of the agrarian question.

defeat – retained the prospect of going much further later. Thermidor is not the restoration. The latter occurred in France, not with Napoleon, but only beginning in 1815. Still, it should be remembered that the restoration could not completely do away with the gigantic social transformation caused by the revolution. In Russia, the restoration occurred even later in its revolutionary history, with Gorbachev and Yeltsin. It should be noted that this restoration remains fragile, as can be seen in the challenges Putin must still confront. In China, there has not been (or not yet!) a restoration.[6]

A NEW STAGE OF MONOPOLY CAPITAL

The contemporary world is still confronted with the same challenges encountered by the revolutions of the twentieth century. The continued deepening of the center/periphery contrast, characteristic of the spread of globalized capitalism, still leads to the same major political consequence: transformation of the world begins with anti-imperialist, national, popular – and potentially anti-capitalist – revolutions, which are the only ones on the agenda for the foreseeable future. But this transformation will only be able to go beyond the first steps and proceed on the path to socialism later if and when the peoples of the centers, in turn, begin the struggle for communism, viewed as a higher stage of universal human civilization. The systemic crisis of capitalism in the centers makes this possibility a potential reality.

In the meantime, there is a twofold challenge confronting the peoples and states of the South: (1) the lumpen development that contemporary capitalism forces on all peripheries of the system has nothing to offer three-quarters of humanity; in particular, it leads to the rapid destruction of peasant societies in Asia and Africa, and consequently the response given to the peasant question will largely govern the nature of future changes;[7] and (2) the aggressive geostrategy of the imperialist powers, which is opposed to any attempt by the peoples and states of the periphery to get out of the impasse, forces the peoples concerned to defeat the military control of the world by the United States and its subaltern European and Japanese allies.

The first long systemic crisis of capitalism got underway in the 1870s. The version of historic capitalism's extension over the long span that I have put forward suggests a succession of three epochs: ten centuries of

---

[6] See Hobsbawm (1990); also see the works of Florence Gauthier. These authors do not assimilate Thermidor to restoration, as the Trotskyist simplification suggests.

[7] Concerning the destruction of the Asian and African peasantry currently underway, see Amin (2012).

incubation from the year 1000 in China to the eighteenth-century revolutions in England and France, a short century of triumphal flourishing (the nineteenth century), probably a long decline comprising in itself the first long crisis (1875–1945) and then the second (begun in 1975 and still ongoing). In each of those two long crises, capital responds to the challenge by the same triple formula: concentration of capital's control, deepening of uneven globalization, financialization of the system's management.[8] Two major thinkers (Hobson and Hilferding) immediately grasped the enormous importance of capitalism's transformation into monopoly capitalism. But it was Lenin and Bukharin who drew the political conclusion from this transformation, a transformation that initiated the decline of capitalism and thus moved the socialist revolution onto the agenda (Bukharin, 1915 [1973]; Lenin, 1916 [1969]).

The primary formation of monopoly capitalism thus goes back to the end of the nineteenth century, but in the United States it really established itself as a system only from the 1920s, to conquer next the Western Europe and Japan of the 'thirty glorious years' following the Second World War. The concept of surplus, put forth by Baran and Sweezy in the 1950–60 decade, allows a grasp of what is essential in the transformation of capitalism. Convinced at the moment of its publication by that work of enrichment to the Marxist critique of capitalism, I undertook as early as the 1970s its reformulation, which required, in my opinion, the transformation of the 'first' (1920–70) monopoly capitalism into generalized-monopoly capitalism, analysed as a qualitatively new phase of the system.

In the previous forms of competition among firms producing the same use value – numerous then, and independent of each other – decisions were made by the capitalist owners of those firms on the basis of a recognized market price which imposed itself as an external datum. Baran and Sweezy observed that the new monopolies act differently: they set their prices simultaneously with the nature and volume of their outputs. So it is an end to 'fair and open competition,' which remains, quite contrary to reality, at the heart of conventional economics rhetoric! The abolition of competition – the radical transformation of that term's meaning, of its functioning and of its results – detaches the price system from its basis, the system of values, and in that very way hides from sight the referential framework which used to define capitalism's rationality. Although use values used to constitute to a great extent autonomous realities, they become, in monopoly capitalism, the object

---

[8] I discuss here only some of the major consequences of the move to generalized monopolies (financialization, decline of democracy). As for ecological questions, I refer to the remarkable works of John Bellamy Foster.

of actual fabrications produced systematically through aggressive and particularized sales strategies (advertising, brands and so on). In monopoly capitalism, a coherent reproduction of the productive system is no longer possible merely by mutual adjustment of the two departments discussed in the second volume of *Capital*: it is thenceforward necessary to take into account a Department III, conceived by Baran and Sweezy. This allows for added surplus absorption promoted by the state – beyond Department I (private investment) and beyond the portion of Department II (private consumption) devoted to capitalist consumption. The classic example of Department III spending is military expenditure. However, the notion of Department III can be expanded to cover the wider array of socially unreproductive expenditures promoted by generalized-monopoly capitalism.[9]

The excrescence of Department III, in turn, favors in fact the erasure of the distinction made by Marx between productive (of surplus value) labor and unproductive labor. All forms of wage labor can – and do – become sources of possible profits. A hairdresser sells his services to a customer who pays him out of his income. But if that hairdresser becomes the employee of a beauty parlor, the business must realize a profit for its owner. If the country at issue puts ten million wage workers to work in Departments I, II and III, providing the equivalent of 12 million years of abstract labor, and if the wages received by those workers allow them to buy goods and services requiring merely six million years of abstract labor, the rate of exploitation for all of them, productive and unproductive confounded, is the same 100 percent. But the six million years of abstract labor that the workers do not receive cannot all be invested in the purchase of producer goods destined to expand Departments I and II; part of them will be put toward the expansion of Department III.

GENERALIZED-MONOPOLY CAPITALISM (SINCE 1975)

Passage from the initial monopoly capitalism to its current form (generalized-monopoly capitalism) was accomplished in a short time (between 1975 and 2000) in response to the second long crisis of declining capitalism. In 15 years, the centralization of monopoly power and its capacity for control over the entire productive system reached summits incomparable with what had until then been the case.

---

[9]   For further discussions of the Department III analysis and its relation to Baran and Sweezy's theory of surplus absorption, see Amin (2013a) and Foster (1984).

My first formulation of generalized-monopoly capitalism dates from 1978, when I put forward an interpretation of capital's responses to the challenge of its long systemic crisis, starting from 1971–75. In that interpretation I accentuated the three directions of this expected reply, then barely underway: strengthened centralization of control over the economy by the monopolies; deepening globalization (and the outsourcing of the manufacturing industry to the peripheries); and financialization. The work that André Gunder Frank and I published together in 1978 drew no notice probably because our theses were ahead of their time. But today, the three characteristics at issue have become blindingly obvious to everybody (Frank and Amin, 1981).

A name had to be given to this new phase of monopoly capitalism. The adjective 'generalized' specifies what is new: the monopolies are thenceforward in a position that gives them the capability of reducing all (or nearly all) economic activities to subcontractor status. The example of family farming in the capitalist centers provides the finest example of this. These farmers are controlled upstream by the monopolies that provide their inputs and financing, and downstream by the marketing chains, to the point that the price structures forced on them wipe out the income from their labor.

Farmers survive only thanks to public subsidies paid for by the taxpayers. This extraction is thus at the origin of the monopolies' profits! As likewise observed with bank failures, the new principle of economic management is summed up in a phrase: privatization of the monopolies' profits, socialization of their losses! To go on talking of 'fair and open competition' and of 'truth of the prices revealed by the markets' – that belongs in a farce.

The fragmented, and by that fact concrete, economic power of proprietary bourgeois families gives way to a centralized power exercised by the directors of the monopolies and their cohort of salaried servitors. For generalized-monopoly capitalism involves not the concentration of property, which on the contrary is more dispersed than ever, but the power to manage it. That is why it is deceptive to attach the adjective 'patrimonial' to contemporary capitalism. It is only in appearance that 'shareholders' rule. Absolute monarchs, the top executives of the monopolies, decide everything in their name.

Moreover, the deepening globalization of the system wipes out the holistic (that is, simultaneously economic, political and social) logic of national systems without putting in its place any global logic whatsoever. This is the empire of chaos – the title of one of my works, published in 1991 and subsequently taken up by others: in fact, international political violence takes the place of economic competition (Amin, 1992).

FINANCIALIZATION OF ACCUMULATION

The new financialization of economic life crowns this transformation in capital's power. In place of strategies set out by real owners of fragmented capital are those of the managers of ownership titles over capital. What is vulgarly called fictitious capital (the estimated value of ownership certificates) is nothing but the expression of this displacement, this disconnect between the virtual and real worlds.

By its very nature capitalist accumulation has always been synonymous with disorder, in the sense that Marx gave to that term: a system moving from disequilibrium to disequilibrium (driven by class struggles and conflicts among the powers) without ever tending toward equilibrium. But this disorder resulting from competition among fragmented capitals was kept within reasonable limits by management of the credit system carried out under the control of the national state. With contemporary financialized and globalized capitalism those frontiers disappear; the violence of the movements from disequilibrium to disequilibrium is reinforced. The successor of disorder is chaos.

Domination by the capital of the generalized monopolies is exercised on the world scale through global integration of the monetary and financial market, based henceforward on the principle of flexible exchange rates, and giving up national controls over the flow of capital. Nevertheless, this domination is called into question, to varying degrees, by state policies of the emerging countries. The conflict between these latter policies and the strategic objectives of the triad's collective imperialism becomes by that fact one of the central axes for possibly putting generalized-monopoly capitalism once more on trial (Amin, 2015).

THE DECLINE OF DEMOCRACY

In the system's centers, generalized-monopoly capitalism has brought with it generalization of the wage-form. Upper managers are thenceforward employees who do not participate in the formation of surplus value, of which they have become consumers. At the other social pole, the generalized proletarianization that the wage-form suggests is accompanied by multiplication in forms of segmentation of the labor force. In other words, the 'proletariat' (in its forms as known in the past) disappears at the very moment when proletarianization becomes generalized. In the peripheries, the effects of domination by generalized-monopoly capital are no less visible. Above an already diverse social structure made up of local ruling classes and the subordinate classes and status groups there is placed a dominant superclass emerging in the wake of globalization. This super-class is sometimes that of 'neo-comprador insiders,' sometimes that of the governing political class (or class-state-party), or a mixture of the two.

Far from being synonyms, 'market' and 'democracy' are, on the contrary, antonyms. In the centers a new political consensus-culture (only seeming, perhaps, but nevertheless active) synonymous with depoliticization has taken the place of the former political culture based on the right-left con-frontation that used to give significance to bourgeois democracy and the contradictory inscription of class struggles within its framework. In the peripheries, the monopoly of power captured by the dominant local super-class likewise involves the negation of democracy. The rise of political Islam provides an example of such a regression.

THE AGGRESSIVE GEOSTRATEGY OF CONTEMPORARY IMPERIALISM: THE COLLECTIVE IMPERIALISM OF THE TRIAD; THE STATE IN CONTEMPORARY CAPITALISM

In the 1970s, Sweezy, Magdoff and I had already advanced this thesis, for-mulated by André Gunder Frank and myself in a work published in 1978. We said that monopoly capitalism was entering a new age, characterized by the gradual – but rapid – dismantling of national production systems. The production of a growing number of market goods can no longer be defined by the label 'made in France' (or the Soviet Union or the United States), but becomes 'made in the world,' because its manufacture is now broken into segments, located here and there throughout the whole world.

Recognizing this fact, now a commonplace, does not imply that there is only one explanation of the major cause for the transformation in ques-tion. For my part, I explain it by the leap forward in the degree of central-ization in the control of capital by the monopolies, which I have described as the move from the capitalism of monopolies to the capitalism of gen-eralized monopolies. The information revolution, among other factors, provides the means that make possible the management of this globally dispersed production system. But for me, these means are only imple-mented in response to a new objective need created by the leap forward in the centralized control of capital.

The emergence of this globalized production system eliminates coher-ent 'national development' policies (diverse and unequally effective), but it does not substitute a new coherence, which would be that of the globalized system. The reason for that is the absence of a globalized bourgeoisie and globalized state, which I will examine later. Consequently, the globalized production system is incoherent by nature.

Another important consequence of this qualitative transformation of contemporary capitalism is the emergence of the collective imperialism of the triad, which takes the place of the historical national imperialisms (of the United States, Great Britain, Japan, Germany, France and a few others). Collective imperialism finds its *raison d'être* in the awareness by the bourgeoisie in the triad nations of the necessity for their joint management of the world and particularly of the subjected, and yet to be subjected, societies of the peripheries.

Some draw two correlates from the thesis of the emergence of a globalized production system: the emergence of a globalized bourgeoisie and the emergence of a globalized state, both of which would find their objective foundation in this new production system. My interpretation of the current changes and crises leads me to reject these two correlates.

There is no globalized bourgeoisie (or dominant class) in the process of being formed, either on the world scale or in the countries of the imperialist triad. I am led to emphasize the fact that the centralization of control over the capital of the monopolies takes place within the nation-states of the triad (United States, each member of the European Union, Japan) much more than it does in the relations between the partners of the triad, or even between members of the European Union. The bourgeoisie (or oligopolistic groups) are in competition within nations (and the national state manages this competition, in part at least) and between nations. Thus, the German oligopolies (and the German state) took on the leadership of European affairs, not for the equal benefit of everyone, but first of all for their own benefit. At the level of the triad, it is obviously the bourgeoisie of the United States that leads the alliance, once again with an unequal distribution of the benefits. The idea that the objective cause – the emergence of the globalized production system – entails ipso facto the emergence of a globalized dominant class is based on the underlying hypothesis that the system must be coherent. In reality, it is possible for it not to be coherent. In fact, it is not coherent and hence this chaotic system is not viable.

In the peripheries, the globalization of the production system occurs in conjunction with the replacement of the hegemonic blocs of earlier eras by a new hegemonic bloc dominated by the new comprador bourgeoisie, which are not constitutive elements of a globalized bourgeoisie, but only subaltern allies of the bourgeoisie of the dominant triad. Just like there is no globalized bourgeoisie in the process of formation, there is also no globalized state on the horizon. The major reason for this is that the current globalized system does not attenuate, but actually accentuates conflict (already visible or potential) between the societies of the triad and those of the rest of the world. I do indeed mean conflict between *societies* and, consequently, *potentially* conflict between states. The advantage derived from the triad's dominant position (imperialist rent) allows the hegemonic bloc formed around the generalized monopolies to benefit from a legitimacy that is expressed, in turn, by the convergence of all major electoral parties, right and left, and their equal commitment to neoliberal economic policies and continual intervention in the affairs of the peripheries. On the other hand, the neo-comprador bourgeoisie of the peripheries are neither legitimate nor credible in the eyes of their own people (because the policies they serve do not make it possible to 'catch up,' and most often lead to the impasse of lumpen development). Instability of the current governments is thus the rule in this context.

Just as there is no globalized bourgeoisie even at the level of the triad or that of the European Union, there is also no globalized state at these levels. Instead, there is only an alliance of states. These states, in turn, willingly accept the hierarchy that allows that alliance to function: general leadership is taken on by Washington, and leadership in Europe by Berlin. The national state remains in place to serve globalization as it is.

There is an idea circulating in postmodernist currents that contemporary capitalism no longer needs the state to manage the world economy and thus the state system is in the process of withering away to the benefit of the emergence of civil society. I will not go back over the arguments that I have developed elsewhere against this naive thesis, one moreover that is propagated by the dominant governments and the media clergy in their service. There is no capitalism without the state. Capitalist globalization could not be pursued without the interventions of the US armed forces and the management of the dollar. Clearly, the armed forces and money are instruments of the state, not of the market.

But since there is no world state, the United States intends to fulfill this function. The societies of the triad consider this function to be legitimate; other societies do not. But what does that matter? The self-proclaimed 'international community,' that is, the G7 plus Saudi Arabia, which has surely become a democratic republic, does not recognize the legitimacy of the opinion of 85 percent of the world's population!

There is thus an asymmetry between the functions of the state in the dominant imperialist centers and those of the state in the subject, or yet to be subjected, peripheries. The state in the compradorized peripheries is inherently unstable and, consequently, a potential enemy, when it is not already one.

There are enemies with which the dominant imperialist powers have been forced to coexist – at least up until now. This is the case with China because it has rejected (up until now) the neo-comprador option and is pursuing its sovereign project of integrated and coherent national development. Russia became an enemy as soon as Putin refused to align politically with the triad and wanted to block the expansionist ambitions of the latter in the Ukraine, even if he does not envision (or not yet?) leaving the rut of economic liberalism. The great majority of comprador states in the South (that is, states in the service of their comprador bourgeoisie) are allies, not enemies – as long as each of these comprador states gives the appearance of being in charge of its country. But leaders in Washington, London, Berlin and Paris know that these states are fragile. As soon as a popular movement of revolt – with or without a viable alternative strategy – threatens one of these states, the triad arrogates to itself the right to intervene. Intervention can even lead to contemplating the destruction of these states and, beyond them, of the societies concerned. This strategy is currently at work in Iraq, Syria and elsewhere. The *raison d'être* of the strategy for military control of the world by the triad led by Washington is located entirely in this 'realist' vision, which is in direct counterpoint with the fashionable view of a globalized state in the process of formation (Amin, 2014a).

RESPONSES OF THE PEOPLES AND STATES OF THE SOUTH

The ongoing offensive of United States/Europe/Japan collective imperialism against all the peoples of the South walks on two legs: the economic leg – globalized neoliberalism forced as the exclusive possible economic policy; and the political leg – continuous interventions including preemptive wars against those who reject imperialist interventions. In response, some countries of the South, such as the BRICS (Brazil, Russia, India, China, South Africa), at best walk on only one leg: they reject the geopolitics of imperialism but accept economic neoliberalism. They remain, for that reason, vulnerable, as the current case of Russia shows (Amin, 2010, 2014b).[10] Yes, they have to understand that 'trade is war,' as Yash Tandon (2015) wrote.

All countries of the world outside the triad are enemies or potential enemies, except those who accept complete submission to its economic and

---

[10]   The choice to delink is inevitable. The extreme centralization of the surplus at the world level in the form of imperialist rent for the monopolies of the imperialist powers is unsupportable by all societies in the periphery. It is necessary to deconstruct this system with the prospect of reconstructing it later in another form of globalization compatible with communism understood as a more advanced stage of universal civilization. I have suggested, in this context, a comparison with the necessary destruction of the centralization of the Roman Empire, which opened the way to feudal decentralization.

political strategy. In that frame, Russia is 'an enemy' (Amin, 2010, 2014c). Whatever our assessment of what the Soviet Union was, the triad fought it simply because it was an attempt to develop independently of dominant capitalism/imperialism. After the breakdown of the Soviet system, some people (in Russia in particular) thought that the 'West' would not antagonize a 'capitalist Russia' – just as Germany and Japan had 'lost the war but won the peace.' They forgot that the Western powers supported the reconstruction of the former fascist countries precisely to face the challenge of the independent policies of the Soviet Union. Now, this challenge having disappeared, the target of the triad is complete submission, to destroy the capacity of Russia to resist. The current development of the Ukraine tragedy illustrates the reality of the strategic target of the triad. The triad organized in Kiev what ought to be called a 'Euro/Nazi putsch.' The rhetoric of the Western medias, claiming that the policies of the triad aim at promoting democracy, is *simply a lie*. Eastern Europe has been 'integrated' in the European Union not as equal partners but as 'semi-colonies' of major Western and Central European capitalist/imperialist powers. The relation between West and East in the European system is in some degree similar to that which rules the relations between the United States and Latin America!

Therefore, the policy of Russia to resist the project of colonization of the Ukraine must be supported. But this positive Russian 'international policy' *is bound to fail* if it is not supported by the Russian people. And this support cannot be won on the exclusive basis of 'nationalism.' The support can be won only if the internal economic and social policy pursued promotes the interests of the majority of the working people. A people-oriented policy implies therefore moving away, as much as possible, from the 'liberal' recipe and the electoral masquerade associated with it, which claims to give legitimacy to regressive social policies. I would suggest setting up in its place a brand of new state capitalism with a social dimension (I say social, not socialist). That system would open the road to eventual advances toward a socialization of the management of the economy and therefore authentic new advances toward an invention of democracy responding to the challenges of a modern economy.

Russian state power remaining within the strict limits of the neoliberal recipe annihilates the chances of success of an independent foreign policy and the chances of Russia becoming a really emerging country acting as an important international actor.

Neoliberalism can produce for Russia only a tragic economic and social regression, a pattern of 'lumpen development,' and a growing subordinate status in the global imperialist order. Russia would provide the triad with oil, gas and some other natural resources; its industries would be reduced to the status of subcontracting for the benefit of Western financial monopolies. In such a position, which is not very far from that of Russia today in the global system, attempts to act independently in the international area will remain extremely fragile, threatened by 'sanctions' that will strengthen the disastrous alignment of the ruling economic oligarchy to the demands of dominant monopolies of the triad. The current outflow of 'Russian capital' associated with the Ukraine crisis illustrates the danger. Reestablishing state control over the movements of capital is the only effective response to that danger.

Outside China, which is implementing a national project of modern industrial development in connection with the renovation of family agriculture, the other so-called emergent countries of the South (the BRICS) still walk only on one leg: they are opposed to the depredations of militarized globalization, but remain imprisoned in the straightjacket of neoliberalism.[11]

REFERENCES

Amin, Samir (1992). *Empire of Chaos* (New York: Monthly Review Press).
Amin, Samir (2010). 'Russia in the World System', in *Global History: A View from the South* (London: Pambazuka Press, chapter 7).
Amin, Samir (2012). 'Contemporary Imperialism and the Agrarian Question', *Agrarian South: Journal of Political Economy* 1 (1), April, 11–26.
Amin, Samir (2013a). *Three Essays on Marx's Value Theory* (New York: Monthly Review Press, pp. 67–76).
Amin, Samir (2013b). 'China 2013', *Monthly Review* 64 (10), March, 14–33.
Amin, Samir (2013c). *The Implosion of Capitalism* (New York: Monthly Review Press, chapter 2).
Amin, Samir (2014a). 'Contra Hardt and Negri', *Monthly Review* 66 (6), November, 25–36.
Amin, Samir (2014b). 'The Return of Fascism in Contemporary Capitalism', *Monthly Review* 66 (4), September, 1–12.
Amin, Samir (2014c). 'Latin America Confronts the Challenge of Globalization', *Monthly Review* 66 (7), December, 1–6.
Amin, Samir (2015). 'From Bandung (1955) to 2015: New and Old Challenges for the Peoples and States of the South', Paper presented at the World Social Forum, Tunis, March.
Bukharin, Nicolai (1915 [1973]). *Imperialism and the World Economy* (New York: Monthly Review Press).
Foster, John Bellamy (1984). 'Marxian Crisis Theory and the State', in John Bellamy Foster and Henryk Szlajfer (eds), *The Faltering Economy* (New York: Monthly Review Press, pp. 325–49).
Frank, André Gunder and Samir Amin (1981). 'Let's Not Wait for 1984', in André

---

[11]   Concerning the inadequate responses of India and Brazil, see Amin (2013c, 2014c).

Gunder Frank (ed.), *Reflections on the World Economic Crisis* (New York: Monthly Review Press).

Hobsbawm, Eric J. (1990). *Echoes of the Marseillaise: Two Centuries Look Back on the French Revolution* (London: Verso).

Kautsky, K. (1899 [1988]). *The Agrarian Question*, 2 vols (London: Pluto Press).

Lenin, Vladimir (1916 [1969]). *Imperialism, The Highest Stage of Capitalism* (New York: International Publishers).

Roberts, Geoffrey (2007 [2014]). *Stalin's Wars: From World War to Cold War, 1939–1953* (New Haven, CT: Yale University Press). French edition published in 2014, *Les guerres de Staline: De la guerre mondiale à la guerre froide* (Paris: Éditions Delga).

Tandon, Yash (2015). *Trade is War* (New York: OR Books).

Conclusions*

Piotr Dutkiewicz

The authors of this book agree that the contours of a 'different' economic and political order are emerging as China is in the process of overtaking the USA as the world's largest economy, and a few other East and South Asian countries are steadily increasing their presence in global markets. The West is effectively struggling to hold on to its global pre-eminence, but the torch is slowly (albeit uncertainly) passing to a new generation of international players. Some version of a new multilateral order is emerging. It is one that is both different from the previous one, but also marked by multiple and significant continuities. This in itself is perhaps not surprising, and in this volume we set out to address several key questions that might help us better understand the directions, depth, consistency, long-term consequences and durability of this shift. In asking these questions, we also became, perhaps unavoidably, entangled in a side debate on the concept of development, as most authors have their own version/vision of it – as per Robert Shenton and Michael Cowen, the 'belief that the powers of productive force . . . could be controlled'[1] and reshaped by the deliberate actions of the state, people and capital.[2]

Our goal was to go 'beyond' (as the title of the book suggests) the new fashion of simply analysing, inventing and/or supporting new dividing lines within the global system. We did not follow – as Andrei Kortunov put it – 'The flavour of the season,' that is, 'the West versus the Rest' paradigm where

> The declining West is trying to preserve its global domination, while the rising Rest is fighting for an alternative world order denying the universalism of the Western institutions, principles and values. Russia and China are leading

---

* We agree that the notion of the 'West' is quite ambiguous. The authors focused on the heuristic of industrial, advanced, developed countries that might share certain fundamental political ideologies, including those of liberal democracy, the rule of law and individualist approach to human rights. The term 'Western world' is sometimes interchangeably used in this volume with 'developed country.'

[1] M. Cowen and Robert Shenton, *Doctrines of Development*, London: Routledge, 1996, p. 472.

[2] The central questions here being 'What state?' and 'Whose state?'

the rebellion of the Rest with Moscow questioning the US security hegemony and Beijing challenging the West-centered economic and financial system.[3]

Our main puzzle was rather to discuss why the income gap between the West and the Rest, which had been growing for nearly half a millennium, has started to close for some among 'the Rest' and increase for others. Is this a temporary or enduring phenomenon? As rising powers have different socio-economic and cultural foundations of development, this begs the second question of how the so-called 'Beijing Consensus' or 'Ankara Consensus' can influence international economic/political relations and ways we think about 'the state and market.'

This book advances three main arguments. The first group of arguments, based on evidence from three macro regions, are focused on reasons for a successful/unsuccessful economic convergence (see chapters by Popov and Sundaram, Popov, Lin, Ghosh, Ocampo). The second major argument – related to state-market relations in the Rest – proposes that a 'new developmentalism' should go beyond the reductionist approach of two dominating economic schools – structural (where the state rules) and neoliberal (where the unconstrained market dominates) toward a blend of both in a so-called 'dual-track approach' to secure accelerated growth (Popov, Lin, Bresser-Pereira). The third group of arguments advances ideas on policy measures and processes to improve the 'well-being of the Rest' (Popov, Lin, Patnaik, Ocampo, Sakwa, Amin).

THE CONVERGENCE VERSUS DIVERGENCE ARGUMENT

Economic history is a story of 'catch-up' attempts[4] and our book also begins (Popov and Sundaram) with a thick brush stroke picture of global shifts in the accumulation of wealth since the fifteenth century, when the ratio of average per capita income in the West (Western Europe) and the Rest (all other countries) was approximately 1:1. By the early twentieth century, the ratio of average per capita incomes in the West (Western Europe and its former settler colonies in North America and Australasia) and the global South (the now so-called developing countries) had increased dramatically – by 1900, the ratio of average per capita incomes in the West

---

[3] Andrei Kortunov, *The Inevitable Weird World*, 2016, http://russiancouncil.ru/en/inner/?id_4=7930#top-content (accessed 22 September 2016).

[4] Daniel Chirot (ed.), *The Origins of Backwardness in Eastern Europe, Economics and Politics from the Middle Ages until the Early Twentieth Century*, Berkeley, CA: University of California Press, 1991.

and the global South had increased to 6:1 – and remained at around that level for the next century. It is only from the second half of the twentieth century that the Rest closed the income gap. Together with the recent acceleration of growth in India, Bangladesh and some other developing countries, this seems to signify a partial end to the Great Divergence. It may well be that in the twenty-first century, the world will experience a gradual global convergence in income levels, with the gap between the North and the South narrowing.[5] Although, as Prabhat Patnaik warned, GDP as the only measure might obscure a more nuanced picture of 'growth,' the fact remains that the high growth in India has been accompanied by such an increase in economic inequality and such a process of 'social retrogression' that the country faces the real threat of social disintegration.

Our authors noted, however, that recent convergence is a fragile and uneven regionally distributed one (Latin America – see Ocampo), prone to backward movement (Patnaik) and dependent on many factors beyond the control of 'the Rest' (as the locus of dominant capital is still in the West – Bresser-Pereira). We devoted a separate chapter to how this fragile convergence may face a major reversal (Karatasli et al.).

In short, the bigger picture shows – nevertheless – that for the first time in half a millennium, from the economic perspective, the average gap in per capita GDP has stopped widening, and started to close – at least for several major emerging economies (Popov and Sundaram).[6]

Puzzling questions arise then on how enduring is this trend and whether economic convergence is reflected in a parallel process of political convergence (polity/policy/governance) or are both a reflection of the same global, neoliberal imperative to make (at a certain level – regional/local) twin convergence inevitable but at a lower level of growth for the Rest (Sakwa). We think that the endurance of the trend is an open-ended question and conditioned by a set of processes (see chapters by Karatasli

[5]   There are significant exceptions to the trend of catching up (in the GDP sense) especially in sub-Saharan Africa, as well as Eastern Europe and the former Soviet Union that have not been catching up, with some even falling behind, especially in the 1980s and 1990s. See J.A. Ocampo, J.K. Sundaram and Rob Vos (2007), 'Explaining Growth Divergences', in J.A. Ocampo and J.K. Sundaram (eds), *Growth Divergences. Explaining Differences in Economic Performance*, Hyderabad: Orient Longman. Similarly, some countries in Latin America and the Middle East experienced growth spurts and seemed to be catching up with the West in the second half of the twentieth century, but most of such growth spurts did not last (Ocampo). From the 1950s to the 1970s, many developing countries in Latin America experienced relatively fast growth, but most lost momentum after the debt crises of the early 1980s (Popov and Sundaram, Ocampo).

[6]   But we also highlight a cautious note by Jayati Ghosh in this volume that 'while the world economy has changed over the past three decades, this change should not be exaggerated for most developing regions, or even for most countries in what is apparently the most dynamic region of Asia.'

et al., Popov, Lin, Ghosh, Ocampo) that I shall discuss in the third section (on policies). As for political convergence (in the area of cross-national polity/policy/governance) we observed growing similarities in both governance structures and policies in the center and its periphery.[7] Based on a limited number of cases, we came to a tentative conclusion that there may be a convergence taking place between liberal democracies and non-liberal democratic regimes. Obviously, regime convergence does not mean that they are becoming the same but they are closer than they were (in our research time frame of two decades) in certain clearly defined areas (particularly in economic policies). The 'convergence' regime thesis may also explain why different regimes (in both West and the Rest) are displaying similar features.[8] The argument is that a neoliberal world order is creating the same kind of pressures for a hollowed out state (the process that can be best described as 'politics without a center'), whose main function is to create stability and order for market economies. But what does it mean for the process of economic convergence? This component of the puzzle is not researched sufficiently in the book. But based on this volume's evidence we may suggest (adding to the criticism of neoliberalism) that the economic catching-up process (or, in other words, the process of economic convergence) actually requires less political/policy convergence ('divergence' from the current global trend) as there is agreement among the authors that accelerated growth requires stronger state (and its institutions) and greater policy flexibility, reflecting the local/regional and social/civilizational and geographic environment (Popov, Lin, Patnaik).

DEVELOPMENT – STATE–MARKET

As described in the previous section, the debate about economic convergence/divergence (Karatasli et al, Lin, Bresser-Pereira, Ghosh, Ocampo) is intimately linked to the discussion about the *state of the state* and its economic role (see Sakwa on the European Union (EU)). The dominant (neo)liberal argument is that economic liberalization is identified with a race to the bottom by the 'competition state.'[9] This requires the

---

[7] Vincent DellaSala and Piotr Dutkiewicz, 'Politics Without a Centre: Political Change and Stability in Russia and Italy', www.researchgate.net/publication/281897628_Politics_Without_a_Centre_Political_Change_and_Stabilit y_in_Russia_and_Italy (accessed 22 September 2016).

[8] https://ecpr.eu/Filestore/PaperProposal/a5e52a9a-d9a3-4b38-aa61-9686712fcea9.pdf (accessed 17 February 2017).

[9] 'The transformation of the Nation State into a "competition state" lies at the heart of political globalization. In seeking to adapt to a range of complex changes in cultural, institutional and market structures both state and market actors are attempting to reinvent the state

state first to act as a quasi-entrepreneur and second, using agreed, globally unified policies.[10] For most authors of this volume, the state (and its
institutions) are key vehicles in enabling catching up, but our faith in an
activist state comes with a strong warning: the state (and its institutions)
may be both helpful (Southeast Asia) and damaging (Latin America) to
economic growth. The reason is, as Vladimir Popov writes,

> Reforms that are needed to achieve success are different for countries with
> different backgrounds and at different stages of development. Manufacturing
> growth is like cooking a good dish – all needed ingredients should be in the right
> proportion; if only one is under- or overrepresented, the 'chemistry of growth'
> will not happen . . . Fast economic growth can materialize in practice only if
> several necessary conditions are met at the same time.

Can we detect those 'ingredients' and 'right moments' to apply the 'right
policies'? Can the experience of those developing countries demonstrating
fast growth (such as China and East Asian economies) be replicated in the
Rest?

Four main clusters of lessons – in breaking with peripheral economic
status – seem to emerge from the regional experiences analysed in this book.
The first suggests that there is no 'model' of economic growth that can be
taken from any existing developmental toolboxes. Reliance either on the
market (neoliberal approach) or the state (structuralist theory) in imitating
the success of others has proved to be a false recipe. Both the invisible hand
of the market and a very visible hand of the state – rigidly applied – have
failed to achieve the intended goals (Ghosh, Patnaik, Ocampo).

This failure suggests the need to have a mix of both. Justin Lin writes,
'The few success economies have something in common: they were a
market economy or transiting to a market economy, as emphasized by
neoliberalism, while their governments also intervened actively in the
economy, as emphasized by structuralism.' East Asia serves as an example.
China's dual-track reform continued to protect and subsidize non-viable
state-owned firms in the old prioritized capital-intensive industries, while
liberalizing the market for labor-intensive industries, which had been
repressed. Economies 'that experienced stability and rapid growth in the
transition, like Cambodia, China, Vietnam and Mauritius, all followed
the gradual, dual-track reform approach' (Lin). It seems, however, that
the main danger on that road and potential check on further growth in

---

as quasi "enterprise association" in a wider world context . . .'. Philip G. Cerny, *Government
and Opposition*, **32** (2), April, 1997, p. 251.
[10] Policy diversity is, as we argue, a *condicio sine qua non* for locally defined developmental tasks harmonized with their historical cum cultural cum social environment (Popov, Lin,
Patnaik).

the region is the increase in income and wealth inequality which has been rising since the 1980s (Popov and Sundaram). That – in turn – could result in 'social upheavals in countries [in fact in most of the developing world] where social tensions rise due to growing inequalities.' Prabhat Patnaik supports this observation by arguing that 'high growth [in India] has been accompanied by such an increase in economic inequality and such a process of "social retrogression" that the country faces a real threat of social disintegration.' Thus, the argument we repeatedly pursue in this volume is that economic growth alone does not guarantee success if the state is unable to transform it into a more equitable society.

Second, as Justin Yifu Lin argues, in engaging simultaneously the market and the state, the role of the state is that of a strategically pro-grammed insurance company, infrastructure manager and institutional facilitator (with a component of social protection) that, on the one hand, limits the risks of those local market participants that are engaged in pio-neering technological and structural change (so-called first movers) and, on the other hand, provides infrastructure and strong institutional support for them to became globally competitive (Popov, Patnaik). Additionally, of crucial importance to East and South Asia has been pursuing the so-called dual-track approach.[11] Based on the East Asian experience, Justin Yifu Lin concludes that 'By spontaneous market forces alone without the government playing a facilitating role, the structural change will not happen at all or will happen very slowly.' Simultaneously, the danger is that an overgrown state over the longer term (after initially being very suc-cessful in state-led industrialization – see Ocampo on the Latin American experience) may suffocate development.[12] Hence, the sequence of reform/support to the technological/industrial market-based projects and timing becomes one of the key factors in successful developmental projects.[13]

Africa – with a few exceptions – can serve as another warning signal of state-dominated economies (particularly until the mid 1980s), where 'development' interventions were conditioned by the 'central and direct involvement of the state in the appropriation of surplus value from producers'[14] that led to the process of 'etatization' and the crisis of

---

[11] 'China's dual-track reform continued to protect and subsidize non-viable state-owned firms in the old prioritized capital-intensive industries while liberalizing the market for labor-intensive industries, which had been repressed' (Lin).

[12] The region's share in world GDP increased up to 1980, from 1.9 percent in 1820 to 9.5 percent in 1980; it then fell to 8.0 percent during the lost decade, and has remained around that level since then.

[13] 'The few success economies have something in common: they were a market economy or transiting to a market economy, as emphasized by neoliberalism, while their governments also intervened actively in the economy, as emphasized by structuralism' (Lin).

[14] James Fergusson, *The Anti-politics Machine*, Cape Town, 1990, p. 267.

'diminished reproduction'[15] in which the main beneficiaries were in most cases ruling groups using the state for – almost a sole purpose – their own social reproduction.[16] Later in that decade – in a swing change and with just a few exceptions – African countries adopted the recipes of the Washington Consensus[17] with similar negative impact.[18]

Third, bringing us to another link between state and development, is the leadership. We have already noted that using the state as a lever, insurer, infrastructure and security provider raises the question of the role of leadership and social participation in development (if not the more general issue of the democratic process in the Rest). These are closely linked in emerging economies in disturbing ways, in which achieving strong governance/state, liberal democracy might not be an imperative, as we see in East Asia or Russia. Business in emerging economies is caught in an existential dilemma – to have a weak state seems to be good for business (not paying taxes, ability to corrupt officials, ability to bypass the rules and so on), but to have a very weak state is bad for business too. The main problem is that the state – the neoliberal version of it – is in fact too weak to secure/protect the gains of the dominant capital and secure property rights. There emerges a distinct need by the local/international capital to find the ideal individual/collective holder of the trusteeship. In other words, the questions are: Who is to lead society into development and progress? Who can be entrusted to lead the change? In their brilliant book on development (see footnote 1), Shenton and Cowan observed that a 'handful of chosen men' could now assume the mantle of the 'active spirit' to become the inner determination of development regardless of the system of governance and its ideological dress. As James Fergusson rightly observed, 'The State', in this conception, 'is not the name of an actor, it is the name of a way of tying together multiplying and coordinating power relations, a kind of knotting or congealing of power.'[19]

---

[15]   Piotr Dutkiewicz and Gavin Williams, 'All the King's Horses and All the King's Men Couldn't Put Humpty-Dumpty Together Again', *IDS Bulletin*, **18** (3), Sussex University, 1987, pp. 1–6; Piotr Dutkiewicz and R. Shenton, 'Etatisation and the Logic of Diminishing Reproduction in Africa', *Review of African Political Economy*, **2**, 1986, p. 108–16.

[16]   'Like corruption, inefficiency in establishing and managing state enterprises . . . rather than preventing the social reproduction of this ruling groups, was an absolute prerequisite for it' (Dutkiewicz and Shenton, 'Etatisation', p. 108).

[17]   The original ten tenets of the Washington Consensus were: (i) fiscal discipline; (ii) reordering public expenditure priorities; (iii) tax reform (broad base with moderate rates); (iv) liberalizing interest rates; (v) competitive (not overvalued) exchange rates; (vi) trade liberalization; (vii) liberalization of inward foreign direct investment; (viii) privatization; (ix) deregulation; and (x) property rights (for the informal sector) (Lin).

[18]   James Fergusson, *Global Shadows: Africa in the Neoliberal World Order*, Durham, NC: Duke University Press, 2006.

[19]   Fergusson, *The Anti-politics Machine*, p. 269.

The enabling condition for steering such governance arrangements is to make society apolitical first and vividly consumerist second. It seems that we spent little time in this volume discussing whether such an outcome (treating the state as a form of trusteeship and pushing 'democracy' down the priority list of the developmental agenda) is a fair price or casualty of the new wave of catching up (development).

DEVELOPMENTAL MATRIX

This book does not propose another 'model for development.' Instead we – collectively – propose a complex matrix of 'developmental processes/policies' (varying from case to case) that might accelerate the catching-up process in emerging economies. Based on the diverse regional experiences represented by our contributors, the proposed 'developmental processes' are based on the (a) dual-track, gradual change that is (b) led by both state and market in (c) selected areas chosen for the presence of natural and human resources and (d) implemented in a given country-specific timeline and culture. Our authors differ in their priorities regarding these factors. For example, Justin Lin argues that a country's economic structure at any specific time is endogenous to its given factor endowments, that is, the amounts of capital, labor and natural resources, and posits that the 'economy's factor endowments is the starting point for development analysis for two reasons. First, they are an economy's total budget at that time, and second, the structure of endowments determines the relative prices of factors: prices of relatively abundant factors are low, while prices of relatively scarce factors are high.' For Vladimir Popov, the key factor is a state's institutional capacity. For Bresser-Pereira, of primary importance is mobilization of domestic savings and positive current account of the balance of payments. For Jayati Ghosh, industrialization and diversification is an essential part of development but only if financial liberalization is kept in check. Prabhat Patnaik stresses the role and quality of political elites in overcoming inequalities as one of the policy priorities.

I would like to conclude this section by briefly discussing two major constraints on the development trajectory. The first is the notion of a so-called 'asymmetry of rationalities'[20] and the second the consequences

[20] 'Improper sequence of liberalization and the global logics ability to inject institutions and procedures that are rational from its own perspective but not from the perspective of the level of development (historical time) of peripheries lead to unsteerability and incomplete capitalism of the latter.' Jadwiga Staniszkis, 'The Asymmetry of Rationalities (Power of Globalization)', *Polish Sociological Review*, 3 (143), 2003, p. 275.

of a diminishing state sovereignty for economic development (with limited available policy choices[21]).

From a macro sociological perspective Staniszkis's notion of 'asymmetry of rationalities' can be fruitful in explaining – at least partially – why many in the Rest were not able to implement relevant policies in the process of catching up. She writes:

> Improper sequence of liberalization and the global logics ability to inject institutions and procedures that are rational, from its own perspective, but not from the perspective of the level of development (historical time) of peripheries lead to unsteerability . . . This leads to a situation within which – even when all the institutional networks are based upon the economic rationality of the market – there is one logic for the local, 'young' market (whose overriding directive is the accumulation of capital, and whose institutional infrastructure is poorly developed) and another logic for the mature market, one poised for expansion.[22]

Along the same lines, some of our authors (Patnaik, Ghosh, Lin) have highlighted that in many cases (Southeast Asia, Latin America) massive imitation of Western economic models, policies and institutions that are not synchronized with local endowment and 'level of development' lead to economic failures. Bresser-Pereira argues that the Rest will be able to catch up and grow faster than the West only if they go against a 'received truth,' namely, that capital-rich countries should transfer their capital to capital-poor countries. Jayati Ghosh comes to a similar conclusion in analysing a 'market stability factor' that 'may play and indeed has played a positive role in some phases of global capitalist growth [but] such stability may actually serve to cement existing unequal divisions of labour in various ways,' thus impeding further growth. Justin Yifu Lin writes about the failure of an import-substitution strategy used in Latin America in an attempt to develop the advanced industries prevailing in the West and defy the comparative advantages of the 'periphery.'

The last variable in the 'best policy choice' debate in our volume is an issue of (state) sovereignty. As described earlier,[23] the general trend seems to be the erosion of the authority of a political center in the form of a sovereign power. As that power evaporates from the state and shifts its locus (Sakwa),[24]

---

[21]   As Sakwa convincingly shows in this book based on relations, for example, between the postmodern EU versus 'modern' Russia.

[22]   Staniszkis, 'The Asymmetry of Rationalities'.

[23]   https://ecpr.eu/Filestore/PaperProposal/a5e52a9a-d9a3-4b38-aa61-9686712fcea9.pdf (accessed 17 February 2017).

[24]   In analysing EU 'behavior', Sakwa points to 'the struggle between universalist representations of global engagement [such as the EU] against particularist articulations of

becoming freer from political control[25]), the 'capacity' (or 'power') to intervene in the economy is diminishing, thus creating an additional layer of challenges for the Rest at a time when such interventions are necessary (Popov, Lin, Ocampo).

CONTOURS OF THE NEW WORLD ORDER IN THE TWENTY-FIRST CENTURY

T.E. Lawrence – in David Lean's masterpiece movie *Lawrence of Arabia* – told Sherif Ali 'Nothing is written.'[26] The authors of this volume share this view about the contours of the new order. We have offered a conceptualization of a new approach to economic convergence but stopped short of suggesting that it forms a new 'developmental model' to be imitated. Instead, we propose a process of change rooted in reinforced relations between state and market based on positive evidence coming from Southeast Asia (Popov and Sundaram, Popov, Lin, Ghosh).

Thus, we predict that there is a high probability of successful catch-up development of East and South Asia and MENA countries, whereas Latin America, Russia and sub-Saharan Africa may be falling behind for some time. 'However, it may well be that states would transit from one institutional trajectory to another – countries with low inequalities and strong institutions can join the opposite group and vice versa' (Popov).

We are also in agreement (Popov and Sundaram, Lin, Patnaik, Ocampo) that the main locus of growth is – at the moment – East and South Asia. Although nascent so far, the rise of China (among others) may trigger profound reforms to international financial and economic relations as it offers a set of specific policies to other emerging economies that goes beyond economic orthodoxy.[27] The result may be more favorable conditions for

national identity in the international sphere, which can also be interpreted as the tension between critical geopolitics and uncritical normativism.'

[25]   Zygmunt Bauman, 'Re-create the Social State', in P. Dutkiewicz and R. Sakwa (eds), *22 Ideas to Fix the World*, New York: SUNY, 2013, pp. 186–202.

[26]   Sherif Ali responded later, 'Truly for some men nothing is written unless they write it.'

[27]   For instance, exchange rate undervaluation despite accumulation of foreign exchange reserves, export-oriented industrial policy, prudential management of international capital flows and other heterodox measures can become more legitimate tools for catch-up development. There may be reforms to intellectual property rights to facilitate affordable technology transfers, new regulations for the international trade in energy and resources, new monetary arrangement, new agreements for cutting undesirable emissions and so on. See Manuel Montes and Vladimir Popov, 'Bridging the Gap: A New World Economic Order for Development?', in C. Calhoun and G. Derluguian (eds), *Aftermath: New Global Economic Order*, New York: SUNY, 2011, pp. 119–47.

catch-up development of all countries in the South and lower disparities between the world's 'rich' and 'poor.'[28]

We may also witness – as a result of newly acquired economic power – development and strengthening of new international institutions initiated by the regional players and based on different developmental logic that may lead to the democratization of international economic relations and form a counterweight/alternative to the World Bank and International Monetary Fund. For instance, the BRICS New Development Bank, the Asian Infrastructure Investment Bank and the Eurasian Economic Union may start such a process.

This volume offers some crucial warnings that a reversal of fortune for those so far successful in 'catching up' is possible or that it might be limited to just a few. Those warnings are scattered throughout this volume and the chapter by Karatasli et al. concludes that 'In sum, in the early twenty-first century, there is no "catching up" with core locations but instead another reconfiguration of the hierarchy of wealth among non-core locations.'

We believe that this book will revitalize a substantial international debate about global developmental paths.

---

[28] The precondition for a developing country to use the advantage of backwardness is to follow the comparative advantage determined by its own factor endowment in the industrial upgrading and technological innovation in a market economy with a facilitating state ... Regrettably, under the drive of nation building and the influence of prevailing structuralism, the governments in most developing countries adopted an import-substitution strategy attempting to defy their comparative advantages and jumping directly to develop the advanced industries prevailing in the West. (Lin).

Index

absolute poverty 132, 134
abstract labor 186
accountability 30
accumulation 60–61, 63
    cycles of 24–5, 29, 34
    primitive 130, 131–2
Acemoglu et al. 45
affirmative action 134
Afghanistan 45
Africa 12, 14, 29, 33, 40, 85–6, 184,
        201–2
    decolonization 9
    see also MENA countries; sub-
        Saharan Africa
agrarian reform 156
agriculture 76, 105, 106
    China 183, 194
    India 116, 117, 129–30, 131
    Latin America 140, 144
    Soviet Russia 182
aid, foreign 39
Akyuz, Yilmaz 98
Ambedkar 126–7
America see Latin America
Amsden, Alice 7
Andean Group 143
Ankara Consensus 197
anti-colonial struggle 125–6, 129
    see also colonization
Argentina 10, 93, 144, 148, 154,
        156
armament 182
Armenia 170
Arrighi et al. 31, 32
Arrighi, Giovanni 24–5, 26, 29, 32, 34,
        35
Asia 14, 17, 18–20, 29–30, 32, 33, 40,
        49, 93, 106–19
    decolonization 9
    exporting manufactured goods to
        the West 71–2

global GDP, share in 97–8
    inequalities, decline of 50
    and peasantry 184
    per capita income 100, 102
    PPP GDP 15, 16
    and Russia 171, 177
    savings-investment ratio 47, 48
    see also East Asia
Asian financial crisis (1997–98) 106–7,
        111, 112
Asian Infrastructure Investment Bank
        206
asset bubbles 113
'associated dependency' theory 80
Association Agreement 166
asymmetry of rationalities 203, 204
Atlantic Charter 174
Atlanticism 5
authoritarianism 135, 168
availability, per capita 130, 133

backwardness 61, 67
Bagchi, Amiya 92
Baker Plan 79
balance of payment crises 86
the Balkans 164, 175
Bangladesh 8, 198
banks 39, 72, 102, 103, 119
Beijing Consensus 197
Belarus 164, 170
Bértola, Luis 138, 151
beta-convergence 7
Big Push 12
bimodal global wealth distribution 26,
        27, 30–31
'Black Legend' 151
Bolivia 144, 148
Botswana 14, 17
Bourbon reforms 138
bourgeoisie 124, 190
Bourguignon, Francois 27

Brazil 16, 75–6, 138, 139, 140, 151
  and direct foreign direct investment 87
  exports 71, 79, 141, 146
  growth 12, 14, 154
Bresser-Pereira et al. 75–6
Bresser-Pereira, Luiz Carlos 6, 84, 203, 204
Brexit vote 172
BRICS 176, 192, 194, 206
Britain 26, 31–2, 181
British Empire 30, 32
budgets, balancing 57
Bukharin, Nikolai 181–2, 185
Burgess, J. Peter 174

Cambodia 58
capital 12, 73, 76, 188, 204
  abundance 60
  accumulation 60–61, 63, 130, 131–2
  centralized control of 189, 190
  globalized finance 128
capital account surpluses 104
capital flows 49, 50, 104–5
capital inflows 85, 87, 103, 104, 105, 106, 107
capital-intensive industries 60, 62, 63, 64–5
capitalism 4–5, 6, 49, 124–5, 131, 191
  crony 39
  historical 29, 34, 181, 184–5
  history of 24–5
  a 'spontaneous' system 128
  state 193, 194
capitalist world-economy 31
Capital (Marx) 25, 130, 186
capital outflows 87, 114
Cárdenas et al. 138
Carr, E.H. 173
caste system 125, 126, 133, 134, 135
Central America 33
Central American Common Market 143
Central Europe 39, 40
centrally planned economies 11–12, 64
Chang, Ha-Joon 80–81
Charter of Paris for a New Europe 161
Chechen wars 169
Chile 63, 144, 145, 156, 157

China 3–4, 6, 14, 16, 17–20, 26, 48–9, 53, 55, 94, 112–16, 191–2, 205
  decline 32
  dual-track reform 58, 64, 67, 200
  family agriculture 194
  and foreign direct investment 38, 87
  GDP 54, 96–7
  liberalization 40
  revolution 183–4
  and Russia 170, 171, 177
  trading partner of Latin America 147
classical developmentalism 72–3, 88
coffee 138, 140, 144
collective imperialism 190, 192
collective property 50
collectivist institutions 46, 48, 49
collectivization 182, 183
Colombia 140, 141, 154
colonization 5, 32, 45, 47, 53, 88, 126, 137
  India 125
  Latin America 138–40
  and primitive accumulation of capital 130
commercial banks 119
commodities 143–4, 146, 147, 149, 151
commodity prices 5, 137, 145, 146, 152–3
commodity processing 141
commodity producer 5, 137
Common European Economic Space (CEES) concept 166
Common European Home 168
Commonwealth of Independent States (CIS) 40
communism 14, 184
comparative advantages 60, 61, 63, 64, 67, 71, 76, 146
  Latin America 204
  Taiwan 65
competition 185
competitive advantage 60
Concert of Powers 175
conditionality 164
Conference on Security and Cooperation in Europe (CSCE) 161
conflicts 49, 50, 191
Confucianism 66

construction 114, 119
consumer debt 112
consumption, credit-driven 118
convergence 6, 7–21, 23, 95, 121, 154, 197, 198, 199
Copenhagen criteria 166
copper 144
Costa Rica 138, 140
Coudenhove-Kalergi, Richard 168
Council of Europe 169
counter-cyclical policies 153
Cowen, Michael 196, 202
credit-driven consumption 118
crime rates 49, 50
Croatia 175
crony capitalism 39
CSTO (Collective Security Treaty Organization) 169
Cuba 139, 140, 144, 146, 154, 155
currency
    devaluation 65
    overvalued 87
current account balance 4, 82, 86, 203
current account deficits 72, 73, 74, 75, 77, 82, 83–4, 86–7
    in East Asia 107
    in India 117, 118
    and political economy 88
    and private domestic investment 104
current account surplus 74, 82, 83–4, 85, 86
Customs Union 170
cycles of accumulation (SCAs) 24–5, 29, 30, 34
Cyprus 42

debt 77, 88, 112, 113, 119
debt crisis (1980s) 138, 151, 156, 157
debt-financed overinvestment 57
debt–GDP ratio 113
debt ratios 153
debt servicing 79
decolonization 9
    see also colonization
Deep and Comprehensive Free Trade Area (DCFTA) 166–7
deflation 105
de-industrialization 103, 125, 145, 151–2

democracy, decline of 189
democratic revolution 123, 124, 125
demographic dividend 150
Deng Xiaoping 66, 183
Departments I, II, III 186
dependency theorists 24
deregulation 57, 102, 103, 117
developing countries 4, 7, 47, 62, 63, 197–8
    and current account deficits 77
    and factor endowments 60
    and growth cum foreign savings policy 80
    limited by the West 81
    and technological innovation 55
    see also global South
development banks 119
development economics 55–7, 71, 72, 79, 80
development planning 158
development project 33
Diaz-Alejandro, Carlos F. 142
diminished reproduction 202
direct investment 73, 78, 86
dirigiste economic regime 128–9
disintegration 123, 124, 135, 198
divergence 7, 8–9, 149, 154
    see also Great Divergence
diversification 121, 203
Doing Business Index 63
domestic investment 75, 104, 107
domestic savings 4, 76, 77, 84, 85, 103, 203
    and investment 108, 112
domestic savings rates 75, 107
Dominican Republic 140, 146
drain of surplus 125, 130
Drangel, Jessica 26
dual-track reform 58, 64, 67, 197, 200, 201
Dutch disease 82–3, 85, 86

EaP (Eastern Partnership) 163, 166, 175
East Asia 2, 3–4, 11, 12, 14, 17, 29, 32, 33, 40, 49, 53, 55, 58, 63–8, 85–6, 205
    China 18–20
    and exports 93
    and foreign investment 79

GDP per capita 54
  growth 13, 14, 200
  and industrialization 152
  inequalities, decline of 50
  and liberalization 107
  savings-investment ratio 47, 48
Eastern Europe 29, 32, 49, 169, 193
ECHR (European Convention on
  Human Rights) 169
ECLAC (United Nations Economic
  Commission for Latin America
  and the Caribbean) 143
ECLA (Economic Commission for
  Latin America) 142
economic convergence 6, 7–21, 23, 95,
  121, 154, 197, 198, 199
economic development, definition 61
economic growth 11–13, 59, 67, 117,
  200
  Latin America 149, 150, 152, 155
  per capita 74, 75
  and stability 92
  and wages 120
economic inequality 4, 123, 133, 198,
  201
economic liberalism 73
economic liberalization 38, 157, 158,
  199–200
economic nationalism 72, 73
Economic Survey of Latin America 142
ECtHR (European Court of Human
  Rights) 169
Ecuador 158
education 133–5, 151, 154, 155, 157
elites 71, 76, 80, 87, 88, 118, 132, 151
  militant 173
  political 203
  and rentism 158
employment 39, 100, 121, 132, 133
endowment structure 60, 61
ENP (European Neighbourhood
  Policy) 163, 167–8
entrepreneurs 61, 62
equality 156
Erten, Bilge 144
Estonia 164
etatization 201
Ethiopia 45
Eurasian Economic Union (EEU)
  170–71, 177, 206

Eurasian integration 175–6
Eurasian Union (EaU) 170
Europe 29–30, 32, 40, 49
  Western 7, 14, 19, 27, 59
European Commission 171
European External Action Service
  (EEAS) 171
European Union (EU) 5, 6, 161–77,
  190, 192
exchange rate populism 80
exchange rates 57, 64, 82, 83, 84, 86,
  103
  capital inflows, affect of 85, 105
  in East Asia 107
  flexible 188
export-led industrialization 121
export-oriented development strategy
  58
exports 71, 79, 93, 107
  China 112, 114, 116
  diversification 143
  Latin America 140–41, 146–7, 149,
  151, 152–3
export substitution 64
external governance 162

factor endowments 60, 63, 67, 203
factor prices 60
family farming 187, 194
farmers 187
'Feldstein–Horioka puzzle' 75
Fergusson, James 202
fictitious capital 188
finance 72–88, 119, 152, 153
financial crises
  Asian (1997–98) 106–7, 111, 112
  Global (2008–09) 112, 163
financial deregulation 117
financial intermediaries 103
financialization 72, 81, 94, 187, 188
financial liberalization 80, 99, 100, 102,
  103, 120, 121, 203
  and Asian crisis 107, 108, 111
  and bias towards deflationary
  macroeconomic policies 105–6
  in India 118
Findlay, Ronald 91–2
first movers 61–2
First Opium War 32
fiscal discipline 151, 152

fiscal populism 80
foreign aid 39
foreign banks 72
foreign capital 76, 121
foreign debt 77, 88
foreign debt crisis (1980s) 79, 80
foreign direct investment 38, 57, 77, 78,
   87–8, 147–8
foreign finance 72–88
foreign savings 4, 75–7, 84, 85, 88, 107,
   111
Former Soviet Union (FSU) 40, 42
   see also Russia
France 171
Frank, Andre Gunder 32, 187, 189
free markets 57
free trade 38
French Revolution 183–4
Furtado, Celso 72

Gala, Paulo 84
Gandhi, Mahatma 126
Gaullist idea 168, 175
GDP (gross domestic product) 2, 123
   China 53, 114
   global 95–8
   growth rates 18, 113
   India 118, 123, 132
   Latin America 140, 152, 153
   Malaysia 108
   and Patnaik 198
   per capita 7, 8, 40–41, 54, 55, 149,
   150
   and shadow economy 40
   world 149
   see also PPP GDP (purchasing
      power parity gross domestic
      product) per capita
generalized-monopoly capitalism
   186–7, 188, 191
Genoa 29, 30
geography, impact on growth 45
Georgia 165
Germany 162–3, 171, 190
Gerschenkron, Alexander 67, 143
Ghosh, Jayati 203, 204
global financial crisis (2008–09) 112,
   163
global hierarchy of wealth 26
global income inequality 8–9

global inequality 2, 26
globalization 3, 6, 49, 50, 95, 150–51,
   154, 156, 174, 187
   capitalist 191
   and inequality 156
   militarized 194
globalization project 33
globalized bourgeoisie 190
globalized finance capital 128
globalized neoliberalism 192
globalized production system 189–91
global North 9
   see also the West
global South 7, 8, 9, 38, 40, 47, 197–8
   see also developing countries
global wealth 26–7, 30–31
Gold Standard 93
Gorbachev, Mikhail 168, 184
governance, external 162
government sector 134
Gramsci, Antonio 35
Great Britain 181
Great Depression 3, 50, 126, 129, 138,
   141
Great Divergence 8, 23, 24, 30, 198
greater Asia 177
greater Europe 5, 167, 168, 171, 172,
   174–5, 176, 177
Greece 14
gross national income (GNI) 26
Grossraum 174
growth 11–13, 14, 48, 59, 99–106
   Asia 67, 112, 200–201, 205
   China 113, 114
   and current account deficits 82
   fastest growing countries 18
   and foreign savings 75, 76–7
   GDP 123, 152, 153
   India 117, 198
   and inequality 128–9
   Latin America 155
   per capita income 21, 23, 24, 59, 74,
      75, 99, 100, 121, 149,
   Russia 42, 47
   and stability 92
   and wages 120, 121
growth cum foreign indebtedness 73,
   78, 81, 83
growth cum foreign savings 72, 76–7,
   79, 80, 81–2, 83–5, 88

growth rates 38–50, 79–80, 128, 149,
    150, 152

hacienda system 140
Haiti 138
hard infrastructure 59, 60, 62
healthcare 134
heavy industries 65
hegemonic stability 177
hegemony 2, 26, 30, 31–2, 33, 34
hexie 66
Hindu religious right *(Hindutva)* 135
Hirschman, Albert 80, 142, 143
Holland 25, 26, 29, 30
Hong Kong 7, 14, 15, 58, 64, 71
housing 112, 118
Human Development Report, 2013 23

illiteracy 155
immigration 156
imperialism 88, 181, 182, 183, 184, 190,
    192
import protectionism 121
imports 114, 116
import substitution 3, 57, 58, 62, 67,
    120, 143, 204
    from primary to secondary 64
import substitution industrialization
    57, 80, 138
income 60, 63
    distribution 155–6, 157
    gap 196
    inequality 3, 8–9, 19–20, 46, 47, 49,
        132, 201
    see also per capita income
indebtedness 78
India 4–5, 8, 14, 16, 17, 26, 31, 116–19,
    123–35, 181
    GDP 97, 98
    growth 198
    industrialization 93
Indian National Congress 126
Indian reservations 140
Indonesia 14, 16, 98, 108, 110, 111
industrial equilibrium 83
industrialization 73, 93, 99, 121, 141–7,
    152, 182, 203
    state-led 138, 149, 150, 151, 154, 155,
        156, 158
industrial revolution 59

industrial upgrading 55, 59, 60, 61, 62,
    64, 65, 67
    and Chile 63
    and Taiwan 65
inequality 3, 5, 48, 156, 203
    decline 50
    economic 4, 123, 133, 198, 201
    global 2, 26
    income 3, 8–9, 19–20, 46, 47, 49, 132
    institutional 125, 127
    low 49, 205
    under neoliberalism 128–9
    social 133–4
inflation 65, 79, 83, 151, 152
information revolution 189
infrastructure 59, 60, 61, 62, 119, 158
*An Inquiry into the Nature and Causes
    of the Wealth of Nations* (Smith)
    59
instability 93–4, 191
institutional capacity 2, 3, 40, 41, 42–3,
    45, 50, 203
institutional change 121
institutional development 2
institutional inequality 125, 127
institutions 2–3, 38, 40, 43–9, 61, 62,
    205, 206
interest rate 65, 82, 83
interest rate caps 57
intermarium 164, 165
international institutions 206
International Monetary Fund (IMF)
    79, 206
international regime 177
international trade 4, 49, 50
investment 73, 79, 86, 106
    capital inflows, affect of 85
    in China 113, 115
    and domestic savings 108, 112
    foreign direct 57, 77, 78, 147–8
    in India 118–19
    in Indonesia 110
    in Malaysia 109
    private domestic 104
    and UN 87–8
investment rates 75, 107, 111
Ireland 14
    Northern 42
Israel 14
Italy 171

Japan 11, 13, 14, 17, 38, 45, 58
  in the 1970s 39
  and changes in comparative
    advantages 64
  and collective imperialism 192
  and per capita income 2
  and PPP GDP 8, 15, 19
jiefangsixiang 66
Juncker, Jean-Claude 171

Karachi Resolution 126, 135
Karatasli et al. 206
Kautsky, K. 182
Kazakhstan 170
Keohane, Robert O. 177
Keynesianism 127–8
Keynes, John Maynard 55
Khodorkovsky, Mikhail 169
Korea, South *see* South Korea
Kortunov, Andrei 196–7
Kronstadt sailors 182
Kyrgyzstan 170

labor 61, 186
labor-intensive industries 64
labor mobility 140
labor productivity 55, 59, 60
labor productivity growth rates 11, 12,
  132
labour reserves 132
Latin America 5, 12, 27, 29, 32, 33, 39,
    40, 47, 48, 49, 85–6, 137–58, 205
  and 'associated dependency' theory
    80
  and colonialism 88
  and development economics 72
  and exporting manufactured goods
    79
  and global GDP, share in 97
  and import-substitution strategy 204
  and inequalities, decline of 50
  and lack of state capacity 40
  and PPP GDP 19
  and Washington Consensus 57
Latin American Free Trade Area 143
'Latin American manifesto' 142
Latvia 164
leadership 202
the Left movement 125, 126
Lenin, Vladimir 124, 181–2, 185

Lesotho 14
liberalism 73, 157–8, 174
liberalization 38, 40, 65, 79, 88, 157,
    158, 199–200
  see also financial liberalization
life expectancy 46, 47, 154–5
lifetime employment 39
Lin, Justin Yifu 201, 203, 204
liquidity 105
Lithuania 171
loans 77, 78, 88, 102, 119
Londoño, Juan Luis 156
The Long Twentieth Century (Arrighi)
    24–5
longue durée 26–7, 34
Love, Joseph L. 142

macroeconomic discipline 151
macroeconomic policies 81, 152–3
Mahmood, S. 64
Malaysia 14, 16, 98, 108, 109, 111
malpractice 102
Malthusian trap 47
manufacturing 46, 72, 100, 105, 114
  in Latin America 79, 80, 142, 143,
    145, 146
Mao Zedong 66, 183
maquilization 80
market economies 58, 64, 200
market reforms 57, 79, 145, 158
  Latin America 146, 147–8, 149–50,
    152, 155, 158
Marx, Karl 25, 59, 130, 186
Mauer, Rainer 7
Mauritius 58
Medvedev, President Dmitry 173
MENA countries 3, 40, 47, 48, 49, 97,
    205
MERCOSUR 146
Merkel, Angela 171
mestizo population 139, 140
metals 141
Mexico 16, 143, 144, 145–6, 148
  exports 71, 79, 140
  growth 154
  and maquilization 80
microeconomics 81
Middle East 12, 14, 33
middle-income countries 74
'middle income trap' 120

migration 149, 162–3
militarized globalization 6, 194
military dictatorships 157, 158
military expenditure 186
Millennium Development Goals 39
minerals 140, 144, 148
mining 76, 144
Minsk peace process 172
MITI (Ministry of International Trade
    and Industry)/Japan 39
Mogherini, Federica 171
monetary union 163
Monet, Jean 174
monitoring, financial 100, 102
monopolies 181
monopoly capitalism 185–7, 189
Monroe Doctrine 174
Montenegro 14
Morris, Ian 46
Morrisson, Christian 27
mortality rates 45, 50
mulatto population 139
multinational corporations 73, 78
murder rates 3, 40–41, 42, 44, 49, 50
Muslims 133, 134, 135

NAFTA (North American Free Trade
    Agreement) 145, 146
Nanjing Treaty 32
Napoleonic wars 139
nationalism, rise of 3, 49
nationalization 144
National Rural Employment
    Guarantee Scheme 129
National Sample Survey 133
national state 191
NATO (North Atlantic Treaty
    Organization) 169, 176
natural resource-based manufactures
    143
natural resource curse 83
natural resources 146, 147, 148, 152,
    158
neighbourhood policy 163–4, 167–8
neoclassical theory 80
neoliberal capitalism 4–5
neoliberalism 6, 56–7, 58, 62, 67, 80,
    127, 199
  and the BRICS 194
  in Chile 63

definition 197
and economic inequality 128–33
globalized 192
in India 131–2, 134, 135
and Russia 193–4
neo-revisionism 173, 177
NEP (New Economic Plan) 182
Netherlands 25, 26, 29, 30
new developmentalism 4, 6, 81–5, 197
New Development Bank 206
newly industrialized countries (NICs)
    71
new structural economics 58–63, 67–8
non-tradables 103–4, 107
norms
  contested 173
  and space 164, 165
North Africa 14, 40
Northern Ireland 42
Nurkse, Ragnar 73
nutritional deprivation 133

Ocampo, José Antonio 138, 144, 151
ODIHR (Office of Democratic
    Institutions and Human Rights)
    169
Odysseos, Louiza 174
oil 97, 140, 143, 144, 148, 154, 155, 193
Oman 14
Opium Wars 32, 48
Organisation for Economic Co-
    operation and Development
    (OECD) countries 75
Organization of Petroleum Exporting
    Countries (OPEC) 144
Oriental school 45–6
O'Rourke, Kevin H. 91–2
OSCE (Organization for Security and
    Co-operation in Europe) 169

PACE (Parliamentary Assembly of the
    Council of Europe) 169
Palat, Ravi Arvind 33
Panama 146
Park Chung Hee, President 65
'Partnership for Modernisation'
    programme 173
Patnaik, Prabhat 92, 198, 201, 203
peasantry 126, 129–30, 131, 182, 183,
    184

per capita GDP 7, 8, 40–41, 54, 55, 98,
    149, 150
per capita income 2, 7, 12, 14, 59, 121,
    197–8
  Asia 100, 102
  Latin America 149, 154
  Russia 10–11
Peru 140, 141
Peter the Great 10
Petitio, Fabio 174
petty production 129, 131
planned economies 58
Poland 163
political authoritarianism 135
political convergence 198, 199
political economy 81, 86–8, 120–21
political elites 203
political liberalism 157–8
political parties 158
Pombaline reforms 138
Pomeranz, Kenneth 30
Popov, Vladimir 200, 203
population growth 149–50
Portugal 14, 29
poverty 132–3, 134
poverty reduction 39, 155–6
PPP GDP (purchasing power parity
    gross domestic product) per capita
    8, 9, 14, 17, 19, 98, 99
  Asia 15, 16
PP (purchasing parity) income 74, 75
Prebisch, Raúl 72, 142
Prebisch–Singer law 78
precious metals 138
prices of factors 60
primary export/import substitution
    64
primitive accumulation 130, 131–2
private domestic investment 104
private sector 134
privatization 57, 79, 80, 134, 147–8
pro-cyclical macroeconomic policies
    152–3
Prodi, Romano 163
production
  factor costs 60
  globalized system 189–91
productive labor 186
productivity
  capital 11, 12, 46

labor 11, 12, 46, 55, 59, 60, 100, 116,
    132, 186
  total factor (TFP) 11, 12
profits 78, 82, 117, 186
proletarianization 188
property 103–4, 107, 113, 119
  rights 57
protectionism 3, 38, 50, 57, 121, 142,
    144
protections 62–3, 63
public property 50
public services 134
public spending 117–18
Puerto Rico 139
Putin, Vladimir 166, 167, 170, 171,
    172, 177, 184, 192

Qing dynasty 32
quadrimodal global wealth distribution
    27, 33, 34–5

Ranis, G. 64
real estate 102, 103–4, 107, 113, 119
redistribution through fiscal means 129
refugees 162–3
regime convergence 199
Reinert, Erik 80–81, 92
rentism 158
re-primarization 79–80
resource mobilization 65
respatialization 174
restoration 184
retail credit boom 117
revolutions 181–2, 183–4
Ricardian comparative advantage 76
Ricardian rents 83
rich country status, losing 10
rightist political groups 49
Rise of the South (UNDP) 95
Rodrik, D. 45, 152
Rodrik et al. 39, 45
rural poor 157
Russia 5, 6, 13, 18, 182, 205
  and collectivist institutions 48–9
  enemy of the triad 192, 193–4
  and the EU 161, 163, 164, 165,
      166–7, 168–73, 174, 175, 176–7
  growth 10–12, 42, 47
  revolution 181–2, 183–4
Russo–EU summit, 2014 172

Saakashvili, Mikheil 165
savings 4, 103, 104, 105–6, 107, 108,
    203
  in China 114
  foreign savings and growth 75–7
  foreign versus domestic 84, 85
  in India 118
  in Indonesia 110
  in Taiwan 65
savings displacement 76
savings-investment rate 47, 48
savings rates 107, 111
Schengen regulations 162
Schmitt, Carl 174
schooling 154
Schuman proposals 174
science and technology 152
Second Opium War 32
Second World War 142
securities 102
serfdom, elimination of 10
services 116, 146
shadow banking 113
shadow economy 3, 40–41, 43
Shanghai Cooperation Organization
    (SCO) 176
Shanghai Stock Exchange 115
Shenton, Robert 196, 202
shishiqiushi 66
shock therapy 58, 64, 67
sigma-convergence 7
Silk Road 177
Silk Road Economic Belt (SREB) 170
Silver, Beverly J. 35
Singapore 7, 14, 15, 58, 64, 71, 72
Single Economic Area 170
slavery 139–40, 156
slowdown 154
smaller Europe 167
Smith, Adam 58–9
social development 154–8
social disintegration 123, 124, 135,
    198
social equality 156
social inequality 133–4
socialism 49, 50
social reform movement 125, 126
social services 158
social spending 155, 158
social transfer mechanism 158

soft infrastructure 59, 60, 61, 62
South Africa 32
South America 33
  see also Latin America
South Asia 2, 17, 20, 33, 40, 49, 205
  savings-investment ratio 47, 48
Southeast Asia 8, 14, 16, 93
Southern Cone countries 140–41, 145,
    151, 154, 155, 156, 157
Southern Europe 32
South Korea 8, 11, 38, 64, 72, 120,
    121
  exporting manufactured goods to
      the West 71
  and export-oriented development
      strategy 58
  financial liberalization 107
  global GDP, share in 97–8
  growth 13, 14
  heavy and chemical industry drive 65
  and PPP GDP per capita 15
  and structural change 99–100, 101
sovereign democracy 167
sovereignty 174, 175, 203–5
Soviet Union 10–12, 13, 18, 193
  former republics 40, 49
space
  greater 174
  and norms 164, 165
Spain 14
Spanish America 139
  see also Latin America
Spanish-American war, 1898 139
spending
  public 117–18
  social 155, 158
Sri Lanka 14
stability 63, 92, 93, 183, 204
stagnation 154
Stalin, Joseph 181, 182
Staniszkis, Jadwiga 203, 204
the state 191
  economic role 199–200, 201–2
  India 128
  institutional capacity 2, 3, 40, 41
  interventions 56
  and the market 158
  protecting peasant agriculture
      129–30
state capitalism 6, 193, 194

state-led industrialization 138, 150,
    151, 154, 155, 156, 158
  anti-export bias 143
  and rapid economic expansion
    149–50
state-owned enterprises 57, 144, 148
state sovereignty 203–5
stock exchange 115
stock market 107, 113–14
stocks, investment in 102
Stolypin's reforms 10
structural adjustment 79
structural adjustment lending 57
structural change 99–106, 109, 111,
    117, 132
structural economics 6, 197
  new 58–63, 67–8
structuralism 56, 58
sub-Saharan Africa 14, 27, 32, 33, 39,
    40, 49, 205
  global GDP, share in 97
  poor growth 47, 48
subsidies 62–3
sugar 138, 141
superclass 189
Surkov, Vladislav 167
surplus absorption 186
Suslov, Dmitry 170
Sweden 163
Székely, Miguel 156

Taiwan 8, 14, 15, 64, 72, 120, 121
  exporting manufactured goods to
    the West 71
  and export-oriented development
    strategy 58
  growth 11, 13
  heavy industries 65
Tandon, Yash 192–3
tariffs 78, 142, 151
taxation 105
tax breaks 57
technological cum structural change
    132
technological innovation 55, 59, 61,
    62, 67
technology and Latin America 146,
    147, 150, 152
technology-intensive industries 62
Tetlock et al. 45

textile industry 142
TFP (total factor productivity) growth
    rates 11, 12
Thailand 14, 16, 45
'The rise and decline of development
    economics' (Hirschman) 80
Thermidor 183, 184
tin 144
tradables 103, 104, 107
trade 4, 43–4, 49, 50, 77–8, 121
  liberalization 65, 88
trade openness 43, 44
trade surplus 116
trade unions 132
the triad 190–94
Triffin, Robert 93
trimodal global wealth distribution 26,
    27, 31–2, 33, 34
Trotsky, Leon 182–3
truncated convergence 154
Tunisia 14, 17
Turkey 16, 45, 171, 174, 175
*Two Tactics of Social Democracy in
    the Democratic Revolution* (Lenin)
    124

Ukraine 164, 176, 192, 194
  crisis 6, 165–6, 170, 171, 174, 175,
    193
unemployment 63, 133
unimodal global wealth distribution 26,
    27, 29, 30–31
United Kingdom 29, 30
United Nations (UN) 87–8, 142
  General Assembly 172
  United Nations Development
    Programme (UNDP) 23
United Provinces/Holland/Netherlands
    29, 30
United States (US)
  in the 1970s 79
  bourgeoisie 190
  and collective imperialism 192
  communism, preventing in Asia 14
  GDP 2
  hegemony 26, 30, 32, 33, 34
  monopoly capitalism 185
  trade agreements 77–8
  trade, attitude to in Asia 121
  as world state 191

unproductive labor 186
urbanization 156
Uruguay 144, 155, 156
use values 185–6
USSR 10–12, 13, 18, 193

Venezuela 138, 141, 143, 144, 154, 157
Vietnam 14, 16, 58, 64, 66, 67

wage-form 188
wage rates 132
wages 116, 119, 120, 121, 186
Waltz, Kenneth N. 173
Washington Consensus 20, 56–7, 58,
      62, 63, 64, 80–81, 202
wealth 2, 26–8, 30–31
   inequality 201
The Wealth of Nations (Smith) 58–9
welfare state 158
the West 2, 81
   demise of 176
   per capita income 197–8
Western Asia 32

Western Europe 2, 7, 14, 19, 27, 30, 59,
      197–8
Westphalian ideas 166, 167, 172,
      175
wider Europe 5–6, 167–8, 174, 176
Witte's reforms 10
Wolf, Martin 23
worker–peasant alliance 182, 183
working class 124
World Bank 63, 72, 79, 206
world hegemony 2, 26, 31–2
world-systems 24
World Trade Organization (WTO) 108,
      131

XI Jinping 170

Yalta ideas 175
Yeltsin, Boris 184
Yukos oil company 169
yushijujin 66

zhongyong 66